THE EPISTLE
TO THE ROMANS

THE EPISTLE
TO THE ROMANS

A Commentary Logical and Historical

By
JAMES M. STIFLER, D.D.
Professor of New Testament Exegesis

MOODY PRESS
CHICAGO

Printed in the United States of America

CONTENTS

PREFACE

THIS BOOK has no other aim than to make the somewhat difficult Epistle to the Romans better understood—to report to the reader what the apostle has written. It is not put forth in the interest of any theological system; it has no theory of any kind to advocate and no point to make, except by dispassionate study to ascertain the meaning of Paul's language. The commentator, even more than the preacher of the gospel, is under solemn obligation not to bear false witness against the sacred penman, not to misinterpret him, not to overlay his thought with personal views; the commentator's work is to follow down the stream of the inspired text, to measure its width and if possible its depth, but not to dig new channels for it and not to divert its flow to water his own garden.

This book is not a hasty product, but the result of many years of labor. The author has had the privilege and pleasure of guiding more than twenty classes of theological students through the Epistle to the Romans, fourteen of these using the original text. The instruction has not been given by means of lectures read or dictated by the teacher. Each word and each idea in the epistle have been discussed with the class, every member of which had the utmost liberty to suggest his difficulty, to ask questions, to oppose, to deny, or to call up the contrary view of any commentator. This book is the outcome of these years of study and discussion.

While the very words written by the apostle have been considered and weighed one by one, the result is not presented in that form, nor with any but the very least reference to the Greek. There is a large class of men, educated men, who, after all, can read a commentary with most satisfaction and profit in English. This book is especially designed for them. The voluminous works of Meyer and Godet, even when translated, of

Alford, of Sanday and Headlam, and of others, are serviceable only to those having a fair knowledge of Greek. Of the commentaries that have appeared since the Reformation, Sanday and Headlam enumerate thirty-five, very few of which can be used by any but scholars. They have their place, and are invaluable in the cloisters of the erudite. But accurate and even expert knowledge can be conveyed in vernacular speech, as is made very apparent in the excellent commentaries of J. A. Beet, of H. G. C. Moule, of M. B. Riddle,—the latter not included in Sanday and Headlam's list,—and of E. H. Gifford in the *Speaker's Commentary*. There is room for more such, in which dry and arbitrary technicalities are not exhibited, in which only the house appears and not the tools, the noise, the dust, and the process of erection. To the commentators above mentioned and to others the author is indebted, and in the body of this work at the appropriate place due credit has been given, Sanday and Headlam, being referred to by the first of the two names only. The King James Version is used as the basis of this commentary, because it is the one still more commonly read, and also because it is less presumptuous to criticize it than the other. But the (English) Revised Version is constantly cited, and its better renderings are always given.

In preparing this book two things have been kept steadily in view. First, Paul's point of view. A commentary cannot be called strictly historical unless its exposition is vitally connected with the thought of the times in which the text was written. It is the theologic current and the religious questions of Paul's day, and not those of the present or of any other day, that must furnish the key to the epistle. He wrote in the face of that imposing system of Biblical interpretation that claimed Moses for its foundation, that found defenders in every synagogue from Jerusalem to Rome, and that was sure that it knew the way of fellowship with God. The only orthodox people were the sons of Israel, who must not be judged alone by their narrow Pharisaism; they were sure that by their law they were the sole custodians of the truth of God. The rabbi was not merely zealous; he was often able. In every line that Paul wrote he had Judaism in mind. The historic attitude of the epistle has been one of the guiding lines in preparing this commentary.

The other and second point constantly aimed at is to give the course of thought without a break. Commenting in the strict sense of the term has not been thought of, except in so far as it was required to show the logical connection. As the language of the epistle is so compact, not a little verbal exposition was found necessary; but it has been sought to make it strictly subsidiary to that which is of prime importance—the apostle's argument. He used words not for their sake, but for the sake of what he had to say, and in the latter sense they have been studied.

To Dr. Henry G. Weston, who has made the New Testament a daily study for more than half a century, and whose knowledge of it is as profound as it is comprehensive, I am greatly indebted; for while he is not responsible for the views of this commentary, he has kindly read the proof-sheets while the book was going through the press, made suggestions, and permitted the use of his name on this page.

JAMES M. STIFLER

Crozer Seminary, Chester, Pa.

INTRODUCTION

1. THE ORIGIN OF THE ROMAN CHURCH is historically obscure. There is no record, and little from which a record can
be constructed, either of the date of its beginning or of the
agent or agents of its founding. When the Epistle to the
Romans was written the church had already a world-wide reputation (1:8). But little can be inferred from this as to the
length of time which the church had already existed. In five
years it might have become known "throughout the whole
world." The Thessalonian church in less than a year after
Paul's first visit was widely known; for Paul writes them from
Corinth (A.D. 52 or 53): "In every place your faith to God-
ward is spread abroad; so that we need not to speak anything"
(I Thess. 1:8). That the Roman church was not much if any
older than the earlier Gentile churches is probable. It was a
Gentile church. It is not easy to conceive how such a one
could have come into existence before the church in Antioch
in Syria (Acts 11:19-21), many years after Pentecost. And
this first Gentile church did not get its authority to be strictly
such until after the council in Jerusalem (A.D. 50). The matter
and the spirit of the Epistle to the Romans show that the latter
were thoroughly settled on the question of their right to be just
what they were—a Gentile church, grounded on faith in Christ.
Now who made them such? Who was qualified to teach them
that in Christ there was no distinction between Jew and Gentile, a doctrine that was not promulgated before Peter's visit
to the household of Cornelius (Acts 10), and that did not gain
authoritative recognition until a "good while" (Acts 15) afterward? It seems almost necessary to believe that the Roman
church was founded by teachers from some of the Gentile
centers, and that, too, after such teachers had come to clear
vision of the intent of the gospel for Gentiles as such, and that

11

they could be saved as Gentiles. The Gentile character of the church is now pretty generally admitted, and this admission makes necessary the other, that its founders must have been men of Paul's way of presenting the gospel.

This disposes of two theories in reference to the establishment of the gospel in the imperial city. First, it could not have been carried thither by the "strangers of Rome, Jews and proselytes" (Acts 2:10), who were present at Pentecost. How could these men have founded a Gentile church? The door to the heathen was not opened until years after the descent of the Spirit. It would be a much better guess to say that some from the household of Cornelius (Acts 10) carried to Rome the news of a Saviour for the Gentiles.

Again, there is no reason for saying that Peter evangelized the Romans. He was not the apostle to the uncircumcision (Gal. 2:7, 8). The sentiment that guided Paul in choosing his fields of labor (15:20) precludes the belief that Peter had been at Rome before him. "It is equally clear," says Dr. J. B. Lightfoot, "that no other apostle was the founder." How the seed came to be dropped that sprang up in this Roman church, or from whose hands, remains in obscurity; but it is safe to say that it was the gospel as Paul preached it that gave the Romans their first knowledge of Christ. It is equally safe to say that that gospel could not have been preached until some years after Pentecost—not until it was formulated. The "many years" mentioned by Paul in 15:23 need not mean more than eight or ten (see Acts 24:17); and it is difficult on account of his history, as given in the Book of Acts, to see how they can embrace any more.

2. THE TIME AND PLACE of the writing of the epistle are well known. The data are furnished in the Book of Acts and in the epistle itself and in others written near the same time. Paley (Horæ Paulinæ) says the time and place are found, "not from the epistle nor from anything declared concerning the time and place in any part of the epistle, but from a comparison of circumstances referred to in the epistle, with the order of events recorded in the Acts, and with references to the same circumstances, though for quite different purposes, in the two

epistles to the Corinthians." This "comparison of circumstances" Paley draws out in an argument that is unanswerable,
not, indeed, for the actual, but for the relative time. He states
his conclusion thus: "We have these circumstances—each by
some hint in the passage in which it is mentioned, or by the
date of the writing in which the passage occurs—fixed to a
particular time; and we have that time turning out upon examination to be in all the same, namely, toward the close of St.
Paul's second visit to the peninsula of Greece." According to
the system of chronology generally admitted now to be correct,
this "time" was the early spring of A.D. 58, and the place was
Corinth. In this second visit to Greece, Paul's third missionary tour, he stayed three months at Corinth (Acts 20:3). This
must have been in the spring, for when he was about to leave
navigation was possible, and though he was compelled to take
the land route to Jerusalem, "through Macedonia," he reached
the latter country before the Passover (Acts 20:6), and hoped
"to be at Jerusalem the day of Pentecost" (Acts 20:16). This
gives us the season of the year to which the writing of the
epistle belongs, for it was penned just as he was leaving
Corinth,—"But now I go unto Jerusalem" (15:25),—in the
month of January or February.

It is not the intention to attempt to demonstrate either the
problem of time and place or several others belonging to this
Introduction. This would be simply to repeat what may be
found in every Bible dictionary and in the numerous recent
introductions to the Pauline epistles. Furthermore, there is
little need of proving what is nowhere seriously disputed.
What Lightfoot wrote about Romans more than a quarter of a
century ago is undisputed to-day: "The date of this epistle is
fixed with more absolute certainty and within narrower limits
than that of any other of St. Paul's epistles" (Smith's *Dictionary of the Bible*, article "Romans"). He might have spoken with equal confidence about the place.

3. THE AUTHENTICITY AND GENUINENESS of the epistle are
both beyond doubt. No book in the New Testament is better
attested. The external testimony begins with Clement of
Rome (A.D. 96), who is followed by Ignatius (A.D. 115), Poly-

carp (A.D. 116), Marcion (A.D. 130), the Muratori canon (A.D. 170), and others, both friends and foes, to the number of nineteen, before the end of the second century. Of the beginning of the same century Sanday, in the Introduction to his commentary, page 80, section 8, says: "Assuming, then, as we are entitled to do, that the apostolic fathers represent the first quarter of the second century, we find the Epistle to the Romans at that time widely read, treated as a standard authority on apostolic teaching, and taking its place in a collection of Pauline letters." Neither the heretic Marcion in that ancient time nor the rationalist Baur in our day has been able to deny that Paul wrote epistle, and that we possess in its present form what the apostle wrote. Such a denial has not been attempted until within the last ten or fifteen years, when certain Dutch and German critics—Steck, Michelsen, Voelter, and others—have made it. They ignore the undisputed testimony of the apostolic fathers, and put nothing in its place but impossible theories based on their own subjective views. Their criticism has hardly created a ripple in the smooth current of clear testimony to the canonicity of the epistle. Sanday, who examines some of these views and acknowledges his indebtedness to Knowling's *The Witness of the Epistles*, concludes: "It has been somewhat tedious work enumerating these theories, which will seem probably to most readers hardly worth while repeating, so subjective and arbitrary is the whole criticism."

But Marcion, unequivocal in his witness to the genuineness of Romans, assailed its integrity. He did not deny that Paul wrote the last two chapters, but denied for some reason that they belonged to this epistle. It was not until Baur's day and that of his followers that they were declared spurious. From some cause they are not found in many cursive manuscripts, the doxology (16:25-27) being appended at the end of chapter 14.

Baur's objections, somewhat plausible as to chapter 16, are not formidable. The question is noticed in the body of this commentary at the head of chapter 15, and briefly in the notes on the last chapter. It remains to say against the cursive manuscripts that all the great uncials, together with the Syriac and Vulgate versions and all the Latin fathers, place the doxology just where it is found in our King James Version. The textual critics, from Lachmann to Westcott and Hort, do the same; so, too, Weymouth and the Canterbury revision. One of the objections to chapter 16, that Paul could not have known so many persons in Rome, is scarce worth noticing. And lastly, Paley, in the same section quoted above, in making eight points in favor of the genuineness of the epistle, finds most of them in these two chapters. In proving the epistle he proves the genuineness of these two chapters, and he does it with a lucidity and a weight of logic that no subjective criticism can possibly overthrow, unless a subjective objection is made to outweigh a solid argument.

4. THE OCCASION AND OBJECT of the epistle are not clearly apparent on its pages. These are not hard to find in some of the other Pauline letters. No one had come to Paul to report disorders and divisions at Rome such as moved him to write to the Corinthians (I Cor. 1:11), and he had not received a letter of inquiry from Rome (I Cor. 7:1). The Romans were neither divided nor disorderly. Their faith was world-wide in its reputation (1:8), and they were full of goodness (15:14). The Romans were in no danger from Judaizing teachers as were the Galatians, so that Paul, in sore apprehension, must write them not to abandon the liberty in Christ (Gal. 5:1) for the bondage of the law. There is scarce a hint, or but one hint, that the Romans were in any danger from false teachers (16:17-19). Again, as to the Romans, Paul need not send to know their faith, as in the case of the Thessalonians (I Thess. 3:5), and to exhort them to remain steadfast in the persecutions that had come upon them, for the Romans were not persecuted when the epistle to them was written.

(a) The date (A.D. 58) and the place of writing (Corinth) being settled, the occasion becomes apparent. Paul had long desired to see Rome, as he declares twice in the epistle (1:13; 15:23) and once in Acts (19:21). He was now at their very doors, but still could not make the intended visit; other work must be done first (15:25), and only "after that" could he see

Rome (Acts 19:21). An explanation is also due the Romans for his long-continued delay in coming to them (1:9, 10; 15:22). The next best thing can be done. Phebe is about to make a journey to Rome, and Paul will take this opportunity to write to the Roman church.

(b) In seeking the object of the epistle, the topics discussed, the contents, and the argument must be kept in view. The topics are sin, grace, law, and brotherly love. There is but a word about the Person of Christ; resurrection (see notes on 1:5, p. 18) is assumed; eschatology, as it appears in other epistles, is wanting; the church as such is mentioned but once in the epistle, and that almost at its close and incidentally (16:23). In its topics the epistle is far from comprehensive.

As to its contents, there are four grand divisions. After the salutation (1:1-7) and the introduction (1:8-15), leading up to the theme of the epistle (1:16, 17), these follow: 1. Sin (1:18—3:20); 2. Righteousness (3:21—8); 3. The Theodicy (9—11); 4. Christian Walk (12—6).

The argument is readily discovered in the epistle. On the main points there can be little difference of opinion among exegetes, and no serious conflict in the details. The *Explanatory Analysis of St. Paul's Epistle to the Romans* (1893), by Canon H. P. Liddon, is minute and exhaustive. Sanday's analysis is, however, more practical, being, as it is, compact and clear. But in studying the object of the epistle minuteness is not as necessary as clear and broad outline. We may follow, with some changes, that of Professor M. W. Jacobus in his article (*Presbyterian Quarterly*, January, 1893), "Paul's Purpose in Writing Romans," a discussion both comprehensive and satisfactory:

I. The first general division, viz., the dogmatic presentation of the gospel righteousness as opposed to the alleged law righteousness (1:18—8:39), which division is subdivided into two parts:

1. The necessity of the gospel righteousness (1:18—3:20), which necessity is evidenced by the impossibility of a law righteousness.

(a) On the part of the heathen (1:18-32).

(b) On the part of the Jew (2:1—3:20).

Having reached this conclusion, the apostle is ready to give:

2. The positive presentation of this gospel righteousness (3:21—8:39), arranged in the following order:

(a) The historical fact of the provision of this gospel righteousness (3:21-26), that excludes all boasting (3:27-30).

(b) Its agreement with the Old Testament Scriptures (3:31—4:25).

(c) Its surety for the present and all the future (5:1-21).

(d) Its result in the sanctification of the individual believer (6:1—8:39).

i. He is dead to sin (6:1-23).

ii. He is freed from the law as a means of sanctification (7:1-25).

iii. He has the power of the Spirit (8:1-39).

Then follows:

II. The second general division, viz., the presentation of the facts in the case regarding Israel's present rejection (9:1—11:36).

1. God is righteous in rejecting, free in electing (9:1-33).

2. Israel's responsibility in the rejection (10:1-21).

3. God's gracious plan in His present dealing with Israel (11:1-36).

III. The epistle concludes with a presentation of the Christian conduct flowing from gospel righteousness (12:1—15:13), which presentation subdivides as follows:

1. Conduct as a member of the Christian body (12:1-21).

(a) In exercising special spiritual gifts (12:1-8).

(b) In the requirement of love (12:9-21).

2. Conduct as a subject of the state (13:1-7).

3. Conduct toward the other subjects of the state (13:8-14).

4. Conduct in questions of conscience (14:1—15:13).

That which remains (15:14—16:27) is epistolary, like 1:1-17, and does not belong directly to the argument.

Now to recall what Paul has not said in this epistle, and to observe the trend and climax of his argument, must lead to the discovery of his main design in writing. The theodicy is the striking peculiarity of the epistle. The climax of the argument is the close of the eleventh chapter (verses 28-36), God's interaction between the two permanent divisions of mankind, with a view to the future salvation of both. The theodicy is not an episode; it is that toward which the argument moves from the start. Paul begins (1:2) with the assertion that the gospel accords with "the Holy Scriptures." Beginning the third chapter, he declares (3:2) that these "oracles" pertain peculiarly to the Jews. This assertion alone made the theodicy necessary, and it was already sighted from this point. The fourth chapter, which shows the agreement between the Old and New Testament justification, seems at first sight to be strikingly like Galatians 3. But there is one marked difference. Galatians makes very clear that Abraham is the father of the Gentiles; the fourth chapter of Romans insists on the other point, that he is also father of the Jews, which is not found in Galatians except by implication. In Romans Paul from first to last preserves an even balance between Jew and Gentile; they are sinners alike (1:18—3:20); the heads of the race, Adam and Christ (chap. 5), embrace Jew and Gentile alike; the law can sanctify neither Jew nor Gentile (chap. 7). When the argument reaches the eighth chapter we find a striking peculiarity, a detailed prediction of the glorification of creation (8:19-23). Only an argument that leads to the demonstration of the salvation of the Jew nationally can make necessary this section about glorified creation, for the Jew's oracles did not promise him heaven, a word which occurs but twice in the epistle—once to tell of the "wrath . . . from heaven" (1:18), and again to forbid ascent thither for justifying help (10:6). The Gentile salvation (Phil. 3:20, 21) may be unlike that of the ancient oracles; but the latter are still living, to be made good to the Jew.

Paul's evangelistic work was well-nigh done. It needed but the capstone of his visit to Rome, from which city, in less than four years after this epistle was written,—and two of those years were consumed in getting there,—he sends out the triumphant message that the gospel "was preached to every creature which is under heaven" (Col. 1:23). Indeed, before this it had "prevailed" (Acts 19:20) with the close of the apostle's work at Ephesus. The time has come to survey the field. Paul is standing in thought on the platform of Judaism. His outlook is from Jerusalem, where every one of his missionary journeys terminated. He sees the danger—a danger, alas! long ago realized—that a gospel of grace that reduces the Jew for salvation to the level of the Gentile, in blotting out Judaism as a means of approach to God may blot out the Jew. What does it mean that at the very beginning he reminds these Romans that this salvation in Christ is "first" to the Jew? Outside the present grace Jew and Gentile are kept wholly separate from beginning to end of the epistle. Let the Gentile not boast. This is his day; that of the Jew is coming. Paul must insist that no man, Jew or Gentile, can now or ever hereafter be saved, except by faith. This was good for all, but hard for the Jew to accept. God's plan is to bring him to an acceptance of it, that He may have mercy on him as He has had on the Gentile; and meanwhile let the Gentile remember not only that this is coming, but that his own ultimate triumph cannot come until mercy to the Jew appears.

To this view of the object of the epistle modern thought is coming. Jacobus says in the article cited above: "Paul's purpose was to correct the attitude of the Gentile element in the church at Rome. They were exalting his Gospel at the expense of the Jew. His plan in writing the epistle, therefore, was to take up this gospel of his . . . and show that, after all, it did not ignore the Jew either as an essential element in the Christian church or as the still unbelieving people outside of it; in other words, that his Gentile Gospel was not to be overpressed and placed in opposition to all the revelation and work of God so far."

Sanday comes to substantially the same conclusion: "Clearly this question belongs to the later reflective stage of the controversy relating to Jew and Gentile. The active contenting for Gentile liberties would come first, the philosophic or theologic assignment of the due place of Jew and Gentile in the divine scheme would come afterward. This more advanced stage has now been reached." Salvation by grace is final. There never will be any other means of saving men. But the results so far seen are far from final, and let not the Gentile confound these two. Grace for the present has saved him and left outside the nation from which it first went abroad. The theodicy, the culmination of the epistle, tells why the Jew is thus left for the present, but it sees his glory in the future. Let the Gentile not shut his eyes to it.

5. THE PECULIARITIES of the epistle demand attention. The first that strikes one is its world-wide view—its universalism. In all time and in all nations men are sinners. God's wrath is not a flash of lightning; it gleams from the whole heaven. Sin and grace are traced to their ultimate sources in Adam and in Christ. The law as a means of salvation is swept away at one stroke. The salvation is considered not in its relation to a single soul or even a single church, but in its relation to the creation itself and to every nation in it. When it comes to duties, they are also comprehensively treated. Love is the universal principle, and the believer is looked at in his relation to the state, to the church, to his neighbor, to his brother, and to himself.

The eloquence of the epistle cannot be overlooked. Other epistles have eloquent passages, like I Corinthians 13 and 15 or Ephesians 3:8-21; but in this epistle there are such passages in almost every chapter (1:16-23; 2:4-11; 3:21-26, etc.), but notably the conclusions of both chapter 8 and chapter 9. The whole epistle is marked by a sustained elevation of thought and sentiment. This universalism and eloquence befit an epistle to the world's capital—an epistle that deals with the world's destiny through its two divisions of men, Jew and Gentile.

In its style the epistle is marked by great energy, but not with vehemence. It is the resistless flow of a broad, deep river, noiseless, but ever onward. But this is true of the argument rather than of the words that convey it, which move rapidly and are often warm with the writer's earnest feeling. His feeling throughout is more uniform than in some of his other epistles; not as calm as in Ephesians, but more so than in Galatians; but sometimes, as in 9:15; 11:33-36, it rises to great intensity. The epistle is the masterpiece of the apostle, in which the Gospel in its strictest sense is methodically unfolded and shown in its widest connection. All men, Jew and Gentile, are lost, "being justified freely by his [God's] grace through the redemption that is in Christ Jesus" (3:24).

CHAPTER 1[1]

THE OUTLOOK

A S PAUL WAS THE PREACHER of a world-wide Gospel, a
Gospel suited to every moral and national condition, he
comes before the Romans in this character. The first chapter
gives a wide survey. It glances at the Scriptures as a whole,
recalls their ancient promise of a Saviour, outlines Paul's extended labors, and presents the religious history of the Gentile
world from the beginning. It has three topics: (1) the salutation (vv. 1-7); (2) Paul's fraternal introduction (vv. 8-17);
(3) the guilt of the Gentile world in all time (vv. 19-32). In
discussing this last topic, the course of thought is that (a)
God's wrath is revealed against the sins of all men (v. 18),
because (b) all men know His will (v. 19a); (c) they know it,
for He Himself has revealed it in nature (vv. 19b, 20); (d) men
rejected the light given, and in devising their own came into
darkness (vv. 21, 22); (e) in this darkness they fell into idolatry (vv. 23-25), sensuality (vv. 26, 27), and every other kind
of immorality (vv. 28-32).

1. In the salutation (vv. 1-7) the writer first identifies himself. At the time he wrote he was already so well known at
Rome that he need give only his name, Paul. As to his relation
to Jesus Christ, he was a bond-servant. As to his office, he was
one sent forth, an apostle. As to his right to his office, his
authority, he was specifically called. As to the limits of his
work, he was separated from everything else and confined to
the Gospel, the message from God. His duty was narrow, excluding even the administration of the initiatory ordinance
(I Cor. 1:7).

---

[1]The divisions in this book are, both as to the chapters and verses, those
of the epistle itself.

2. With the second verse he begins the exaltation of his sub-ject—the message from God. It is not novel. God promised it long before by means of "his prophets." The latter get their dignity and authority in the little word "his." They were God's own. How much would have been lost if, instead of "his," Paul had used the word "the"! The prophets were not an evolutionary product of their times—there were many such (II Chron. 18; Matt. 7:22, 23)—but men endowed with God's Spirit to foresee the Gospel message. It was recorded in Scrip-tures which are "holy." The emphasis is on the word "holy." It calls attention to the character of these writings. By means of two words "his" and "holy," Paul shows the lofty and unique origin of the Gospel message. If any should accuse him of promulgating a new gospel his answer is that his mes-sage was foretold for hundreds of years. It is in harmony with the Bible of that day. And this is not a mere ad hominem argu-ment against the Jews. He virtually declares that their Bible was itself a supernatural product. The Old Testament is the documentary defense of the Gospel.

3. To show still further the glory of the Gospel, he mentions its exalted theme. It is concerning God's Son, Jesus Christ. The first word in this verse joins it either with the end of the first verse, "gospel of God," or with the word "promised" in the second verse. The sense is about the same with either connection.

Jesus Christ, the theme of the Gospel story, is declared to be preëminent both on His human and on His divine side. The antithesis in the phrases "according to the flesh" and "ac-cording to the spirit" does not lie in the sphere of His person, but in His relations. He was one person, but He belonged to two realms. According to the flesh, looked at in His con-nection with the race, His origin was the very highest. He was princely, being descended from the royal family of David. According to the spirit of holiness—that is, looked at in His connection with the realm above—He was higher than all angels (Heb. 1:4); He was the Son of God. The relation of the two natures in Christ's person is not thought of. That question was not raised in Paul's day. Neither would it suit the context. Paul is magnifying the theme of the Gospel. It is about a being the most exalted, whether viewed in His human or in His divine relations. The twofold antithetic statement shows its significance when applied, as it well can be, to another. It could be said of David, as to his flesh, as to his origin as a man, he was the son of Jesse, or even the son of Judah; as to his relation to God, he was the declared and acknowledged king of Israel. It would be absurd to ask now, about the person of David, what part was merely natural or human and what was royal or kingly. He was a man and a king both at the same time. And so of Jesus: He was the son of David and the Son of God. Of course the latter relation involved an appropriate nature, but that nature is not the question here.

4. Because the terms "flesh" and "spirit" designate not what was in Christ as constituent of His person, but two external and converging agencies, at whose point of contact He appeared historically, it is not Paul's purpose to show what Christ is, but how He was declared to be what He is. His resurrection powerfully asserted His Sonship. The rising from the dead did not create Him a Son. This very passage says He was born so. The Gospel according to the text is about "his [God's] Son, who was born." The word "made" of the King James Version is abandoned by recent translations. The three phrases beginning at "with," "according," and "by" give respectively the manner, the measure, and the means or cause of the declaration of Christ's Sonship.

5. But Paul mentions the resurrection for an additional purpose—to give the source and character of his own apostolic grace. Immediately upon this mention he adds, "through whom"—through this raised Christ—"we received grace and apostleship." This is all-important. It gives at one stroke the point of view from which Paul will discuss the Gospel; not from the side of the incarnation, but from the side of the resurrection (II Cor. 5:16). It is not always noted that this is the epistle of the resurrection, resurrection not of the body—alluded to only twice in the epistle (4:17; 8:10), and both times by an unusual word—but resurrection as the central potency

of salvation. Both justification and sanctification are secured by it. "He was raised again for our justification." We are "married to another, even to him who was raised from the dead," that we might bring forth fruit unto God . The subject is mentioned in 1:4; 4:17, 24, 25; 5:10; 6:4, 5, 9; 7:4; 8:11, 34; 10:9; and possibly 11:15. But this occurrence of the word is but the outcropping here and there of the granite ledge that lies everywhere underneath the epistle and on which it is based.

In verse 5, Paul has come around to that with which he started in the first. There he was an apostle. Here now, by means of what intervenes, he shows the dignity and character of his apostleship. It is from a raised Christ, who was promised in the Scriptures. Hence the Scriptures predict the resurrection, and hence, too, the Gospel according to Paul is universal. It is not Jewish, but world-wide, a Gospel for the Gentiles, for by resurrection Jesus transcended all Jewish connection and became the world's Saviour, a Saviour not by obedience to law which was Mosaic, but by the power of an endless life. Life is universal. Thus Paul, by linking his apostolate with the raised Christ, gives first the character of this epistle, and second its scope. It is the epistle of divine life in Christ Jesus for all nations, on the condition of faith.

6, 7. After his profound prelude, Paul, in the sixth verse, reassures his readers, declaring that they are embraced in the intent of the Gospel; then comes the salutation proper. It connects with the first verse, that which lies between verses 2 and 6 being, so to speak, parenthetical.

Two things may be observed in this salutation. First, like most of them (see esp. Gal. 1:1-5), it involves the germ of all that follows. It has four items: the writer has a message in accord with the Scriptures; it is from the risen Christ; it is universal; and it is for obedience to the faith. These are the leading thoughts of the epistle.

Second, this salutation is striking in that it implicitly asserts the cardinal points of the Gospel history, "the fundamental facts of Christianity." The epistle was written within thirty years after Jesus Christ trod the earth. This cannot be denied. It is generally admitted. And this salutation asserts now that the main facts of the Gospel were in accord with Old Testament prediction; it asserts the incarnation and the resurrection, and that these Romans, qualified to weigh the facts, had responded with implicit faith in them. What they trusted then men may safely trust now.

Having addressed the Romans formally and officially, Paul now writes personally. One cannot fail to see between the lines that the Romans had expected him to visit them before this time, and that Paul is justifying himself for his failure to meet that expectation. Rome was the capital of the Gentile world, and Paul was the Apostle to the Gentiles; why did he not come to them? Why spend years in the provinces? Once before he had been at their very doors (Acts 18:1-18) and had turned away from them, and now he was about to do so again (cf. Acts 19:21 with 20:3; Rom. 15:25). This introduction has this state of things in full view.

8-13. He is not indifferent about the spiritual welfare of the Roman church. He thanks God by means of Jesus Christ for their faith, already known throughout the Roman Empire. This wide reputation implies that at this date there was a general diffusion of the Gospel. And since there is no other to testify, he calls God to witness that he makes unceasing prayer for them. He prays also that God would prosper him in a journey to them. He longs to see them, that he may help them and may be helped by them. He declares to them the fact that he has again and again tried to come to them, but was hindered. He covets the same fruit among them that he has found among other Gentiles. All this is neither the spirit nor the conduct of one not their friend.

14. It is not without some vehemence—there is no connecting word introducing this verse—that he professes his obligation to men of every tongue, "Greeks and Barbarians," and to men of every degree of culture, "wise and foolish." In these categories his readers would be classed with the Greeks and the wise, for the word "Greek" in the New Testament is not strictly an ethnic term (Acts 7:26).

15. In accordance with this acknowledged obligation Paul declares his readiness to preach at Rome. He is master of his purpose, but not of his circumstances.

16. "For I am not ashamed of the gospel of [concerning] Christ." If anyone in Rome either said or thought that Paul did not come to the capital because he distrusted the Gospel for that field, this is his answer. And the reason he is not ashamed of it is because it is God's power effecting salvation in every believer. Power of any kind is in honor among men, and divine power can put no man to the blush. In this brief sentence Paul has packed three rich facts: first, the effect of the Gospel—salvation; second, the extent—it is world-wide, to "every one"; and third, its condition—faith in Jesus Christ. Paul contemplates men of every land and of every degree of culture. If they have discovered or if they can discover any other means of salvation than the Gospel, it has nothing to boast of; it no longer stands alone. But he is not ashamed to present it to the civilized and the learned, for culture has not brought them salvation, nor even the means of it.

17. This verse gives the very point of the effectiveness of the Gospel. Certainly he is righteous before God who follows God's means of righteousness. And the Gospel alone reveals this righteousness. In what it unveils lies its power. Righteousness means conformity to the divine claims on man. This conformity is reached by means of faith. On man's part faith is the righteousness (4:5). The phrase "from faith to faith" is to be joined not with the verb "revealed" but with the word "righteousness." The apostle is not concerned here with the mode of the revelation, but with the character of that which is revealed. It is a by-faith righteousness. So far as the message of the Gospel is concerned, the revelation is purely objective. To connect the phrase in question, as many able commentators do, with the verb "revealed" makes the power of the Gospel lie in the manner in which it discloses salvation, rather than in what it discloses, and the Gospel itself to be unknown but by an experience of it. Paul is first of all and most of all describing the righteousness objectively, and only incidentally showing how it is to be attained. The latter he does further on.

The phrase "from faith to faith" is, literally, "out of faith into faith." The righteousness provided by God is seen to be one that springs out of faith; it is one adapted only to (into) faith. The phrase might be rendered "by faith for faith," in which its simple meaning is seen that it is a righteousness wholly by faith; just as it might be said of a healing ointment, it is a remedy by rubbing, a remedy for rubbing, and not a remedy for or by any other use.

As this means of salvation involves the chief element in the Gospel, and the point at which it departs from the Pharisees' teaching of Paul's day, he quotes their own Scriptures to show that he is not inventing something new. As in Habakkuk's day, so now men live by faith. It is not a proof text, but it indicates decisively that there is harmony between the Gospel and the law.

With the eighteenth verse of this first chapter the discussion begins. Under the first topic, the universality of sin, Paul begins with the Gentile world. There is not much argument on this point. A mere statement of the facts was sufficient to gain the consent of all his readers. When he comes to speak of the sinfulness of the Jew (chap. 2) he resorts to proofs.

18. The "for" is not specific but comprehensive. It looks at all that Paul has just been saying. He is not ashamed of the Gospel. The Gospel would be nothing if men were not guilty and in need of the rescue which the Gospel alone can afford. The Gospel alone reveals the means of salvation, for everywhere else there is no revelation except of wrath. The eighteenth verse, about wrath, gives significance to the preceding two, about grace. Sin is the measure of salvation. Only they know what it is to be saved who know what it is to be lost. All heresy has its source in wrong or feeble conceptions of sin. "As with churches, so with individuals, the estimate of sin determines everything" (*Hulsean Lectures*, 1874, p. 14).

The power of the Gospel need not shame one, for everywhere else God's wrath, from which it can save, is revealed.

This wrath or holy anger is universally revealed, "from heaven." Men in all ages have been aware that the Power above frowned upon them for their deeds. These deeds fall under two heads: "ungodliness," a denial of the character or essence of God, and "unrighteousness," a denial of His rule. The blackness of their sin is that they "hold" or withhold the truth in unrighteousness.

19. The assertion that they so withhold the truth and are amenable to God's wrath is justified on the ground ("because") that what may be known of God—that is, "the truth" —is manifest in them. They know the truth. They know it because God has showed it to them. They have had a teacher who could not fail in his work. The steps so far are three: God's wrath is righteously revealed against men; it is so revealed because men know and will not do; they know because God himself was their instructor. Their sin, then, is willful opposition to the revealed truth about God and from God.

20. This verse tells first how the revelation was given—"by the things that were made." Creation is revelation. Second, it tells how long the revelation has been in existence—"from the creation of the world." God created man, and from the beginning the Creator could be known by that which He created (Acts 17:29). Third, the verse tells what has been revealed—"the invisible things of him," that is, "his eternal power and Godhead," or divinity. There never was a time when the divine personality did not reveal Himself to men. God's works constitute His earliest and His universal Bible. It was open and legible. "The dim light of nature" is a phrase of fiction, not of fact. His invisible things are "clearly" seen. That first Bible in the sky above (Ps. 19), the earth beneath, and in the heart of man was not written, but it was read, read to men by God himself: "God hath showed it unto them," so that they are without excuse. It was not from lack of knowledge that men sinned, but in spite of it. Sin was not an infirmity, not an inability from lack of development in primitive

men, but a willful refusal to conform to the teaching given
by God.

21. The last verse closed with the statement that men in
all ages, the Gentiles, were without excuse under the wrath of
God. This verse restates and expands the reason: "Because
that, when they knew God, they glorified him not as God,
neither were thankful." This is the "ungodliness and unrighteousness" of the eighteenth verse. They knew Him; this is
plainly asserted; but they did not respect His person by giving
Him worship, neither did they acknowledge His benefits by
giving thanks. They withheld the truth, the knowledge of
God, in their unrighteousness; and a negative or neutral position before God is impossible. As they refused to follow the
light, they were brought to folly in their thoughts—"became
vain in their [corrupt] reasonings, and their foolish [senseless]
heart was darkened." The intellectual revolt against what they
knew to be right was attended by a darkening of the whole
understanding. The refusal to accept the truth destroys the
power to discriminate between truth and error.

This is Paul's general survey of the religious history of the
race from the beginning. In his earlier days man was mono-
theistic. His development has not been upward, but downward, not toward God, but from Him. The prime error lay
in seeking to know God while denying the evidence which He
himself has given of His character and personality. God manifested Himself unmistakably; but instead of worship and
praise, the two eyes without which God cannot be seen, men
betook themselves to vain reasoning. "The world by wisdom
knew not God" (I Cor. 1:21). God knows how to reveal
Himself in nature, and today in His Word. He is qualified to
give evidence of Himself. In man's estimation it may be in-
sufficient and even absurd; he may see no evidence of God in
nature, and nothing but patchwork in the Bible; but one word
from either source is worth more than all human speculation.
"The foolishness of God is wiser than men" (I Cor. 1:25).

22. "They became fools." This is the writer's, not to say
God's, estimate of the philosophers and religious leaders of
the race. He knew the boasted wisdom of the Euphrates and

of the Nile, the learning of Hellas and of Rome. We know it today. But there is this difference: there are those in our time who see no generic difference between these ethnic sages and the prophets of God, while Paul declares the former to be but "fools."

23. This verse gives the evidence of their folly. The glory of God, that admirable and effulgent representation of Himself which glowed in all that He had made, this they changed in the likeness of an image—"the uncorruptible God into an image made like to corruptible man." The odiousness of idolatry is not alone in the immorality to which it leads, but that it is a caricature of God and a slander. It belongs to His glory that He is imperishable. He was likened in that which is corruptible. The very material of the image was a dishonor, as if one should erect a statue to a distinguished man today not in marble or bronze, but in chalk or putty. To liken God to man is idolatry. Men were to make no image of Him. Had they preserved their original conception of Him they would not have attempted it. In due time He gave an image of Himself in a sinless being who was animated with eternal life, "the brightness of his glory, and the express image of his person" (Heb. 1:3). If Jesus was not more than a mortal, He was an idol.

These professed sages did not stop with likening God to man; they figured Him as a bird, then as a quadruped, and finally as a reptile. There was the Apollo of the Greeks, the eagle of the Romans, the bull of the Egyptians, and the serpent of the Assyrians. Paul may be giving in this verse the historical development of idolatry, from its highest phase to its worst; or he may be setting it forth in climactic form; but certain it is that all these phases of the sin existed.

In this review of the world's religion from the beginning, Paul teaches that man at the first was not an idolater. The origin of this sin is not contemporaneous with the appearance of man on the globe. Man did not work his way from fetishism through polytheism up to monotheism and the worship of the true God. His course was the reverse. From the beginning he did not grow better religiously, but worse. The Bible

gives no evidence of idolatry among the antediluvians. Men
in that age called on the name of the Lord (Gen. 4:26). The
earliest mention of idolatry belongs to the days of Abraham
(Josh. 24:2). Paul here gives the history and origin of idolatry. Men knew God and refused to worship Him. Idolatry
followed as a psychological necessity. If there is a force of development inherent in man, a force tending upward, the Gospel of the grace of God is an impertinence, and Paul might
well be ashamed of it. And why has not this force manifested
itself somewhat in the last two thousand years in Africa, in
India, and in China? The idolatry of today is no better than
that which grieved Paul.

24-27. This is the next long step downward. From idolatry
sprang sensuality. Originally man was chaste, but when he
cast God off, his animal passions were unchained. It was God's
infliction of punishment for the sin of idolatry. He punished
one sin by the imposition of another. Twice in these verses
we are told that "God gave them up," not passively, but actively. The reason is again given: "Who changed the truth of
God into the lie" of idolatry. They did not change a lie into
truth. Man's course was not in that direction. They took "the
truth of God" which He gave them and perverted it to the
falsehood of idol-worship. This was the cause of that vileness
whose hideous description we have here. "For even their
women." There is point in that word "even." Woman is the
purer, the more modest, of the sexes, has propensities less
ardent; but even she became worse than beastly and equaled
vile man in his depravity. The corruption that got into the
blood of the race by the Fall did not show itself at once. The
earlier families and tribes of the world were pure; God kept
them so. Whatever morality there is in the world is due not
to human nature, but to the restraining power of God. When
God "gave them up," the original corruption in the blood
showed itself in foul moral ulcers, and human virtue proved
to be less than that of the beasts of the field, among which
the barriers of sex are not crossed.

28-31. Again we are told that "God gave them over," and
again for the same reason. As they did not like to retain God

in their knowledge, He smote their mind to work abnormally and wickedly. They failed not only in their passions, but also in their thought. They practiced not only sensuality, but every other kind of immorality. Paul gives an appalling catalogue of their crimes.

32. The last verse in the chapter sums up everything written from the eighteenth, and restates it with unmistakable plainness. Men in all time and in all ages knew the "judgment" of God against sin, that it was death; but, in defiance of His wrath, they not only continued to practice these foul deeds, but to applaud those who did them. The lowest stage in depravity is to take pleasure in those who exhibit it. It is with this thought that Paul brings the discussion of the Gentiles' sin to a close and a climax.

Many salutary lessons are taught in this sad recital:

First, God gives in the works which He has made sufficient knowledge of Himself for adoration and gratitude. This knowledge is accessible to the heathen of today. The first verse in Genesis, repeated in almost every other book of the Bible, is vital. God is before all things, and created them. It is vital, for He is "understood by the things that are made."

Second, man's religious evolution is not upward, but downward. Men had sufficient light, and refused it. In their darkness the descending steps were three: the growth of elaborate systems of idolatry, the loss of all restraint upon the animal passions, and the complete violation of all the commands of the second table. The list of sins in verses 29-31 looks to this second table; for the words "haters of God," the only exception in the list, ought to be "hateful to God."

Third, God punishes sin with sin. This is His "wrath." If men will not honor Him, He takes away from them the power of chastity and morality. Indeed, the section teaches that these sins come as a punitive infliction from God. This wrath against the race can never cease while men as a whole refuse to glorify Him "as God." The attempt to rid the unbelieving world of the moral ills that afflict it is to attempt to change God's judgment of wrath. The world has deliberately and finally cast God off. It is well-nigh two thousand years since

this sad list of sins was set down by the pen of Paul. Let candor say which one of them has ceased to have existence among
men. They came in God's wrath then because men refused
the light of nature. The light today in Jesus Christ is many
times more intense, and men still refuse.

Fourth, we now have Paul's point of view, and can see what
he means in calling the Gospel a "power" and in declaring
that he is not "ashamed" of it. It can rescue the believer from
this judgment of God upon his sin. Paul did not expect the
flow of God's wrath against the world to change any more than
we may expect a change in gravity; he knew that that burning
torrent would continue to the end (II Thess. 1:6-9); but he
was also assured that through Jesus Christ men could be
snatched from this flood and reconciled to the God whose
wrath was once upon them. God himself so loved the world
against which His anger burns—the contradiction is too great
for human understanding—that He sent a lifeboat into the
judgment-tide that He himself created. The tide will not
leave the world, but men may leave the tide; He will save
them that believe. When Israel rebelled against God in the
wilderness (Num. 21:4-9), He sent fiery serpents that bit the
people, "and much people of Israel died." When in repentance
they prayed that God would "take away the serpents," He did
not answer them in this form. The serpents were not taken
away. God's punishment of their sin could not be so lightly
removed. But a remedy was provided in the brazen serpent
upon the pole, so that "he who looked upon it" lived. Who
would esteem the remedy if the judgment of the presence of
the serpents could be removed? The cross and the resurrection
are as great an outrage to human wisdom as is the serpent upon
the pole; but when men learn that there is no other escape
from the wrath of God, they will not be "ashamed" of the
Gospel. No reform can permanently succeed, for God never
ceases to punish the world's sin with sin. Therefore the
Gospel is glorious, for it and it alone (Acts 4:12) is God's
power for salvation.

CHAPTER 2

THE JEWS EQUALLY GUILTY
WITH THE GENTILES

IN DEPICTING THE SIN of the Gentile in the first chapter, Paul did not name him. It was not necessary. The picture was so true to life that no one could fail to see who sat for it. The author has been assured more than once by returned missionaries from China and India that when this first chapter was read to intelligent natives of these heathen lands they have hesitated to believe that it was from the missionary's sacred Book, suspecting that the missionary had written it himself as a description of what he had seen since he came among them.

In this second chapter Paul has no one but the Jew in view. He does not mention his name until the discussion has advanced some distance. It was easy to prove the Gentile a sinner. He claimed nothing for himself, and his immorality was patent to every eye; Paul had only to point to the facts. But in the case of the Jew all was different. He had a divinely given system of religion. In the letter it was never better observed than when Paul wrote. The Jew as a son of Abraham considered himself righteous by the law. To convince him of sin was no easier than it is today to convince a hollow Christianity of its fatal error. Paul has still his statement in view, that the Gospel is the only power of God for salvation, and nothing to be ashamed of. If Judaism can save men, the Gospel is an impertinence; hence the radical failure of the Jew must be shown.

Before he directly assails the Jew Paul lays down in verses 1-16 of this chapter the principles of the judgment. These are four, found in verses 2, 6, 11, 16. The judgment will be according to "truth" (v. 2), according to "deeds" (v. 6), without "respect of persons" (v. 11), and "according to my gospel" (v. 16). This section (vv. 1-16) constitutes what is virtually an indisputable major premise. Hence but one of the points (v. 11) is argued.

1. "Inexcusable, O man, whosoever thou art that judgest." This verse comes as a deduction from the preceding section about the Gentile. At the first blush it seems to be illogical, for the inference is wider than the premise. Paul has proved the Gentile a sinner amenable to God's wrath, and now he seems to imply that every other man is so if he judges. But the failure in logic is only momentary, for he at once adds that he who judges does the "same things" that he condemns in the wicked heathen. This is the proposition to be proved in this chapter. A part of the Jew's righteousness consisted in condemning the Gentile (Gal. 2:15), and Paul, well aware of this, wrote the sentence in this form to suggest what reader was aimed at. The verse, then, contains both an inference and a proposition. The inference is true; the proposition will be proved so when the four principles of the judgment in which all must stand are unfolded.

2. A better rendering of the phrase "we are sure" is "we know"—know that the judgment of God is according to truth. The connection is in contrast with man's partial judgment mentioned just before. Truth here has a shade of meaning different from that in 1:18, 25. There it means the revealed fact, that which is known about God; here it means the actual condition of the man judged—just what he is. When gold is assayed, the test considers only the metal which is under it; it does not ask whence it came, whose it is, but what it is. God's judgment proceeds on just what the man or the deed before him is in itself, apart from birth or race or religious connection.

3. The second verse begins with "we know." What is known requires no proof. The statement of verse 2 is self-evident. Hence the connection is not in the way of argument; it is rather an appeal against a false and perilous reckoning.

You do the very things you condemn in others, but irrationally think that you will escape their punishment. This delusive self-estimation is always found in the false religionist.

4. The case may be worse than a vain, false estimate; the man may despise God's means to win him to a better life. Against this contempt the apostle makes another appeal, that ends in a solemn warning. God has not only shown some "goodness" to the Jew; He has been rich therein. He chose the Jew in the past; His providence watched over him; He sent him great kings and prophets, and finally the Messiah, and made him the leading nation of the world. Toward the Jew's waywardness and unthankfulness God was patient ("forbearance"). This patience extended not only over all the former times of Jewish history, but especially in the latter years when the Messiah was rejected and His messengers slain. It is this continued patience which is called "long-suffering." All this goodness the Jew despised, looking upon it as his desert, and ignoring the fact that it ought to lead him to repentance. The case is going hard against the Jew, though he is not yet named. The Gentile had none of this mercy to move him, and yet was a condemned sinner; the Jew had it and treated it with contempt. What is he?

5. This verse answers. In accordance with ("after") his hardness and impenitence of heart, though judgment did not at once come, he was heaping up for himself daily a treasure of wrath in that treasury of wrath, the day of the righteous judgment of God. The blackest of sins is not rights violated, but mercies despised, and such sins were accumulating against the Jew on that record which can neither be evaded nor disputed. God's is called "righteous" judgment to contrast it with the Jew's.

6. After this solemn appeal under the first principle of the judgment, Paul brings in the second, "to every man according to his deeds." This really constitutes the closing sentence in the appeal, and thus shows that a judgment according to truth and a judgment according to works or "deeds" are practically the same thing. The former is abstract; the measure applied in the judgment will be reality. This (v. 6) is concrete. That which is measured will be what is done, "deeds." The judgment will embrace "every one." That there is to be a judgment was not denied by the Jew; it cannot be denied by any sober man; and therefore Paul brings no proof in evidence. In that judgment, sure to come, God will render to every man according to his deeds.

7-10. The first principle was followed by an appeal. This second one is followed by an appositional sentence in exposition of what "deeds" appear in the judgment, and their awards. It is quietly implied that there are but two classes of men, and consequently but two kinds of deeds. These are set forth in a striking antithetical parallel, as is shown by the Rev. John Forbes, LL.D. (*Analytical Commentary*, pp. 7, 146), from whom we adapt:

"Who will render to every man according to his deeds:

Good
1. To them who by patient continuance in well-doing [character]
2. Seek for glory and honor and immortality [pursuit],
3. Eternal life [award]:

Bad
4. But unto them that are contentious [character],
5. And do not obey the truth, but obey unrighteousness [pursuit],
6. Indignation [shall be] and wrath [award],

Bad
7. Tribulation and anguish [award],
8. Upon every soul of man that doeth evil [pursuit];
9. Of the Jew first, and also of the Gentile [character];

Good
10. But glory, honor, and peace [award],
11. To every man that worketh good [pursuit];
12. To the Jew first, and also to the Gentile [character]."

There is a wealth of parallelism here which nothing but careful inspection can discover. The thought is given in four triplets, balanced against one another. The first two are introversively paralleled with the second two, and the lines in each pair of triplets show the same feature. This gives us first the statements about the good and the bad, followed by similar statments about each party in the reverse order, the reversal being not only in the triplets, but in the lines composing them. The three lines in each stanza, for such they may be called, give first the character, then the purusits, and finally the appropriate awards, both of the good and of the bad. This is the order in the first couplet.

In the second couplet we have it reversed: first the award, second the pursuit, and third the character. In the very first line of the first couplet we have character in the patient continuance of well-doing; the pursuit is glory, the award is eternal life. This is followed in the second stanza by the opposite kind of character: contentious, exhibiting itself in an opposite kind of pursuit, obedience to unrighteousness, with its opposite award, indignation and wrath. In the third stanza Paul takes these up in the reverse order and goes over them again: the sad award of tribulation and wrath for him who in his pursuit "doeth evil," whether in character Jew or Gentile, and the glorious award of honor and peace for him who in his pursuit "worketh good," whether in character Jew or Gentile.

By this parallelism richness of exposition is gained, both by the repetition and the contrast of the lines. The exposition of the "deeds" is given in two opposite directions: first from the character of the doer, through his work up to his award, and, conversely, beginning with the award, we go back through the work and reach the character.

In this appositional unfolding of the deeds we see they are more than mere acts. They embrace both the character and the aim of the doer. Every deed has three elements: the source from which it comes, the aim, and the concrete act. The deeds, then, are, first of all, deeds of the heart, patience, and a right aim on one side, and contentiousness and disobedience of the truth on the other. And thus it is seen that the second principle of the judgment, an award according to "deeds," is pretty much the same as the first, an award according to "truth," or what a man is.

Some difficulty has been found as to the harmony between this principle of the judgment and the doctrine of salvation by faith. This difficulty arises from a misconception of Paul's view of faith. He is not speaking here of faith's beginning, but of its completion; not of justification, but of judgment. The deeds that gain a reward clearly imply faith in him who does them. For in the opposite side of the parallel indignation and wrath are said to come to those who do not obey the truth, but obey unrighteousness; that is, this sad award comes to them as a result of their unbelief. Moreover, Paul saw no contradiction here, for he closes the discussion (verse 16) with the declaration that the judgment will be according to his ("my") Gospel.

11. This is the third principle which will hold in the judgment—"no respect of persons." Paul had said that men would be rewarded according to their deeds, whether they were Jews having the law or Gentiles excluded from the law. This verse comes in as a reason for that statement. God will not inquire in the judgment about a man's outward religious connection. If his deeds are right, his being a Gentile will be no detriment; if they are wrong, his being a Jew will be no excuse. This phrase about respect of persons is used in the Bible only in connection with judgment, and so here it is limited to this single point. It will not serve a man in that awful day to claim that he was an adherent of a true system of doctrine.

12. The "for" at the head of this verse introduces it not as a proof—that comes later—but as an explanation of what Paul means by the words "no respect of persons." Those who sinned without law—men can sin where there is no written law—shall also perish without law. Men can sin and perish, too, where God's Word was never heard; but they will perish "without law," that is, without such penalties as must meet those who knew the law and did not do it. And as many as have sinned in the law (of Moses) shall not be saved, but judged by that law.

13. The "for" brings in a proof of the last statement. A man may hear the law read every Sabbath day in the synagogue, but if he does not do the things enjoined by it he fails. For the only virtue in hearing the law lies in hearing to do. This is exceedingly simple. A child might hear his parent's command, might admire the clearness of his voice and the

perspicuity of his words, but what of this approval if he did not obey and do as told? The child could not be held just. In these two verses, 12 and 13, substitute "gospel" for "law" in reading them, and they present the truth and the admonition suited to modern times.

14. "For when Gentiles [omit "the"], which have not the [written] law." This verse clearly shows that hearing or having a holy law cannot recommend a people to God. It is a proof of the statement in verse 13. The argument lies in this, that Gentiles have what is tantamount to the moral law. If having a law will save the Jews, why should the Gentiles not also be saved? This is an *ad hominem* thrust. It struck at a vital part in the Jew's prejudices. If he claims immunity because of his law, the Gentile is equally safe; but that a Gentile as such could be saved the Jew would not for one moment admit.

It must have been generally known that there were among the Gentiles at least some who "by nature" did the things of the law, pure men who knew the right and loved it, who looked upon God as one and a person. Noah and Melchizedek, Abraham and Job, are examples.

15. This verse merely continues the thought of the last— that Gentiles are not devoid of that in which the Jew boasts and trusts. The Gentiles' conscience bears testimony to this fact along with their works. Their inward thoughts are in constant debate one with another, one thought accusing or else excusing another. How could this be unless some standard of right and wrong existed by nature among the heathen?

It must be noted that Paul does not say that the heathen have the law written on their heart, for this is the characteristic blessing under the new covenant (Heb. 8:10). God in regenerating grace certainly gives something more than that which the heathen already have. Paul says they show not the law but its "work" written on their heart. A machine may show the work of intelligence, but it has none.

Again, while Paul asserts that Gentiles may have what is equivalent to the law, he does not say that they are saved by that possession or that they can be; rather the reverse, that if the Jew can be saved by his law, why not the Gentile by that which belongs to him? The discussion comes to just this: that the Jew in his claim for his law is claiming too much. If the law will save him, is not the Gentile saved too? For he has virtually the same. Paul would drive the Jew from his false mooring and leave him at sea. There is nothing else even by implication in the argument.

16. This verse lays down the fourth principle. Paul says, "God shall judge the secrets of men . . . according to my gospel." The connection is not with the twelfth, as some editions of the King James Version would indicate by their parentheses, but with the thirteenth verse. Verses 14 and 15, containing the argument for the third principle, are parenthetic. Without the interruption of this proof matter, the thought runs: "The doers of the law shall be justified in the day when God shall judge the secrets of men."

Here we learn the meaning of the word "justify" on its first occurrence in the epistle, for surely God will not at the judgment-hour make these good who have already shown themselves good by being doers of the law. The word cannot mean "to make," but "to declare good."

We have seen above, under verse 6, that the "deeds" are largely deeds of the heart. Hence Paul speaks here about judging the "secrets" of men. Only the doers of the law will pass the judgment, but the law is not done in God's sight except by the incarnation of it in the heart. Paul is in strict harmony with the Sermon on the Mount. The deeds to be judged are not alone those which are seen in the life, but those which God sees in the hidden chambers of the inner man.

"According to my gospel." There is no antithesis between law and Gospel when both are rightly understood. When Paul says "my" Gospel he indicates the broad and universal turn which he has given to it, unfolding it in a way suited to men of every age and nation. It had its origin in one nation, but it is not a national gospel; it is world-wide. Paul's keenest weapon against the narrow Jewish error lies in this word "gospel." The judgment will not be according to law, which by the Jewish interpretation left relation to Christ out, but according to the Gospel, which makes relation to Him the chief factor in the judgment. The Gospel is the standard of judgment; the Judge, the day, the deed, the standard. The Judge is just, the day is certain, the deed is known, the standard is the Gospel. God judges, but Jesus Christ holds the court. "He hath committed all judgment unto the Son" (John 5: 22; Acts 17:31).

Having now unfolded these four principles of the judgment, Paul speaks directly to the Jew in what may be called the minor premise in the argument (vv. 17-24). The major premise comes to this: that the judgment is of such a character that sinners, no matter who they are, Jew or Gentile, cannot stand in it. This minor premise shows the Jew that he is a sinner, but the proposition which embraces both premises is that the Jew who judges the Gentile does the same things. In proof of this, Paul proceeds in the method used in the first chapter against the Gentile: first, that he knew the truth, but, second, refused it, and so, finally, fell into the sin of idolatry, sensuality, and general immorality. We have the same method and the same three sins.

17-20. These verses show what light the Jew had, the light not of nature only, but the clearer revelation of the law. In five particulars he claimed personal privileges above other men: "restest in the law ... makest thy boast of God ... knowest his will ... approvest the things that are more excellent," and "instructed out of the law." In five other particulars the Jew was "confident" that his knowledge was superior to that of the Gentile. He claimed to be "a guide of the blind ... a light of them which are in darkness ... an instructor of the foolish ... a teacher of babes," having "the form of knowledge and of the truth in the law." In these ten items of the Jew's superiority the law is mentioned three times. On this point of knowledge Paul merely declares of the Gentile that he had it (1:18-21), but when it comes here to the Jew he convinces him out of his own mouth. It was the Jew's claim and boast that he knew.

21a. In the beginning of verse 17 it should read, not "Be-

hold," but "If thou art called." It begins the first member of
a conditional sentence, the second member of which is found
in the first question of the verse before us. Paul does not assert; he only asks a question, a question that can have but
one answer: If you are a Jew, claiming full qualification to
teach blind Gentiles, do you not thereby teach yourself? Do
you not *know?* This is the first point in proving that the Jew
"does the same things" as the Gentile. He knows God, yea,
by his own confession he knows vastly more than the despised
Gentile.

21b, 22. The Jew had all the means extant in his time of
knowing God's will. The verses now in hand show his sad
failure in doing that will. Paul does not assert that the Jew
was guilty of these three sins of idolatry, sensuality, and immorality; he puts it significantly in the interrogative form.
This means that his questions could have but one answer. In
the first chapter, in dealing with the Gentile, he proceeds
from idolatry to immorality. This order is reversed in the case
before us. He proceeds from immorality, "Dost thou steal?"
to idolatry, "Dost thou commit sacrilege?" or, to follow the
Revised Version, "Dost thou rob [heathen] temples?" This
change in the order is easily accounted for. In the first chapter Paul is giving the origin and development of sin among
men: he follows the natural order. But when it comes to the
Jew he writes climactically. Idolatry was forbidden by the
very first commandment. The Jew claimed to be free from
it and professed to abhor it; and yet Paul more than intimates
that he is guilty of this foolish, debasing crime, the worst of
all sins. He mentions it last because it is blackest.

There is not sufficient information today to show what is
meant by Paul's allusion to the robbing of temples. In his
day the Jews did not actually worship idols, and he does not
charge them with the sin in this form. But it seems that they
did not hesitate, in the various heathen lands in which they
lived, to purloin the treasures deposited in these temples (Acts
19:37) and to take the accursed stuff (Deut. 7:25, 26) into
their own houses.

23. Twice now Paul mentions the light-giving law, which, with the question asked, "Dishonorest thou God?" condenses into one compact, condemning whole all that has been said beginning with verse 17. The verse does not advance the argument; it sharpens it and brings it to a focus in the word "dishonorest." This is the odiousness of all sin; it tarnishes the glory of God's name.

24. Five questions have just been asked, the first expanded in the next three, and the last condensing them again to an arrow-point; but Paul does not directly answer them. But this twenty-fourth verse, beginning with "for," gives a reason for asking them, and that reason is the answer. It must be that they are guilty under these three counts, for, just as Isaiah wrote long ago (52:5), God's name is blasphemed among the Gentiles because of the Jews. The latter claimed to be a holy people knowing the true God, and the heathen among whom they dwelt did not stop with contempt of them for their hypocrisy; they exhibited that contempt toward God himself. Says Beet (*Commentary, in loc.*): "Men around think less of God because this man lives among them and calls himself a disciple of God. It were more for the glory of God, and therefore for the good of those who know this man, if he were a professed heathen."

Thus far Paul has shown that the Jew is a sinner like the Gentile. The next step will be to drive him from his refuge in the rite of circumcision. This was the outward mark which distinguished the Jew from his heathen neighbor and showed him to be a descendant of Abraham.

25. "For . . . thy circumcision is made uncircumcision." This first mention of the rite in the epistle comes in abruptly and therefore startlingly. The "for" introduces the discussion as a confirmation of what was said in the two previous verses. You dishonor God and lead the Gentiles to despise Him, for your circumcision is no advantage to you.

Circumcision profits if one keeps the law, for it was not intended to be an atonement for wrong living, but a spur toward right living. It is a seal, and what is the value of a seal when torn from that which it was intended to certify? To be

content with the rite while neglecting that for which it stood
is to behave like him who should take a money sign ($, £)
for the money itself. By wrong living circumcision failed of
its object and became uncircumcision, or exclusion from sonship with Abraham.

26. "Therefore." Here is a fair deduction. If the aim of
circumcision was uprightness, and if a heathen exhibited the
latter—if he has the substance, what odds if he lack the sign?
Bullion is gold, though it has no government stamp upon it.
In the scales of the judgment whose principles have been so
clearly laid down, will he who has the rite without the righteousness outweigh him who has righteousness without the rite?
This question needs no answer.

27. This verse also comes in under the "therefore" above.
"By the letter" ought to read "with the letter," invested with
the letter of the law and with circumcision. Would that be a
judgment "according to truth" in which he who had the law
and the rite should stand after having transgressed both, while
the upright man who never had either must fall? Will the
sinner who has the law pass where the righteous man will fail
because he has not what never was given to him? Yes, if God
were seeking legal rather than real obedience. But since the
latter is his delight, the man who has it under the disadvantage
of no law will be a burning condemnation to him who, despite
the law to teach him, has failed to hear its voice. Cornelius
far outweighs Caiaphas; for Caiaphas with his circumcision
was at heart one with heathen Pilate against Jesus, while
Cornelius without circumcision was at one with Peter in following truth.

The principle involved in these three verses is that a religious rite is worthless unless it is attended with goodness—
"patient continuance in well-doing." (See also John 8:31.)
And this principle is solemnly applicable today in the matter
of baptism. Read the passage above, substituting "baptism"
and "no baptism" for "circumcision" and "uncircumcision"
respectively, and the verses become modern.

28, 29. In describing, as Paul does here, the real Jew, that
he must be such at heart in that which is within, Paul is in

harmony with his fourth principle of the judgment. God will not look on that which it outward, but will judge the "secrets" of men. That circumcision must be of the heart was not Paul's invention; it was as old as the law (Deut. 10:16) and the prophets (Ezek. 44:9). This statement of what constitutes the veritable Jew is made in justification ("for") of the sentiments in verses 25-27. If verse 25 degraded the more formal Jew to the Gentile level, verse 28 tells why; and if verses 26 and 27 elevated the good heathen above the professional Jew, verse 29 presents the substantial reason. He who is right at heart is in God's sight a Jew even though he cannot trace his fleshly descent from Abraham. He is not a Jew who is only one outwardly, in dress, in profession, and in subjection to ceremonials, and circumcision is not accomplished with a sharp knife; but he is a Jew who is right within, where only God sees; for circumcision pertains first of all to the heart, a cutting off of man from all evil. The phrase "in the spirit" serves to define the word "heart." The man must not only intend right in his heart, but he must be right in his spirit. Circumcision is not effected by the "letter" of the law. Some think, however, that by the word "spirit" Paul means the Holy Spirit. In this case the word would give the means rather than the definition of a genuine circumcision, and it would stand in antithesis with the word "letter."

This second chapter, then, in showing that the judgment is concerned wholly with character and not at all with the outward ceremonials of religion, puts the immoral Jew among the sinners of the first chapter, because he does the same things, and his Judaism goes for nothing; circumcision will not shield him. But Judaism is God-given, and it is God who has made the broad distinction between circumcision and uncircumcision, a distinction which Paul seems to obliterate. This starts a serious objection to the line of argument, and this objection is noticed in the beginning of the next chapter.

CHAPTER 3

THE ARGUMENT ON SIN CONCLUDED (Vv. 1-20), AND THE SECOND MAIN DIVISION OF THE EPISTLE— RIGHTEOUSNESS—BEGUN (Vv. 21-31)

PAUL (1) answers an objection (vv. 1-8) and (2) concludes with a scriptural argument for the universality of sin (vv. 9-20). Beginning the second grand division of the epistle, (3) the righteousness that saves is described (verses 21-26), (4) a righteousness that excludes the Jews' boasting (verses 27-31).

1. "What advantage then hath the Jew?" This is one of the profound questions of the epistle. If circumcision in itself does not give righteousness, if uncircumcision does not preclude it, what profit was there ever in it? A distinction that God made among men seems, after all, not to be one. Paul must answer this objection to his argument for the sinfulness of the Jew. He does this fully in chapters 9—11. Here he considers it only briefly and only so far as it blocks his argument about sin. His readers, especially Jewish ones, could not follow him another step until this hindrance in the line of thought is removed.

In asking the question, "What advantage then hath the Jew?" of course he does not mean the true Jew ethically, described in the closing verses of the last chapter, but the Jew nationally. What is the profit of Judaism if in itself it does not save from sin and presents no advantages over heathenism? There are not two questions in this verse; the repetition is a Hebrew parallel, used for the sake of perspicuity.

49

2. "Much every way." This is the answer, brief and unmistakable. It was written at a time when Christianity was
practically established all over the Roman Empire. There
were Christian churches everywhere, and yet Paul says there
is much "advantage" in Judaism. For centuries the religious
world has overlooked this verse and has thought and written as
if Judaism were a mere relic of a dead past. Paul was everywhere planting believing communities composed of Jews and
Gentiles—communities in which these and all other distinctions disappeared (Gal. 3:28); and yet he declares the Jew as
such has "much" left in his favor. Has Paul's view of the matter become obsolete? When in the course of the centuries
after Paul's day did the Jew lose his advantage over Gentile
Christianity?

He tells in what the advantage lies. It is not that Judaism
prepared the way for something better, for we have seen that
that supposed better thing, the Church, was already in existence when Paul affirmed the superiority of the Jew. His advantage was not that God sowed Judaism and the world reaped
Christianity. That blots out Judaism. It was first of all "that
unto them were committed the oracles of God," not that they
were made a mere Bible depository, but that God gave them,
as Jews, promises, not yet fulfilled, and peculiarly their own.
The Old Testament, the record of these oracles, contains not
one promise either of or to the Church as an organization. It
does not predict a Church; it foreshadows a kingdom in which
the Jew shall be head and not lose his national distinction as
he does in the Church. Dr. Adolph Saphir, himself a converted Jew, a man who deserves to be better known both for
his profound scriptural knowledge and his Christlike piety,
says: "The view that is so prevalent, that Israel is a shadow of
the church, and now that the type is fulfilled vanishes from
our horizon, is altogether unscriptural. Israel is not the shadow
fulfilled and absorbed in the church, but the basis on which the
church rests (Rom. 11). And although, during the times of
the Gentiles, Israel, as a nation, is set aside, Israel is not cast
away, because Israel is not a transitory and temporary, but an
integral part of God's counsel. The gifts and calling of God

are without repentance. Israel was chosen to be God's people, the center of his influence and reign on earth in the ages to come. The church in the present parenthetic period does not supplant them. The book of the kingdom awaits its fulfilment, and the church, instructed by Jesus and the apostles, is not ignorant of this mystery" (*Christ and the Scriptures,* p. 64).

3. "For what if some [Jews] did not believe?" The "for" bears on the assertion that the Jew, as such, has much advantage. In spite of his disbelief of the gracious promises made exclusively to him in the Old Testament oracles, Paul asserts his superiority, for the unbelief of "some" will not make God untrue to His promises to the nation. As God's long-given promise to send Israel a Redeemer was not defeated by the nation's deep sin and hypocrisy, so His promise to give the nation headship cannot be made void by their disbelief of the promise. He who could give unbelieving Israel a Saviour can also give the same people that for which the Saviour came, a universal kingdom of righteousness.

4. To the question, "Shall their unbelief make the faith [faithfulness] of God without effect?" Paul replies vehemently, "Let God be true, but every man a liar." Between the terms of this reply and those in the preceding verse there is an instructive change. There he said, what if "some" disbelieved; here he answers, let "every man" do so. Again the unbeliever there is in this verse defined as a "liar," and finally the "faith" of God is reproduced in the word "true." What if some did not believe the oracles intrusted to them? Shall their lying, yea, shall the lying unbelief of the whole nation, so turn God that He also shall not be true to His own oracles? Why does Paul teach that an unbeliever is a liar? It is easy to see how his unbelief makes God a liar (I John 5:10). Unbelief is lying, because it virtually pronounces unworthy of trust that which is the truth of God. And so when God eventually makes good His promises to the nation, not only will the unbelievers be seen to be liars, but God will be "justified" in all His Old Testament sayings, and will "overcome" when He is judged, for He was misjudged. In such an hour—and it is coming—

His faithfulness to His promises will shine with added luster,
because it was kept with those utterly unworthy of it. If Jesus
Christ is not the Son of God, and if through him the Jewish
race is not ultimately redeemed, then His rejectors are the
world's wise men; but if God's plain but far-reaching promises
are made good by Him, then unbelievers will be found liars,
and God's glory will shine the brighter on the dark background
of their unworthiness and sin.

Paul has now answered the Jew's objection which arises
from placing the Jew and the Gentile on the same level in the
church. For the present there is no advantage in circumcision
except the possession of certain national promises which the
Jew alone has. The answer comes to this, that the Jew must
not confine his view to the question of salvation from sin,
where indeed he is on the same plane with the heathen—trust
in Jesus; nothing else, not even circumcision, will avail, but
he must remember that in addition to this salvation God has
promised him a high place of honor in the world. Peter and
Cornelius were both sinners, the one circumcised, the other
uncircumcised, and both were saved from sin by the same
means, the forgiving grace of God. So far they are alike, but
now when saved Peter is made an apostle and Cornelius is
not. Here is a difference. And neither the Old Testament
nor the New can be thoroughly understood until one perceives
the analogous likeness and difference between Jew and Gentile. They are saved alike, but their future standing in the
earth is not alike.

We might start an objection here not noticed by Paul, and
most likely because it is not a real one. To what Jews will
God make His oracles good if all are found liars? The Scripture quoted here from the experience of David (Ps. 51) may
answer. It was not until he was given penitence for his sin
that he could say of that very sin that it justified God in His
sayings and gave Him victory when judged. Repentant Israel
will find the "advantage," and they are promised repentance
(Acts 5:31; Rom. 11:26).

5. But while Paul does not notice such an objection, if indeed it is one, he does see a real hindrance in the way of his

argument. It does not come in abstractly. The context clearly shows that Paul had actually met it in his experience in dealing with the subtle, wily Jew. You have shown, says the opponent, that God's promises, when they come to pass on Israel, will appear all the more gracious on account of the nation's previous unbelief. Our obstinacy has turned out to His glory: why should He punish us for that which has been a favor to Him? "If our unrighteousness commend the righteousness of God," is not God unjust to punish us for that unrighteousness? Paul shrinks in placing these two words "God" and "unrighteous" together, and declares he is not speaking as a believer, but as a "man."

6. His reply to the question comes at one blow—"Then how shall God judge the world?" For the world is unrighteous too, and its sin makes conspicuous God's love toward it. If God may not punish the Jew for the reason here mentioned, neither may He punish the Gentile, for the same reason can be urged in the latter's case. And so all judgment is at an end. This is the *ad hominem* argument again. The Jew could not admit that the wicked Gentile world could go unpunished.

It must not be overlooked that Paul does not let this discussion of sin drift away from the light in which he began it—the light of the judgment. And he still keeps both Jew and Gentile in view. Where the latter can find no cover, neither can the former.

7. This verse does not advance the thought. It individualizes the previous statement about the "world." The world's sin has made God's mercy toward it all the brighter, and so each man in the world might come before God with the claim that His glory had been advanced by the man's lie, and on this ground claim exemption. But while this does not advance the argument, it quietly intimates that not a single sinner will escape the judgment.

8. Paul now with one stroke brings the whole objection to its logically absurd conclusion. If sin enhances the glory of God, and therefore is no longer guilt, why, the more we sin the brighter His grace. Let us do all the evil we can, for the more evil the more praise to His name! Some had affirmed

that this is the apostle's own doctrine. In their righteous condemnation of it they condemn themselves in the claim that God cannot punish sin, because it promotes His glory, for this claim is the very essence of the hateful sentiment. And thus he has come around in most skillful fashion to the assertion with which he began against the Jew: "Thou art inexcusable, O man, whosoever thou art that judgest: for wherein thou judgest another, thou *condemnest thyself*" (2:1). He joins with them in repudiating the godless maxim, but he does not go with them in holding it. They "slanderously report" him who say he does.

9. Here the argument (see (2) above) from Scripture for universal sinfulness begins. In the words, "What then?" the whole course of thought from the beginning (1:18) is looked at, as much as to say, How does the question about sin stand now? Whether the next little sentence should be rendered as in the King James Version, "Are we better?" or as some others, "Have we an excuse?" is not easily decided. The translation of the Revised Version is wide of the mark. The answer to the question, whatever that question is, shows that Paul now has both parties in view, both Jew and Gentile. This would decide against the King James rendering, which can embrace only the Jewish party. In looking back over the argument, as the little interrogation, "What then?" directs, we see that Paul has argued the guilt of both parties. One refuge after another was beaten down. Does any remain? Have we an excuse? Is there no refuge for men? Then comes the sweeping negative, "No, in no wise," and in justification of this negative he refers to what he previously said about both Jew and Gentile, that they are all under sin. Note that he does not say with the King James Version that he before "proved" it; for while he has made it very evident, the clinching proof comes only now, and it comes from Scripture. The selections are from various Psalms, from the Prophets, and one (v. 15) from the Book of Proverbs (1:16). They are arranged to give, first, the character of men, second, their conduct, and finally, the cause of their sin. They can be presented to the eye thus:

1. Character (vv. 10-12).
2. Conduct $\begin{cases} \text{speech (vv. 13, 14),} \\ \text{action (vv. 15-17).} \end{cases}$
3. Cause (v. 18).

10. "None righteous, no, not one." The striking little repetition "no, not one," makes the preceding assertion all-comprehensive. In the divine estimation of the nonrighteousness of the race there is not a single exception.

11. "None that understandeth." The apostle taught before (1:21, 22) that men became "fools." They did "not seek after God," though they sought everything else. The word "seek" implies not that God is concealed, but that man is lost. As these passages are proof texts of sin, the failure to understand and to seek God is sin. A negative attitude toward the truth is positive transgression.

12. "All gone out of the way." They knew the right way, the Gentile by the light of nature (1:20, 21) and the Jew by the law (2:17-20); but they deliberately forsook the path where God's light shone for their own way of darkness. They are "together [without exception, again] become unprofitable." The last is a picturesque word, signifying something that once was good and useful, like meat or milk, but has grown corrupt beyond recovery. As Paul began this section on character with the sweeping statement that there is none good, so he closes it with the equally inclusive statement that no one "doeth good." All their religious works—and they are many—are conceived in sin and are therefore unrighteous.

13, 14. Speech was given to man for his honor and blessing. He turned it to his own shame. See the whispering, back-biting, boasting, in 1:29, 30. "Throat," "tongues," "lips," "mouth," an anatomical order from that which is inward to the outward. The throat over a corrupt heart is like an unfilled grave, with the putrescent corpse lying at the bottom—a terrible picture for a Jew, or for anybody, for that matter; the tongue, a means to praise God, become an instrument of craft; the lips—think of those of Judas—deadly with the old serpent's poison; and the mouth, made to be full of innocent laughter

(Ps. 126:2; Luke 6:21) and joyous praise, befouled with cursing and bitterness.

15. Their action is no better than their speech. "Their feet are swift"—they run eagerly to commit murder and make war.

16. "Destruction and misery are in their ways." What have the old nations that have run their course left in the path behind them? Each empire has built itself up on the ruin of all others. It is an adage, "Blessed is the nation that has no history," for all history is but the annals of strife and human woe.

17. "The way of peace . . . not known." This is the other side of the last verse. Peace is a stranger to the world.

18. "No fear of God before their eyes," for they turned their backs on Him. This lack of reverence for Him and His revelation is the fruitful source of this "mosaic of sin." It is to be noted that what is a subjective condition of heart is here spoken of as if it might be outward, "before their eyes."

19. This plain Scripture proof of man's sinfulness having been adduced, the next step is to show to whom it applies. The Jew might say it is inspiration's estimate of the heathen world, but cannot refer to him. No, says Paul; "we know that what things soever the law saith"—he calls the Psalms and other books from which these quotations are selected, the law —"it saith to them who are under the law," that is, to the Jews. These sentiments about the character and conduct of men and the cause of their sin do describe the Gentiles, but are intended first of all as a condemnation of the men to whom they are spoken and in whose Bible they are recorded. Might it be possible for us to delude ourselves today in a way that Paul would not allow the Jew to do—that these pictures of sin are photographs of that distant age, but not of ours? But have we not the same "law" then possessed by the Jew? And has the principle—it is a principle—failed, that what the law says it speaks first of all to them that have it?

Paul goes on to give the object of his quotations: they are intended to stop "every mouth," that of the Jew especially, and to show a whole world guilty before God. It is a condemned world, condemned by the Judge himself. To save it or any man in it, there can be no means but His mercy.

20. The word "therefore" is a mistranslation. Paul is not drawing a conclusion, as this word would indicate, but is about to demolish the last stronghold of the Jew. For "therefore" read "because." All the world is guilty before God "because" by deeds of law shall no flesh be justified, accounted righteous, before Him. Many Jews were rigorous observers of the law. Paul's own righteousness in it had been perfect (Phil. 3:6).

In proving all men sinners, he was well aware of the Jews' scrupulous attention to the behests of Moses, but he demolishes their last refuge in declaring that law-works cannot save. After all of them are done, they leave a man in sin (Gal 2:15, 16). The reason law cannot save is because it has neither the office nor the power of salvation. In one word Paul gives its office; "by the law is"—not justification—"by the law is the knowledge of sin." It has an office and "is good, if a man use it lawfully" (I Tim. 1:8). But one might as well attempt to cross the river on a millstone as to get into Heaven by works of law. If he would sink without the stone he must sink deeper with it. If the Gentile perishes "without law" (2:12), much more will the Jew, who has it, for it only makes his sin apparent.

It is to be observed that he does not say that only the law has this office, nor that this is the only office of the law. Men have "the form of knowledge and of the truth in the law" (2:20). It is a permanent revelation of divine righteousness. Again, it is said to be "a schoolmaster unto Christ" (Gal. 3:24) and to have been made for the lawless (I Tim. 1:9). The offices of the law are various. On the other hand, sin is revealed not only by the law, but by conscience, as the apostle has already taught (2:15), by the Gospel, and especially by the Holy Spirit (John 16:8, 9). When Paul says here that by the law is the knowledge of sin, he is just asserting in the most emphatic manner that the Jew cannot hope for salvation by its observance. It cannot lift him out of the wide morass of his sin; it only shows him how deep and how hopelessly he is in.

This brief but radical statement about the office of the law would startle the first readers of the epistle, especially the Jewish ones, and lead them to expect something more on the topic. And Paul presents it, but not here. Indeed, the law is a chief topic to be considered. The most serious Jew would ask, Has God given Israel a code that, after all, cannot save? The question confronts the Gospel at the start; Jesus met it (Matt. 5:17-20), and Paul will in due time.

And here it may be as well to notice that this is a characteristic of the epistle, to touch a subject and then drop it for a full treatment farther on. We have had three such instances already. The righteousness by faith was mentioned and at once left at 1:17 for the discussion about sin. It is taken up again as the next topic, and forms the main line of thought to the end of chapter 8. The advantage of the Jew was broached in 3:1-4, but will not be noticed again until chapters 9-11, where it is fully considered. The third case is this one about the law, glanced at again in 5:20 and 6:14, but the full exposition is withheld until chapter 7. Romans 3:21 is the text of chapter 4. Finally there ends with 6:13 a very short exhortation, taken up again in the first verse of the twelfth chapter as the theme for the rest of the epistle. Rigid attention to the course of thought shows the necessity for this first mention and later development, and accounts logically for the place where each comes in.

The first main division of the epistle forms a powerful negative argument for the second, and was evidently so intended. Since man is a sinner with no help in himself and none in the law, what is left to him but to look to the mercy of God? Every son of Adam is not only lost, but condemned. His penalty is continuance in sin not only while he sins, but because he has sinned. This is the wrath of God, the proposition which begins the first main division (1:18) and is proved in it. All the world is "guilty before God." In a court of justice it is only after every defense has failed and the law itself has been shown to be broken, it is only at this point that the appeal is made to the judge for his clemency. The epistle has brought us to such a point.

This division extends to the close of chapter 8, and contains two leading thoughts: first, justification (3:21—5:21), and second, santification (chaps. 6-8). These theological terms are used instead of the more Biblical ones, "righteouness" and "holiness" because Paul embraces under the former both justification and sanctification, both the removal of guilt (3: 21—5:21) and the power of right living(chaps. 6-8). For clearness of thought, theology separates these two and discusses them apart. Paul includes the two in the word "righteousness" and even in the word "justify."

21. With this verse Paul begins the description of that righteousness which avails before God. (See (3) above.) It might read, "An apart-from-law righteousness of God has been revealed." This gives Paul's order of the words. The definite article before the word "righteousness" is omitted in modern translations. He told us in a former verse (1:17) that it is in the Gospel that this righteousness is unveiled, or, as here, stands in clear light. The word "now," meaning as the case, the argument, now stands, shows how gladly Paul turns from the painful matter of sin to its sure remedy. A sigh of relief can be heard in the particle.

Just one point is made so far about the righteousness: it stands apart from the law, has no vital connection with it; its source is elsewhere. Paul says just this in Philippians 3:9. He does not define the word. Something of its contents is given in I Corinthians 15:3, 4. Of course it is not God's attribute, so called, for that is not the special revelation of the Gospel; neither could it be said of that attribute that it is a righteousness by faith. The Gospel tells where this saving righteousness is found—in Christ; on what condition it is gained by a sinner —faith; what are its present fruits—love, joy, and peace; and what is the outcome—eternal life. Paul's readers knew all this, and therefore he limits himself to other points, equally important, found in the paragraph before us.

"Being witnessed by the law and the prophets." While denying one relation between the law and the Gospel, Paul never forgets to insist upon another. There is no breach between the Old Testament and the New. The ceremonies and the prophecies of the Jewish Bible could not give life; they did not develop the Christ; but in His springing "out of Judah," in His being "made under the law," and in His resurrection "according to the Scriptures," they become a powerful and ever-living witness to Him. A shadow never gives birth to substance, but substance to shadow. The shadow of the law answers exactly to the substantial righteousness of the Gospel, from which the shadow arose, and testifies that they belong together. How the ceremonies of the law pointed to Christ is elaborately unfolded in the Book of Hebrews. The tabernacle, the lavings, the sacrifices, all pointed to Christ. The prophets bore direct verbal testimony to righteousness to come just as it did come. The Gospel, when it was first preached and as Paul preached it, must have seemed like a subversion of the ancient documents, so new and radical was it. But Paul found it harmonizing with these same parchments, when read under the new light burning in Christ; and He stands for and stands on the "living oracles" (Acts 7:38).

In this verse, then, Paul has given the first item in describing the new righteousness; it is apart from the law, but not contrary to it.

22. He tells us next the source of this righteousness—it is "of [from] God"; he gives its leading characteristic—it is not a by-works, but a by-faith righteousness; he points to him on whom alone the faith must rest, Jesus Christ, for right faith is faith on the right object; he asserts the universality of its provision—it is a righteousness for all; he gives the condition of its bestowment—it is for everyone who believes. It is to be observed that faith, first the noun and then the verb, is mentioned twice in this verse. Commentators are either silent here or confused. Even Meyer, correct in his exposition of the first mention, but surely wrong at 1:17, says nothing about the second. The lack of clearness arises in not observing that when faith is first spoken of in the verse it belongs to the description of the righteousness, and in the second instance it teaches how the righteousness is attained. The first is objective, the second subjective. As a righteousness by works is secured by works, so a righteousness by faith is secured by faith.

"For there is no difference" between Jew and Gentile. This little sentence gives the reason for saying that the righteousness is for "all." All need it, and no class of men has anything else to present before God for salvation.

23. "For all have sinned." This shows what Paul means in saying there is no difference. He does not mean that they have all sinned to the same degree, but if any man has sinned at all he has failed, and cannot be saved by any other means than faith in Christ. Paul shows next the consequence of universal sinfulness; all sinned and are coming short, in successive generations, of the glory of God. He changes the tense from the past to the present. He does not say that all men come equally short of measuring up to the standard; but the standard is perfection—nothing else can pass before God—and the lack of an inch is as fatal as the lack of twelve. In this world he who sins but little is much better than he who sins much, but at God's bar neither will be accepted. There is "no difference." To sin at all is to lose all and to come short of the glory or praise of God. "Glory" in this place means the same as in John 12:43, where it is translated "praise." For man can have no higher glory than the approbation of God.

What Paul has to say in this and the preceding verse about sin is very brief, for the subject was fully discussed in the first section of the epistle; but this brief mention shows how this section is made vital by that one.

24. "Being justified freely." The subject of this participial clause is the "all who sinned" at the beginning of the last verse. Of course Paul does not mean to say that all sinners are justified. He had just declared that the condition is faith, and he need not say it again. To have inserted the word "faith" would have turned the attention from what he has to say, that sinners without exception are justified not by works, not by any means except those mentioned below. When they are justified, or if they are justified at all, it must be as here described. The present tense of the participle does not show a continuance of the act—justification occurs once for all—but a continuance in its spreading among men and generations that need it.

To justify does not mean to make (inherently) righteous, but to declare or pronounce righteous. (See remarks on 6:1.)

Two cases in which the word has already stood in the epistle show this (2:13; 3:4). In the first, men are said to be justified in the judgment. Can that mean that they are made right in that hour of award? In the next, God is said to be justified at that same time. He that is holiness itself can be declared so, and anything else is blasphemy. (See also I Tim. 3:16; Luke 7:29.) In Matthew (11:19) wisdom is said to be "justified of [by] her children." Her children recognize her excellence, and pronounce it such, but do not make her what she already is. To justify is in some sense a forensic act equivalent to "not condemned"; "he that believeth is not condemned" (John 3: 18), that is, he is justified on his faith. But the peculiarity of the divine court is that the sinner has been proved to be guilty and is known to be guilty—all the world is guilty before God —and after all is freely justified; while in the human court this is impossible. When one is justified or acquitted among men it must be either that his crime was not proved or that there were extenuating circumstances. But before God man is guilty and yet is justified on believing, but not for his believing. Man cannot justify a sinner; God can.

Paul proceeds to give three interesting facts—the very marrow of the Gospel—pertaining to the subject. First, as to the manner. All are justified "freely." It costs the acquitted person absolutely nothing, "without money and without price" (Isa. 55:1). Second, the source of the justification. "By his [God's] grace." This is His favor to the man not after he is justified, but before. It is grace toward the ungodly (Eph. 2:4, 5): He "loved us, even when we were dead in sins." Third, we have the means of the justification of grace. "Through the redemption that is in Christ Jesus." Note the relation of the two divine persons toward the justifying act. It is God who justifies; it is Christ who is the medium. God's grace comes in and through Christ.

25. In this and the following verse there are just two points: first, how Christ became redemption, and second, why. The redemption is from the wrath of God. The Jew had little trouble in understanding this point. As a sinner he knew he was under the divine displeasure, and brought therefore a bloody offering—an ox, a sheep, or a dove—by which to redeem himself from God's displeasure and render satisfaction for his sin. Paul now says God himself has set forth Jesus Christ in His blood as the propitiatory offering through faith. The phrase "in his blood" is to be joined not with the word "faith" immediately preceding, but with the verb "set forth." Philosophy and theology have busied themselves here, without reaching unanimity, on a question which Paul does not hint at—the relation of the sacrifice to its end. The apostle gives only the facts. God freely justifies men by means of the ransom power in Christ Jesus. He is such because God has set Him forth in His blood as a sufficient propitiation. Whatever reason may say about such a sacrifice, Paul is satisfied with it because it is God's own. God is satisfied with the offering, for He provided it. It becomes a propitiation "through faith," because faith says of it just what God does—I accept what God has provided for my sin. That ends the difference between God and the sinner, and they are at one in Christ Jesus. This is justification by faith.

"To declare his righteousness." With this Paul begins to answer the second question, why Christ Jesus was set forth as a redemptive sacrifice in His blood. His answer will not satisfy unless his exposition of sin is accepted. Man's sin is not misfortune; it is guilt. God's wrath burns against it; why should that wrath ever cease? Again the Jew could answer. His law bore witness (v. 21) to the Gospel. The smoking altar where he offered his lamb or his bullock not only testified that God could remit the offerer's sin, but declared also that God was holy. Justice demanded the life of the sinner and a life was given in that of the bloody offering. Justice justified because justice was satisfied.

The word "righteousness" in this sentence does not mean the same as in verse 21. To insist that a word must in every instance of its use have the same signification is subversive of all understanding. Such a notion is contradicted by the facts. The word "glory" has already been used in two widely different senses. Righteousness here looks at God's character as Judge. The question now before us is, How can a righteous

Judge pronounce a guilty sinner guiltless? Paul's answer is that the redemptive sacrifice in Jesus Christ, a sacrifice foreshadowed in the Jewish altar-offerings, declares the divine righteousness in showing mercy. The chief question in saving man is not how the man may be accounted just, but how God may remain so in forgiving his sins.

"For the remission of sins that are past, through the forbearance of God." The Revised Version is preferable: "Because of the passing over of the sins done aforetime, in the forbearance of God." These are not the sins committed by the believer before he came to Christ, but the sins done under the old economy, before Christ came (Heb. 9:15). It is not said that God forgave these sins; not even, with the King James Version, that He remitted them. To all appearances, in all past time He paid no attention to sins; He overlooked them ("winked at," Acts 17:30), without meting out adequate punishment (Ps. 78:38). Sometimes in the history of the race He sent judgments, now against the Jews and now against the Gentiles. The Jews were driven more than once into captivity, and more than one heathen nation had been overthrown; but as judgment for man's sin, this was nothing. Inspiration's just estimate, in spite of these severe visitations, cries that there was on God's part a "passing over of the sins done aforetime," as if the just Judge had not rightly weighed their guilt. There was a thick veil over His righteousness, but the cross removed it and demonstrated His judgment of sin. The terrible tragedy of the cross, on which God set forth His Son in His blood, is His measure of man's demerit. The punishment that man so long escaped fell at last on the Son of Man.

Now, while the death of Christ Jesus looked back thus at the sins of the whole race, and while He died "because of the passing over of the sins done aforetime, in the forbearance of God," it is by no means taught that the race was saved. What is taught is very clear, not that Christ died to secure the righteousness of men, but to rescue the righteousness of God from a misunderstanding. Says Godet (*Commentary, in loc.*): "For four thousand years the spectacle presented by mankind to the whole moral universe (compare I Cor. 4:9) was, so to

speak, a continual scandal. . . . Divine righteousness seemed
to sleep; one might even have asked if it existed. Men sinned
here below and yet they lived. They sinned on and yet reached
in safety a hoary old age. Where were the 'wages of sin'? It
was this relative impunity which rendered a solemn manifestation of righteousness necessary." Jesus died for men, but in
a much more striking way He died for God. What a fathom-
less depth of meaning He gave to the first petition in the
Lord's Prayer, "Hallowed be thy name"! How God hates sin!
For even overlooking it His honor demanded the blood of the
cross; how much more when He forgives it! And it is not
difficult to distinguish between the cross as a demonstration
of God's righteousness on one hand, and a propitiation looking toward man's righteousness on the other. It is a propitiation only through faith; it is a demonstration in itself. In all
time, past, present, or future, only those men are saved by the
cross who belive; but equally in all time the cross honors God
whether men believe or not. The cross, instead of saving all
men, does show, by its declaration of God's righteousness, and
show conclusively, that they are not saved unless they believe.

26. The cross stands midway in the history of the race and
looks in both directions in declaring God's righteousness in
His dealings with men. For this reason the phrase "to declare
his righteousness," in verse 25, is repeated here. The death of
Christ on the cross accomplished one great work and became
the means to another. It showed that God was not slack in
His dealing with the sins of the race in the past; it also declares
His righteousness in His mercy toward the believer now, "at
this time," a phrase in contrast with the word "past" in the
preceding verse. But this phrase conveys also the fitness and
significance of the era of the cross. It was the time foreseen
and chosen by God for His marvelous display of His own holy
character. In after years men came in some sense to recognize
the meaning of this period by dating time from the birth of
Christ. What the Antichrist will at the last attempt to do
(Dan. 7:25) Christ had the right to do—create a new era.

"That he might be just, and the justifier of him which [who]
believeth in Jesus." This is the grand purpose of God in set-

ing forth Christ in His blood. On this setting forth the three main ideas in these two verses depend: set forth to declare God's righteousness in the past; set forth to declare God's righteousness "at this time"; and set forth that He might be just, and the justifier of him who believes in Jesus. But why does Paul mention the retroactive influence of the cross? It is his argument, first of all with the Jew and ultimately with all men, to cut off the Jew from a false reliance on his past history. It explains history. History cannot interpret the Gospel; the Gospel interprets history. Jew's history was not complete, his sacrifices never atoned, until Christ died on the cross, which death showed that God had dealt with men not as they deserved and not strictly in accord with His character as a righteous Judge. The sacrifice on the cross demonstrates for the first time what God is and shows that in times past and present He is the same—"of purer eyes than to behold evil" (Hab. 1:13).

If God set forth Christ in His blood as a redemptive and propitiatory sacrifice in order that He might be just in justifying the believer, then we gain with certainty the meaning of the words "redemption" and "propitiation." God could not be just without the sacrifice of Christ; it was made in order that God might be just; therefore it must be said that Christ died for men and that His blood was their redemption price (Gal. 3:13; I Pet. 1:18, 19). The judge could not release the bankrupt man until his creditor was satisfied. For Christ did not die that God might seem to be just, but that in fact He might be just in the very act of justifying the believer. It is a righteous thing as well as a merciful thing for God to forgive a believer; but the sinner cannot plead this right, since he did not provide the ransom; God did in Christ, but the sinner's Saviour can plead it for him. Justification is an act of righteousness toward Jesus Christ, an act of mercy toward the sinner. If mercy is not made prominent in this description of righteousness, it is because Paul is looking at the primal difficulty in saving men. It is not how to get men to God, but how to get God to men—how a just God is to pronounce a sinner just. The wisdom of men never could have removed this difficulty even if they had seen it. It is completely taken away in Christ Jesus.

The paragraph (vv. 21-26), then, has just two topics: the righteousness that avails, and its bestowment, justification. It may be outlined thus:

Righteousness
1. Its source—"God."
2. Relation to law { (a) "Apart from" it; (b) "Witnessed" by it.
3. Chief characteristic—"Faith in Jesus."
4. Condition—Belief in Him.
5. Its extent—"Unto all."
6. Reason for this extent—"No difference."

Its bestowment
1. How { (a) Manner—"Freely." (b) Cause—"His grace." (c) Means—"Redemption that is in Christ Jesus."
2. Why by blood—"That God might be just, and the justifier of him which believeth in Jesus."

This brief but masterly exposition of righteousness, like the sun, is its own evidence. But it found great opposition at the start, not in heathenism, but in pharisaism. The Jew could claim that his God was the true one, his religion a revealed one, and its documents inspired. (See his boast in 2:17-20.) It is not the false, but the perverted religion that furnishes the chief obstacle to the truth. And Paul begins here to answer the perversion. Indeed, the direct exposition of the righteousness by faith ends with the twenty-sixth verse. If the epistle had ended there it would not have been incomplete. All the rest is a consideration of objections, in which the further unfolding of the righteousness is only incidental.

27. "Where, then, is the boasting" on the part of the Jew? How can he claim anything over the Gentile? Righteousness does not arise from his law; he is a sinner like the Gentile, and the salvation in Christ is universal. "Where, then, is the boasting? It is excluded. By what [kind of] law?" What sort

of institution? One whose chief characteristic is prescribed works? No; where a man does works of law to be saved, he can boast of them and boast of the law that warrants them. Boasting can only be shut out by a law, an institution, whose chief characteristic is faith. For faith says first of all (Luke 18:13) that man is so hopelessly, helplessly a sinner, so guilty even with all his law-works, that God's grace alone can save him in Christ. If a man believes, he cannot boast of that; for even if it is denied that faith is God's gift, it is nothing to a man's credit to trust God. While it is the chief of sins not to do so, trust is every man's bounden duty.

It will be noticed here that Paul claims the same distinction for faith that the Jew does for works; it is a law, a new and wholly different law—not a law of bondage, but a "law of liberty" (James 1:25). He also sets the two in sharp antithesis. Faith and works of law are mutually exclusive.

28. "Therefore we conclude . . ." The Revised Version also reads "therefore," but it is not correct. It ought to be "for." And thus the verse gives the substantial reason for the exclusion of boasting. That reason is that "a man [any man, Jew or Gentile] is justified by faith [the latter is the emphatic word] without deeds of law." The last clause is more forcible by omitting the articles.

But why does Paul thrust so sharply at the Jew's boasting? Is it not because vain pride or prejudice is generally the last and strongest support of a bad case? The Jew's loud boast was his only argument, and it must be silenced.

29. "Is he the God of the Jews only?" The word "or" should precede—"Or is God the God of the Jews only?" This brings up the Jew's boast on another side. His claim that law-works justify involves a position which he cannot maintain— that there must be more than one God, one of the Jews and one of the Gentiles. It is proved now that there can be but one way of justifying men, the way of faith, a way suited to the Gentile and in flat contradiction to the Jew's way of works. Now if the Jew sticks to his course, there must be two Gods, for the same God cannot save men by opposing methods. It is easy to become confused here. Paul is not contending for

justification by faith. That doctrine is settled, settled with the close of the twenty-sixth verse. He is arguing now for its exclusiveness, that it is the only true doctrine. The Jew claims that the works of law will save; Paul has proved that faith saves. If both are true, God is not one. But the Jew admitted that his God was the God of the Gentiles. The Old Testament gives abundant proof of this in the Psalms and in the prophets. (See Jer. 10:7.) It was freely admitted during the ministry of Jesus (Mark 12:32), so that no one would dispute the saying, "Yea, he is the God of the Gentiles also." The Jew's boast in his works denied this, or it was a groundless boast.

30. "Seeing it is one God." The Revised Version changes both the reading and the rendering: "If so be that God is one." The change in reading does not materially alter the sense; the change in translation is a gain in that it brings out the idea of the unity of God. Because God is one there can be but one way of justifying men. A righteous judge could not render contradictory decisions where all are alike guilty, and certainly he could not decide in such a way that his judgment to save some would necessarily exclude others. The unity of God makes salvation by faith exclusive of every other means.

It is to be noted that Paul's argument on this whole subject of justification by faith, beginning with the twentieth verse, is so far theological. It is based on the character of God and on His unity. The Jew admitted His holiness and His oneness, but his deduction that justification came by works of law was utterly inconsistent. He reached this false conclusion because he was ignorant of his sinfulness. It cannot be said too often that a false theology finds its source in inadequate views of depravity.

Paul excludes the works of the law from justification, and yet the Jew's Bible prescribed them, and in a most solemn manner: "The uncircumcised man . . . hath broken my covenant" (Gen. 17:14). The apostle's argument so far is unanswerable; it is based on solid theological data; but from the very start he has claimed that it is also scriptural. It has a documentary defense, being witnessed by the law and the prophets.

31. This last verse of the third chapter serves to bring up this question. Faith excludes works; does it, then, evacuate the Book of works, as the Jew supposed it to be? The negative comes with a shudder—"God forbid." Paul will teach nothing contradictory to what he has already called the Holy Scriptures (1:2). For the word "law" here does not mean the ceremonial or even the moral law, but the whole Old Testament. "We establish the law." The next chapter shows how. He does not confirm it by abstract theological reasoning, but by exegetical exposition of its utterance.

CHAPTER 4

RIGHTEOUSNESS BY FAITH IN HARMONY WITH THE OLD TESTAMENT SCRIPTURES

THIS CHAPTER answers the question raised in the last verse above, and shows the concord between Moses and Paul, between the law and the Gospel. The points are four. (1) Abraham, with whom the Jewish nation began, was justified by faith (vv. 1-5), the method celebrated in song by their greatest king, David (vv. 6-8); (2) Abraham was justified long before he was circumcised (vv. 9-12); (3) the promise that he should be the heir of the world was by means of faith (vv. 13-17a); (4) the faith demanded by the Gospel is none other in character than that which Abraham exercised (vv. 17b-25).

1. "What shall we say then that Abraham . . . hath found?" The variations in the reading of this verse do not seriously affect the sense. As Abraham was the father of the faithful, Paul seeks in the record of his life how he was justified. What did Abraham, our forefather, find or obtain "according to the flesh"? This phrase is to be joined with the verb "hath found" and not with the word "father." It means, What did he find by his own natural efforts in contrast with that which is spiritual? The phrase is almost equivalent to this: What did he gain by religious works? The word "flesh" stands for the whole natural man, body, soul, and spirit, and not for the physical part only. Hence the Scripture can speak of "the will of the flesh" (John 1:13).

2. "For if Abraham was justified by works." The "for" does not give the answer to the question about Abraham, but the

reason for asking it. The Jew rightly assumed, with Paul, that the head of the nation was justified, but the question is, How? by what means? If by works, then he has something of which to boast. He can point to these words; he can "glory." The conditional sentence ends with this word "glory," which is rightly followed, both in the King James and the Revised Version, by a semicolon; for that which follows, "but not before God," is Paul's own solemn assertion. Admitting that Abraham was justified in some way, Paul declares that it was in such a way that the nation's head had nothing to boast of before God. Paul's declaration is the proposition now to be proved.

3. "For what saith the Scripture?" This is Paul's support of his point that Abraham found nothing of his own to glory in before God. In the Scripture, in the law, it is written: "Abraham believed God, and it was counted to him for righteousness" (Gen. 15:6). It was not his natural works but his trust in God that was set down to his account. The history, a part of which is here quoted, leaves no room for works. God made Abraham a supernatural promise, and the patriarch believed it, and that belief was set down to his account for justification. And since there is no merit in believing God, because it is every man's duty to do so, it was God's mercy, God's grace, that "counted" Abraham's act of faith to his credit.

4. Paul might have dropped the question with the Scripture quotation, which clearly proves that Abraham did not work, but believed; but he gives an exposition of the latter part of his quotation almost in syllogistic form. It is a general principle that a worker's "reward" or wages is a "debt" due him for his work. But Abraham's reward, justification, was "counted" to him, was bestowed on him as a favor. It follows, then, that he was not a worker. If he was, the word "counted," implying grace, could not be used. It is no favor to a man to pay him what he is earning. It is a "debt" due him. Dr. Shedd (*Commentary, in loc.*) quotes *Coriolanus* (Act 2, sc. 3) here:

> Better it is to die, better to starve,
> Than crave the hire which first we do deserve.

5. "But to him [anyone] that worketh not [the case of Abraham], but [on the other hand] believeth on him [God] that justifieth the ungodly [individual], his faith [his believing] is counted [to him] for righteousness [justification]." Abraham was justified; this is not disputed. He did not do works to reach this happy position before God; therefore nothing is left to which to ascribe his salvation except his believing. This verse has not the form, but all the force, of a deduction from what precedes. It is the fundamental and guiding principle in obtaining the favor of God. Abraham stood before God in his sins. They were not forgiven. God made him a promise that was against human reason, and the patriarch put his trust in it and relied upon it. And now, on the condition of that trust in God's Word, God pronounced him no longer guilty of sin. He had not uttered a prayer, he had not done a religious deed, he was not a good man, but "ungodly," and yet he was justified. The term "ungodly" does not necessarily mean depraved, but simply without acceptable piety. But after all it is an elastic term and can include the utmost departure from moral rectitude. God's justification reaches believing men in whatever sins it finds them.

It may be said that Abraham was a believer long years before the incident in his life cited here by Paul; and so he was. "By faith Abraham, when he was called, . . . went out, not knowing whither he went" (Heb. 11:8). But it is nowhere recorded that this act of faith justified him. It was not a faith against reason, but a commendable following of the guidance of God. If any kind of faith in God—faith in His existence, faith in His goodness, faith in His almightiness—justified, why, who would not be saved? The faith that saves is narrow, specific, and resting on one single item, the Gospel, as Paul soon shows. Abraham had been a good man and even a believing man, as was Cornelius (Acts 10:1-6), and all this was no hindrance to justification, but in the way of it. Justification, however, did not occur, at least there is no record of it, in the case of Abraham until he believed God's supernatural promise. And Cornelius was not justified by his goodness; he had to hear the Gospel to be "saved" (Acts 11:14).

6-8. "Even as David." Another most eminent man in Jewish history is cited in favor of "righteousness without works." David's testimony would be conclusive with a candid Jew. The introductory words "even as" show his exact accord with Paul's reasoning about Abraham's justification. David uses the same language in describing the felicitation (not felicity) of the man to whom "God imputeth righteousness without works." David is just citing his own case (Ps. 32:1, 2), when he had none but most evil works to show. "This righteousness is not ours, otherwise God would not gratuitously impute it, but bestow it as a matter of right; nor is it a habit or quality, for it is 'without works'; but it is a gracious remission, a covering over, a nonimputation." It is God's sentence of acquittal, pronounced on the sinner when he believes God.

At first sight there seems to be a serious disagreement between what Paul sets out to prove and the citations from David in attestation. Paul's proposition is that God "imputeth righteousness without works." The quotations mention neither righteousness nor works, but speak about sins being covered—the only instance in the New Testament where this language is used—and about "the man to whom the Lord will not impute sin." But to "forgive" clearly implies "without works," and to "cover" implies the presence of the sins at the moment when the mantle of grace falls on them to hide them. They could not be covered if they had not been there when the gracious concealment took place. This is the first point in the proposition of "no works." The second, about "righteousness," follows in the eighth verse, for the nonimputation of sin is necessarily the imputation of righteousness. There is no conceivable state of the heart between the idea of no sin and that of righteousness. Where there is no darkness there must be light.

9. "Upon the circumcision only, or upon the uncircumcision also?" With this verse begins the discussion of point (2) in the concord between the Old Testament record and grace. It is now proved by that record that a man is justified by faith without works. Does this blessed way of saving men belong to the Jews only? "For" it was proved only in the case

of him who is the father of the Jews, Abraham. This puts the question into narrow limits. The universality of justification by faith must now be proved from Abraham's case; and this proof Paul proceeds to furnish.

10. "How was it then reckoned?" Paul is not now inquiring after the condition on which Abraham was justified; for it has already been established that that condition was faith. But what was his own personal or religious standing when he believed and was justified thereby? Was he a heathen or a Jew? Was he circumcised or uncircumcised? Paul declares he was in the latter condition, and submits this assertion without proof, for the history of Abraham was conclusive on the point. In Genesis 15 he was declared just. After this Ishmael was born, and when thirteen years old (Gen. 17:25) he and Abraham were circumcised on the same day; that is, Ishmael was in his fourteenth year, a number very significant in the estimation of Paul's Jewish readers.

This was a tremendous blow to any who claimed that there could be no salvation (Acts 15:1) without this principal Jewish rite. Israel's own father was a justified man fourteen years before it was imposed.

11. "The sign of circumcision." A new question now confronts Paul. If the rite did not confer justification, if Abraham was saved so long before it, what was its office? what did it accomplish? Here is a reminder of the objector's question at the beginning of the third chapter—"What is the profit of circumcision?" In answering Paul deals another heavy blow to the opponent. The rite, instead of conferring righteousness, confirmed that which Abraham already had, in that it was a "sign" and seal of it. Circumcision attested the validity of Abraham's faith—righteousness in uncircumcision. In no dispensation do rites bestow anything; they are the shadow, not the substance; they are a seal. But the seal is worthless apart from the matter or from the document that it attests. The Jew had torn off the seal from the covenant and then vainly boasted of this meaningless imprint.

"That he might be the father." After using circumcision and the relative time when it was given as a telling argument for justification by faith and without works, Paul now shows the divine intent of the rite. Without it Abraham would have been father of the Gentiles only. With it he becomes father of the Jews also. Thus quietly he puts the Jew in the second place so far. Abraham is called father neither in a physical nor in a spiritual sense. He is father in that he is head of the faith clan and so the normal type. He is the head and father in the fact that he was the first in whom God showed how men are to be saved.

"Father of all them that believe, though they be not circumcised; that [in order that] righteousness might be imputed unto them also." In showing that Abraham is father of "all," father of both Jews and Gentiles, he mentions the latter first. The patriarch was saved without circumcision, by simple faith; so may the Gentiles be saved. The subordinate sentence, "That righteousness might be imputed . . ." depends on the word "believe" in the preceding one. Gentiles in their uncircumcision believe in order that righteousness may be reckoned to them, just as Abraham believed to become, in God's purpose, their father and type.

12. "And the father of circumcision." God's gracious thought to save the world antedates, so to speak, His thought of Israel. Israel was the means to the universal end. Hence after Abraham was made the father of the believing Gentile he was circumcised that he might become the first of a circumcised people; thus he was head or father of both classes. But Paul, by adding qualifying statements, carefully excludes the unbelieving Jew from salvation in the Abrahamic descent. If he was justified in uncircumcision he was circumcised in a condition of faith. And faith is the vital element in establishing saving descent from the patriarch. Without faith there is no circumcision (Phil. 3:2, 3); for Paul's qualifying sentences show that Abraham is not father of those "of the circumcision only"; they must *also* walk in the steps of the uncircumcised faith of the patriarch—"that faith of our father Abraham, which he had being yet uncircumcised."

Paul has turned the Jews' boast upside down. It is not the Gentile who must come to the Jew's circumcision for salvation; it is the Jew who must come to a Gentile faith, such a faith as Abraham had long before he was circumcised. Paul's reasoning here has been called a piece of "rabbinical scholasticism." Is it not rather a plain but solid exposition of the historic facts in Abraham's history?

That Abraham circumcised his sons, from one of whom the circumcised Jewish nation according to the flesh sprang, has nothing whatever to do with the point which Paul is here considering. It is Abraham himself and in his belief that is the father and model of all God's people. He was not circumcised to be saved; he was saved by faith and then circumcised for a wholly different purpose, as Paul has shown, that he might be father of a race of circumcised men. Faith saves; nothing else ever did or ever will. Circumcision is a pledge of nationality, because Israel as a race is never to cease. Faith is the condition of life for all men. Circumcision is a token of the headship of Israel among the races of men—a headship to be gained when Israel as a nation adopts also Abraham's faith. Isaac's circumcision when eight days old (Gen. 21:4) was not, as in Abraham's case, a seal of righteousness, for the babe had none. And what did Ishmael's circumcision "seal"? Ishmael and his descent, though circumcised, were never in the Jewish covenant, but "cast out" (Gal. 4:30). Men have never been able to rid themselves of the delusion that circumcision has something to do in securing salvation; but Abraham was a saved man many years before the rite was given. Circumcision secures not salvation, but nationality. Abraham received it to become father of a faithful circumcised nation, Isaac to perpetuate the national promise, and Ishmael because God said, "Of the son of the bondwoman will I make a nation, because he is thy seed" (Gen. 21:13). When Isaac was saved he was not saved by his circumcision any more than was his father before him. God never promised salvation except to faith; He never promised a perpetual nationality except to circumcised men who believe. Abraham is head and father of both kinds of men. Isaac is not; he is first in the national line. Here was the Jew's fatal mistake. He practically took Isaac in his eight-day-old circumcision for the model of a saved man, and not Abraham in his faith.

Another error on this verse is to be avoided—that Paul is showing and explaining how both Jews and Gentiles in his day came together in the church, how Abraham was the father of the church composed of both kinds of people. But the church knows no nationality, and Paul is not considering the church in this epistle. It is not mentioned till the argument has closed. The theme of the epistle and of this verse is world-wide, world-long salvation in Christ, in which all men shall share, and ultimately the Jew as a Jew. It is a defense not of the church, but of faith. The Jew thought circumcision saved; Paul shows that it only points to nationality when the Jew believes.

Can the question still be asked, "What is the profit of circumcision?" Paul has already given one rich word in reply (see on 3:2); here he has conceded that Abraham is the national head of the Jews, and incidentally that their promises, of which the fleshy mark is the token, still stand (11:28). The full answer to the question is postponed, for here his main point is that salvation comes only and wholly by faith.

13. "For the promise, that he should be the heir of the world." The course of thought still depends on the proposition in 3:31, that salvation by faith without works of law establishes the law; it conforms to the law. In proof of this it has been shown from that same law, a part of which is the history of Abraham, that he was saved by faith and he was saved before that prime article in the law, circumcision (Gal. 5:3), was given.

With this thirteenth verse point (3) is taken up. Paul, in verses 11 and 12, had used three times the common Jewish designation for Abraham, "father." Israel's boast and trust was "We have Abraham to our father" (Matt. 3:9). As father he had obtained in promise an inheritance for himself and his posterity, in accordance with which promise Isaac was born. Now it is on his fatherhood in this light that the "for" of this verse bears. Paul admits with the Jew that Abraham is father and thereby heir; but as he becomes father by faith, the thing already proved, so he also becomes heir by faith. This last must be argued, and the word "for" introduces the proof. The patriarch before Judaism existed had obtained the grace of justification not as a Jew, but as a man; but in addition to this favor he also got the promise that he and his seed in time to come should possess the world. The Jews contended, even the best of them (Acts 15:5), that the latter favor was on the ground of law. Paul disputes it. His argument is not drawn from Scripture, but from the faith now proved and from the holiness of God. This thirteenth verse does no more than to deny the false assumption that the promise of heirship to Abraham and to his seed was to be realized by means of the Mosaic law, and to assert that that promise is to be made good by means of a faith righteousness.

14. If the assumption were true, that "they which are of the law," the Jews as such, were heirs, then two impossible things must be conceded to follow: first, faith is out of the question, "is made void;" and second, the promise itself is nugatory or "of none effect." But that there is no righteousness but by faith, that Abraham obtained his righteousness by faith, has already been proved. Paul, therefore, does not argue this point, but proceeds to discuss the next one.

15. Why would the promise be nugatory if conditioned on the keeping of the law? "Because the law" cannot realize any promise based on its observance. It cannot work out a promise to him who is under it, for he does not keep it, and so law only works out "wrath" to him. God is holy and cannot suffer the least infraction of His commands; and Paul has already shown the whole nation under sin (3:9-20).

"For no law, . . . no transgression." Instead of "for" all modern versions read "but." Where there is no written law man is still in sin. God expects nothing else of man, and in His grace can provide for his rescue, and is not hindered by transgression in showing favor. But when man is under law he adds to his sin the aggravation of transgression, and the divine grace is estopped. It is shut out not only by the violation of the law, but by the holiness of God, who must vindicate His law. Therefore the promise of heirship was given to faith outside of law that there might be no transgression to defeat the promise.

16. This verse concludes and so repeats the proposition under debate, adding some amplifying details. It begins with very elliptical language, as the italic words in the King James Version indicate. The case is now so plain that Paul rushes to the conclusion in the fewest words: "Therefore of faith, in order that according to grace." The ellipses can easily be supplied from what precedes. "Therefore [since law cannot realize anything but wrath] it [the promised heritage] is of faith [or "by faith"], that [in order that] it might be by grace [or a gift to believing sinners]." Even if the heritage could have been earned by keeping the written law, none but the Jews had the law, and they only would have been heirs. But as their law only brought wrath and not the promise, the latter could have come to neither party. So God conditioned it on faith, which is possible to all men, "to the end [with the intent] that the promise might be sure [surely given] to all the seed [both Jew and Gentile, as the rest of the verse declares]." In specifying that part of the seed which belongs to the law he does not mention faith again. It was not necessary, because this had just been declared to be the condition on which "all" the seed could inherit. Note that, while the twelfth verse refers to one class, the Jews, with two characteristics, this verse refers to both classes with but one characteristic, faith.

It is not without much hesitancy, even after prolonged study, that at this point the great commentators cannot be followed. Meyer, Forbes, Alford, even Bengel, make this third point to be a further discussion of justification by faith, as though this were synonymous with the words "heir of the world." Godet just once touches on what is the matter here considered, but then immediately drops it: "Believing Jews and Gentiles, we all participate by faith not only in justification, *but also in the future possession of the world.*" The words which we have italicized in this quotation are the key to this third point in the chapter. The subject is not justification; that ended with verse 12. The subject is clearly and unmistakably announced at the head of the paragraph—that

Abraham and his seed had the *promise of heirship of the world* on the ground of faith. The heirship of the world does not mean that Abraham was to have an elect number of believers in all nations, that he was to be "the father, federal head, and pattern of all them that believe" (Forbes). Abraham was set forth as a father and pattern in the second section (vv. 9-12). Why should Paul be supposed to be repeating that, especially when he has pointedly given the topic of this third section?

Furthermore, the topic is not that Abraham by his faith should be a model to his spiritual progeny; both he and they are taken together, and it is declared of the father and the children in common that the heirship of the world is theirs. It is not that Abraham's seed is such only by faith, but that Abraham's seed gets the possession of the world by faith.

It must in justice be said that Meyer (*Commentary, in loc.,* pp. 205, 206, T. & T. Clark) admits this view, but further along he seems to relapse to the other. The Epistle to the Romans must be studied historically and not as a theological thesis on faith. The Jews of Paul's day had a definite and pronounced eschatology, easily ascertained (Luke 2:30-32), based on many clear promises (Jer. 3:17, 18), and it gives the key in more than one place; it is the key here. By the law they hoped not only for salvation, but for universal dominion of the world. Paul no more denies their eschatological hope than he does their hope of salvation. His contention so far is not only that both can be realized by nothing but faith, but that this is the teaching of the law itself. The law promises to Abraham's seed the possession of every nation, but that possession is to be gained by faith.

"Abraham, who is the father of us all." This repetition of what we already had in verses 11 and 12 is brought in here in order to return to that which was the main subject there, faith, whose vital element must be considered now in what remains of this chapter.

17a. "As it is written." The quotation is cited hardly in confirmation of what Paul has said, but to show the harmony between him and the Scripture. The first step was that Abraham was justified by faith; the second, that he was justified in uncircumcision, and, though afterward circumcised, the object was not salvation, but that he might be father of both divisions of men, Gentile and Jew. The third point is that he and the men who make him father are heirs of the world. This heirship is not by law, which could not realize it. And so as a man of faith he is not only father of all, but father of all their hopes for world supremacy. It was to him as a believer that it was said that he should be a father of many nations. Hence Paul's doctrine of faith conflicts with the Jews' Bible neither in the matter of salvation nor in the matter of their world hope. "Father, . . . before him [God] whom he believed." In God's sight he was a father by faith before he had a son. Why should the Jews labor to get into their hands by law what they may have at once in God's purpose by the faith of Abraham?

17b. "Even God, who quickeneth the dead." Here begins point (4) above. These first words show in what character of God Abraham believed in Him. The present tense shows what is always true of God. If a Jew says he believes as sincerely as Paul, it cannot be denied; but suppose he complains that Paul in presenting Jesus as an object of faith is demanding a different faith from that in the Old Testament, this can be shown to be false. Old Testament faith rests on resurrection. Acceptable faith is not merely the conviction that there is a God and that He is benevolent and a just rewarder of the good and evil; this is the world's faith. Abraham's was more; he became the father of many nations by believing in God as one "who quickeneth the dead." He not only believed in God's existence and that He could bless; this is not sufficient; he believed that that blessing could only come from God as now active in nature for spiritual ends—a spiritual creator just as once He was a creator of nature. Faith gets its character from that character in which it accepts God. Abraham looked on Him as one who in spite of nature is making alive the dead. This is the leading thought in this section. God calls the things that are not, not in the possibilities of nature, as if they already were; He calls them into existence. Natural nations come in the course of nature; but when God asked Abraham to look to the stars and said, "So shall thy seed be," did He mean a natural seed and natural nations? Isaac was not a child of nature, but a child of faith, and Abraham's seed are not children of nature.

18. "Who against [all rational] hope believed in hope," the supernatural hope which God's promise awakened. Let the Jew who thinks that he is Abraham's son reflect that Isaac, from whom all sprang, was brought into being by the same power that raised Christ from the dead.

19. "He considered not his own body." The "not" is in dispute; critics are divided on its genuineness. Whether we read it or do not read it, the sense is much the same. In the former view it would be said that Abraham's faith was so strong that he never once looked at the tremendous difficulty in the way of his becoming a father. Weak faith looks at difficulties and scarcely looks to God. Strong faith looks at God who has promised, and does not see the difficulties. In the other view Abraham did "consider" the difficulties, his own body now dead and the deadness of Sarah's womb, but still believed. He estimated the hindrances at their full weight, but did not "stagger" under the load.

20, 21. Abraham's faith was threefold. Two elements are already given: the character of his faith in that it accepted what is tantamount to the resurrection, and the strength of his faith in that it was superior to all hindrances in its way. The third element is its worshipfulness. By it he gave "glory to God"; he did this by trusting God where reason could not follow. When faith's only reason is God himself it honors and worships Him.

These three elements are now summed up in what might be called Abraham's creed. It is simple but comprehensive. The character which he ascribed to God, his estimate of the difficulties, and his worship come to this: a confident persuasion that what God had promised He was able also to perform.

Anyone can believe in God's power abstractly. Everyone who believes there is a personal God believes also that He is omnipotent; but saving faith stands alone in saying that God can make His supernatural promises good. What is not ascribed to God's word is not ascribed to Him; and the heart is only cheating itself into self-deception on one side or superstition on the other that believes something else than what He has revealed. A man's measure of God's Word is the measure of that man's faith in God.

It might be thought that Abraham should have believed in God's willingness rather than in His ability to carry out His promise; that the question is not what the Almighty can do, but what He will do; that the account should read, "that what God has promised he will perform." But God's will is already indicated in the promise to make Abraham a father of many nations; His word is His will. The only question is, Can He bring that supernatural promise to a reality? Any heart can say that God can do natural things; faith says He can do things beyond and above nature. And all God's saving promises transcend nature; they rest on the supernatural.

22. "And therefore it was imputed." The word "therefore" is instructive and impressive. Because his faith stood on the word of God—a word that nothing in nature could explain—because his faith was of this character, it "was imputed to him for righteousness." There is a natural faith that can accept much, and it is beautiful and salutary, but its highest exercise does not attain to justification. It falls far below Abraham's in that he trusted in a personal promise which nothing but the direct activity of the God who gave it could make good. This is supernatural faith, and only such is imputed for righteousness.

23, 24. Paul in citing Abraham's faith declares that its description is not primarily in honor of the patriarch. The story is not written for his sake alone, "but for us also." If the patriarch found righteousness by believing in God as one who quickeneth the dead, is the apostle's insistence upon faith in the resurrection of Jesus an unscriptural demand? Paul asks no more than Abraham exhibited in his life. He asks the same—faith in God who raises the dead. The Jew believed in one God; he did well; but this was not the whole of his great ancestor's faith, who believed also in resurrection. On the

ground of such faith he was saved, and no one can be saved
on any other.

25. "Who was delivered for, . . . raised for." Why was this
twenty-fifth verse added? Why did the story not close with
the twenty-fourth? To show that the faith that saves is not
faith in the act of resurrection, but in its import. He who
is justified must believe not only that Jesus died and rose
again, but why. He died "for our offenses." This word
"offenses" brings to view again the whole somber picture of
the first main division of the epistle, the division about sin.
Sin was such that nothing but the blood of Jesus our Lord
could atone for it. But His death does atone, and therefore
no works of law find any place in justification. And so it
comes to pass that he who believes in the resurrection believes first of all that his own personal sins sent Jesus to the
cross and the tomb, that He was the all-sufficient sacrifice for
sins. It is only painful conviction of sin that can believe in
this way.

But if faith stopped at the tomb it would be only an agony.
It also sees that, while Jesus died for sins, that death was accepted as the ransom price (3:24), and so Jesus was raised
again. He who became surety for the sinner's debt could not
have been released from the prison-house of the tomb unless
the debt was paid. His reappearance from the tomb is an
everlasting proof of the sufficiency of His atonement for our
sins; and he who really believes in the resurrection believes
that the guilt of his sins is canceled. Faith is no longer an
agony but a joy, and the believer's heart is set not merely on
the historic (II Cor. 5:16) but on the raised Christ. That He
was delivered for our offenses is pain; that He was raised again
for our justification is pure spiritual delight.

To believe in the resurrection of Jesus, then, is to accept
the two prime articles in the Christian creed, sin and grace;
sin that slew Jesus, and grace that accepts Him for our justification.

In this sentence, "delivered for, . . . raised for," it is easy
to misunderstand the preposition. This comes because the
mind unconsciously gives a different meaning to the two in-

stances of the same word. "For" means not only "with a view to," but also "because of." It cannot have one of these in one case, and the other meaning in the second; the parallel between the two clauses will not allow this. The first "for" cannot have the meaning "with a view to"; it must be "because of." Hence the second "for" has the same signification; He was raised not with a view to, but because of, our justification, just as He was delivered because of our offenses.

The difficulty raised is in assigning the sinner's justification to the time of the resurrection, and not to the time when he believes; but this is the manner and confidence of Paul. Elsewhere he refers the believer's regeneration, resurrection, and even glorification all to the same moment, and that moment the resurrection and exaltation of Christ (8:30; Eph. 2:5, 6). The difficult language, when resolved, furnishes great gain to faith. To be sure, no man has justification until he exercises evangelical faith; but the moment he does that his faith may be assured of its foundation. It does not rest on its own activity or in any experience, but at once finds its sure basis at the empty tomb; it rests on the Gospel. The man was justified in his believing, but not because of his believing. The cause is the grace of God made sure by the resurrection of Jesus.

But when it is said above that Jesus' reappearance from the tomb is a proof of the atonement, and when it is said just now that the resurrection makes grace sure, this by no means exhausts its office and efficacy in the means of salvation. The penalty of sin is death, and man was under it; he had lost spiritual life. The resurrection restored it, for when Paul says Christ was raised for our justification, he uses the word not in our modern theologic sense, but in an inclusive one that embraces all that is contained in 8:1, 2. (See remarks on Paul's use of this term just above the comment on 3:21.)

It is shown now that the law as recorded in Genesis proves (1) justification by faith, (2) in uncircumcision; (3) the promise of heirship by faith; (4) and that the required faith in Jesus is the same in character as that which Abraham had.

CHAPTER 5

JUSTIFICATION BY FAITH SECURES
THE FINAL SALVATION OF
BELIEVERS

THE RIGID HARMONY in four elementary points between the law and faith having been now exhibited, a new question arises, a question of hope: Will faith save at last, and will it save all, both Jew and Gentile? The two classes of men are not mentioned, but the discussion has a race-wide view that embraces all. In favor of the affirmative Paul makes three points as the sure ground of hope: (1) afflictions will not destroy, but strengthen it (vv. 2-4); (2) it has a sure basis in God's love toward the justified man (vv. 5-11); (3) as man's relation to Adam never fails to bring death on account of his one sin, so the believer's similar relation to Christ cannot fail to secure everlasting life on account of Christ's one righteous act at the cross (vv. 12-21).

Many commentators have entitled this chapter the "Fruits of Justification." This fails in both logic and history. Paul's first readers would be amazed to hear him speak here about fruits. Their cry would be, Is this method safe? Doing no works of law, what assurance does this faith in Christ's work give one for the future? Furthermore, fruits are immediate results in experience and do not need the rigid logical proofs exhibited in this chapter. And what "fruit" is there in the parallel between Adam and Christ?

1. "Therefore . . ." In view of the previous exposition of the doctrine, it can be said of "being justified by faith" that "we have peace with God." For "we have" many read "let us have." In favor of the former stands the American portion

87

of the Revision Committee, as well as Meyer, Godet, and others. Meyer says the imperative is "utterly unsuitable" to the sense. The question turns on the length of a single vowel, and the manuscripts are not trustworthy on this point; they frequently confound long and short o. The logic must decide.

"Peace" does not mean primarily tranquillity of mind, but that state of things ensuing from the cessation of hostilities, freedom from strife (3:17; Acts 12:20). This peaceful state came "through our Lord Jesus Christ," who averted the wrath of God. It is possible by not noting this meaning of the word "peace" that the mode of the verb was changed. For justification gives peace in this sense even when there may be no settled tranquillity of the heart.

2. "By whom . . . access by faith." The "grace" to which Christ gives access is the grace of justification. The first and the second verses both revolve about Christ. Through Him we have the peace; He procured it; and through Him by faith we gained access to justification, wherein the peace exists. The first verse looks at the standing of the believer, and the second recalls the hour of attaining it. The first verse has in view the redemption wrought at the cross; but it is only the justified man who gets it, and this justification is administered by God through Christ in the hour of conversion. The sentiment of these two verses up to this word "stand" is just a repetition of 3:24, a verse, with its context, that clearly implies the "peace" and the standing of justification by faith unfolded in these two. When justified freely by God's grace men have peace, and they have also a permanent standing as acquitted persons before God. The idea of permanence is doubly furnished by the tense of the two verbs "have" and "stand." These two verses up to this point, in unfolding 3:24, do in some sense show what may be called fruits—peace and standing. But this beginning of chapter 5 is, after all, but a repetition, a restatement, of what was given before, that we might start from the same point on a new line of discussion, the permanence of justification already hinted at in the two verbs above, "have" and "stand." Until this latter word is reached there is no advance; it begins with the very next sentence:

"We . . . rejoice in hope of the glory of God." This is the new theme: Is this hope well founded? Is rejoicing in it defensible?

What was said above on the reading "let us have" is equally true here on the wrong reading "let us rejoice." The King James Version is correct.

It is to be noted that the moment this new proposition is reached, after the restatement in verses 1 and 2 of what went before, the proposition that justification by faith is permanent, the word "faith," both noun and verb, is dropped. We have up to this moment had them constantly before our eyes—the verb nine times, and the noun twenty-seven times. Neither occurs again until 9:30, unless for the verb the solitary instance in 6:8 be counted an exception. But it is not, for in this place the word has rather the idea of being persuaded. (See John 20:8, 25, 27.)

The reason for dropping this leading word is obvious. Since it is the permanence of a faith-justification which is to be proved, that permanence must be established by other means than faith. If the latter should even once enter into the question we should have a *petitio principii*, a begging of the question, and the inquiry, But what about my salvation if my faith fails? would be legitimate. Faith is, after all, a personal experience, and the argument cannot be drawn from it. It is itself to be shown in its permanence, and the proofs are all brought from other and higher sources.

3, 4. "Tribulations . . . patience . . . experience . . . hope." For "we glory" in the third verse read "we rejoice," as in the second. The believer not only exults in the glory awaiting him on the ground of his justification, but he exults, too, in the tribulations or afflictions which beset him in the path leading to the glory. The latter rejoicing comes about because he is "knowing" the influence of these. They do not destroy his hope, but, on the other hand, by a regular process strengthen it. The storm-shaken tree roots the deeper. Justification does not give patience, constancy, or endurance; this quality does not come at the hour of conversion, but the trials and buffetings of the way thereafter serve to evoke it. A man with some worthy thing in view, like the glory of God, is prepared to withstand trials; but he who has no hope in the future frets under afflictions or seeks to avoid them.

When tribulations have taught the believer that he can stand, or withstand, there ensues "experience" of the world, but especially of himself. He has learned that he can endure. The first storm may frighten the young sailor in guiding his craft; but after he has passed through a score unharmed and without seeing a timber start, he knows the worst the sea can do, the strength of his vessel to carry him, and his own ability to steer. The man of experience is the proved man. The word "experience" has been translated "approval." Others know him now, but, more than all, he knows himself. The "probation" of the Revised Version is misleading and is not as good as the King James's "experience." When one finds that for the sake of his hope he can suffer pain, and that God is with him all through it, he has gained confidence in himself before God. He knows that this ark to which he has resorted will carry him. And now the hope that he gained in the hour of justification he has gained anew in the discovery that it sustains him in conflict. And it does not make ashamed. Thus Paul has made his first point. The hope of glory through justification by faith cannot be destroyed by tribulations, because instead of overthrowing they strengthen it. This topic, so briefly treated here, is taken up at length in chapter 8. (See p. 134.)

5. "The love of God." This is the second argument in favor of the theme restated now in a new form—"hope maketh not ashamed." The justified man does not blush to profess this hope, because he has a proof that it will not disappoint him at last. Without this proof his hope would be madness; for who is he? A justified man, to be sure, but far from perfect, beset with sin, full of ignorance, and with no act of his life for which he can claim perfection. And yet he hopes to stand before God, to be admitted to His glory, and to be an equal heir with His own Son. It is as if a barbarous and coarse Central African prince should boast that he expects shortly to be son-in-law to the good Queen of England. His claim

would be ridiculed by all knowing people as the raving of delusion. But if the vulgar prince could show on the finger of his black hand that royal gem, the Koh-inoor, presented to him by the queen and brought to him by the third in rank in the government, his boast would be justified. That he has it in his possession is proof that it came to him as a gift; he could neither buy nor steal that costly precious stone. The hope of glory does not make ashamed, because the priceless jewel of God's love toward the sinner is in the latter's possession, poured out in his heart by the Third Person in the Trinity, "the Holy Spirit which is given unto us." This language makes it plain that it is not the justified man's love toward God, but God's love toward the man, that is the proof and pledge of the validity of his hope.

6. "For . . . Christ died." The "for" does not introduce a proof of the possession of the love, but of its nature. The possession need not be proved, being as it is a matter of experience. But if the African prince knows neither the nature nor the value of his gem, if he looks upon it as a common stone, what evidence can it be to him? It is not merely the fact of God's love toward the believer, but its unearthly character, that fortifies hope. The Holy Spirit is the channel through which God is pouring the love of His heart into the sinner's. We are carried now to the fountainhead of the blessed stream to study this love in its source. When "we were yet without strength" to do right this love gave Christ to die. How contemptible is he who lacks the moral ability to do that which is right! Christ died for the pusillanimous. But while sinners were imbeciles for good, they were mighty for evil—"ungodly." In the former condition they excite disgust, in the latter, wrath, and each righteous feeling against them reacts against the other to heighten it. But for just such Christ died "in due time." The timeliness of His death in its averting the wrath due enhances the love manifested at the cross.

7, 8. "God commendeth his love." The sixth verse clearly implies the unearthly character which these two verses now prove. The "for" bears on this unearthliness; the appeal is to

what is known in the history of men. For a "righteous man,"
the man who conforms to the law, one would "scarcely" die.
The "yet" in the seventh verse should be rendered "for," as it
is in the Revision. It explains the word "scarcely." I say
scarcely for a righteous man would one die. I leave room for
an exception, for when the righteous man is that and something more, so that he could be called "good," it might be
that "some [one] would even dare to die." In New Testament
terminology to be good is much more than to be righteous
(Mark 10:18). The former word is rarely used of men, and to
die in behalf of this loftiest form of righteousness is the very
utmost of earthly love, and rare in its examples at that. "But
God"—what a sharp contrast, the difference of earth and
Heaven—gave His Son to die for sinners. His love has no
parallel among men; it is divine. What men can scarcely do
for the good, God has done abundantly for the vile and the
despicable.

9. Having shown what God's love to sinners is, he draws
the necessary and logical inferences. If He could do so much
for them, "much more" now can He save from the "wrath" to
come those who are "justified by his [Christ's] blood." In
the New Testament men are said to be "justified by grace"
(3:24); "justified by faith" (5:1, and many other places);
"justified by works" (James 2:21); but this is the solitary instance in which "justified by blood" occurs. Grace is the
source of justification, faith the condition, works the evidence;
but what is it to be justified by blood, and why did Paul use
this term here rather than his favorite one, "justified by faith"?
The blood is the means, not to say the ground, of the justification, and the phrase is about equivalent to that other in 3:24,
"justified . . . through the redemption that is in Christ Jesus."
Paul could not use the phrase "justified by faith" here for the
reason given above under verse 2. (p. 88), that it is this very
kind of justification that is to be proved. Will it give security
in the hour of God's coming wrath? Yes; for it is made sure
by the redeeming blood. Man's faith does not appeal to God,
but Christ's blood does. The argument, then, comes to this:
If man in his odious sin found the favor of God, how much

more shall that man have His favor whom He accounts right on the ground of redeeming blood!

10. The conclusion in the ninth verse, deduced from the character of God's love, becomes also a proposition to be supported by the argument in the tenth. Hence the latter begins with the causal word "for." The "if" following does not express doubt, but, as in many other places, is equivalent to "since"; it introduces the admitted basis upon which the proof follows. The argument here is in the form of a triple antithesis, like that in Mark 7:8. It can be exhibited to the eye thus:

1.	2.	3.
Enemies . . .	reconciled to God	. . . death,
Reconciled . . .	saved	. . . life.

That is, (1) if God could do so much for His enemies, what can He not do now for those who are in a reconciled state? Again, (2) if God could become reconciled with men when enemies, can He not remain reconciled (which insures their being "saved") now that they have become friends? And once more, (3) if the death of Christ, a negative power, could do so much (reconcile), what will not His life, His active energy on high in their behalf, what will not His ever-living insure? This threefold antithesis in argument is not merely three times as weighty as a single one, but nine times.

The word "reconciled" occurs twice in this verse: "were reconciled to God," "being reconciled." The first does not indicate any change in the feelings of man; it is the equivalent and takes the place of "justified by his blood" in the previous verse. It does not signify that man was active in the reconciliation, but God was, "in that he desists from his claims" (Cremer, *Theol. Lex, sub voce*). He established a new relation with men, exchanging the relation in wrath for the blessed relation in love. He became appeased toward us in the death of His Son. The second occurrence of the word gives the result of the first. The first is God's act, the second the standing into which "we" are brought by means of the first.

The word "enemies" is also passive. It is not that men were inimical to God—in fact, to be sure—but that He was inimical to them. This anger is not inconsistent with His loving them at the same time.

This matter is given in II Corinthians 5:19, 20: "God was [not "is"] in Christ, reconciling the world unto himself. . . . Be ye reconciled to God." He changed toward you; do you change toward Him.

11. "And not only so," not only reconciled, but at the same time rejoicing in God. The change did not stop with that which was outward, in an altered standing; it was and remains accompanied with an inward exultation—the effect of the love shed abroad in the heart. The argument has come around to that with which it began: "we rejoice in hope of the glory of God" (v. 2). This rejoicing is "through [by means of] our Lord Jesus Christ, through whom ["by means of whom" again] we have now received the reconciliation [the changed attitude of God toward us]." It is ours "now." The word "atonement" in its modern signification of propitiation or satisfaction by the death of Christ is not correct here. The original word is the same one used twice in the tenth verse.

It has not been sufficiently noted by expositors that the word "received" is not active, but passive, equivalent to "made recipients of." The argument for the "assurance of salvation secured for the present and the future" (Meyer) is conducted wholly from the divine side; man and his believing do not come into view. If it is objected that, after all, faith is a necessary condition of salvation, and if it fails all fails, why, this very point is secured by the whole argument. If when we were hateful to God He changed toward us, will He—now that we have been made recipients in His grace of that saving change— will He now not insure the condition of its perpetuity? Will God care for everything concerning the believer, support him in trials, shield him in temptation, shed His love abroad in his heart, but leave him to himself in the vital point, his faith? The reconciled man's faith is the first and the chief object of the divine care. The single aim of the argument is the permanence of *justification by faith*.

12. With this verse begins the third (see (3) above) argument in favor of the proposition of the chapter, that justifica-

tion by faith gives a sure hope of the glory of God. The proof is found in the likeness of Adam and Christ in their relation to those who are in them respectively. As Adam's one sin never fails to bring death, so Christ's one righteous act in behalf of sinners never fails to bring the opposite award to those who are in Him. This is the simple course of thought easily traced through this section, but the details present serious difficulties.

"Wherefore," or, as the Revised Version, "Therefore." Literally it reads, "On this account." This shows that the chain of thought is not broken; the topic is the same as in the first eleven verses of the chapter. The connection is this: because through Christ we received the reconciliation and the assurance of eternal salvation, we can say this which follows. Paul goes now to the germ of the disease on the one hand, and of the remedy on the other. He shows anew that salvation is the work of Christ, complete in Him, and in no way to be earned, but simply to be received in its objective perfection. The validity of the argument depends on the immutable relations connecting men with the two sources, Adam and Christ, and this vital connection gives the argument its comprehensive character. The world's history is laid bare at its root, and the key to that history is placed in our hands.

"By one man sin entered into the world." Paul does not even by implication say whether sin had an existence before Adam's fall or not. He says "sin," not "sins." He is looking not at the concrete acts of sin, not at the habit. Adam did not bring sin into the world by setting a bad example; his one act wrought a constitutional change of unholiness within his heart. That act resulted in an innate corrupting principle that transmitted itself just as his natural features did. Because he had two feet rather than four, so all his descendants are bipedal; and as he became a sinner, so is each one of the race sprung from him. Thus it entered into the "world" of men. The material creation was affected on account of Adam's sin (Gen. 3:17), but not by direct connection, and Paul does not contemplate it in the word "world." He means the world of mankind.

"And death by sin." This is the direct outcome and unfailing fruit of that transmissive poison which entered Adam's heart. It is primarily physical death, as is plain from verse 14 below, but physical death as an exponent and sign of that other deeper death of the soul, spiritual death. The two stand in together, and therefore Paul does not sharply distinguish them. (See II Tim. 1:10.)

"For that all have sinned." A better translation is "because all sinned." Death is consequent on sin, and so death passed on all men because all men sin in Adam. "This is proved by the succeeding explanatory context, verses 15-19, in which it is reiterated five times in succession that *one* and *only* one sin is the cause of the death that befalls all men" (Shedd, *Commentary, in loc.*).

This verse, and especially this short concluding sentence, has provoked a world of controversy. The debate arises not so much from facts which must have been plain to Paul's Roman readers, but from the multitude of questions which the facts suggest. Was Adam not created mortal? What is the nature of his relation to posterity? Do men participate in the guilt of his sin? Is its punishment imputed to them? Is natural depravity transmitted from him to the race, and is it culpable? There is no explicit answer to these questions either here or anywhere else in the Bible. The first question is not practical; as to the second we have already indicated our view— the connection is natural, real. If Levi could pay tithes when the tribe was yet unborn in the loins of Abraham (Heb. 7:9, 10), so the unborn race could sin in the loins of Adam. To the remaining questions the answer must be in the affirmative, both for the sake of the parallel with Christ and that Paul's words may be left to stand in their naked plainness.

But now springs up the question of the divine justice. Should millions suffer for the sin of one? Yes, if millions may be saved by the righteousness of one. But, furthermore, if the elemental facts are as above it is presumptuous to raise the question of justice. What God does is the ultimate standard of right.

13, 14. These two verses, the last clause excepted, are intended to show that men die not for their own personal sin, but because of Adam's. It is a fact that sin was in the world all along until the time of the giving of the law at Sinai. It had an actual, practical existence; but this personal, practical sin is not "imputed," not set down to the account of these sinners, and the reason for this nonimputation is there was "no law"—no written or spoken law which they by personal act could break. They sinned without law, but they could not be adjudged worthy of the penalty of that sin before the law was promulgated. The general principle is sin not imputed where there is no law. It comes to this: no written law, no sin, and no sin, no death. But now the fact is that death reigned, had sovereign, undisputed sway, during all the no-law period from Adam to Moses. In all this long period death came to those who had "not sinned after the similitude of Adam's transgression"; that is, they had not broken any formal command. Many more irresponsible babies died in the Flood than men. If, then, death is the penalty of some law broken, and these had none, it follows they broke that first law: they sinned in Adam. And the statement "for that all have sinned" means this. The unwritten law noticed in 2:14 cannot be the cause of death, for babes have not even that. All sinned when Adam violated the Word of God.

"Who [Adam] is the figure [type] of him that was to come." Adam is a figure of Christ in just this respect: that as his one sin brought death to all, even when there was no personal sin, so Christ's one act of obedience brings unfailing righteousness to those who are in Him, even when they have no personal righteousness. Hence the argument of verses 13 and 14 to show that death must be traced to Adam's sole act and not to the sin of his posterity—one side of the parallel.

15. "But not as the offense [the fall of Adam], so also is the free gift [in Christ]." This verse and the next two show in what points the type falls short of the antitype. The type is complete in the outline, but not in some details. This verse gives the difference in intensity between the destructive and the recovering power.

"For if through the offense of [the] one [the] many be dead," or "the many died," as in the Revised Version. The King James, in its failure to give the articles, does not bring out the sharp contrast between Adam and the race. The "if" does not express any doubt; it is argumentative. The "for" brings in what Paul has to say on the inequality between the offense and the free gift. Note that in this sentence, "Through the offense of the one the many" died, he asserts that Adam's sin is the sole cause of death among men. This unsupported statement shows how Paul must be understood in verses 12—14. It needs no proof here, for that has preceded it.

Over against this poisonous fountain in Adam—this fall which brought death to all—stands the healing "grace" of God and the "gift" of justification. These two, the grace and the gift, are found "by grace, which is by [the] one man, Jesus Christ." The Revised Version is preferable here: "Much more did the grace of God, and the gift by the grace of the one man, Jesus Christ, abound unto the many." Over against the fall of the one is the grace of the one, Jesus Christ. Over against the effect of the Fall, the death of the many, is the effect of the grace of the one man, Jesus Christ, namely, that the grace of God and the gift have "abounded unto [the] many." The complex language of the verse becomes plain when it is observed that it sets forth two opposing sources in the two men. followed by two opposite results. This may be seen in transposing the sentence: If the many died by the trespass of the one, much more the grace of God and the gift abounded to the many by the grace of the one man, Jesus Christ. The "much more" is logical—much more certain is it—and not quantitative, for the grace in its extent is here considered to be just as wide and no wider than the death. The many were embraced by both.

Meyer misses the whole point in saying that the grace in the one man, Jesus Christ, is that in which "he found himself moved" to accomplish the redemption; for then there would be in the verse two sources of grace, God and Christ, and the parallel with Adam would be gone. Our guide here must be 3:24. Christ mediates the grace of God; the grace of God that "abounded unto the many" is the very same grace that was "by one man, Jesus Christ." Grace did not abound by grace, but grace abounded in grace, the grace of God in the grace of Christ. "God was in Christ, reconciling the world unto himself" (II Cor. 5:19). And now the argument can be restated: If man, a creature, can do so much against the race by his fall, what cannot God do for the race by His grace in Jesus Christ? It is well-nigh a double antithesis: God in Christ over against man, and divine grace over against a fall.

The whole verse is objective; the first member, "by the offense of the one the many died," surely is. The question is not one about salvation, but about the power to effect it; and this power resides in Christ for all men, or "unto the many."

16. "And not as it was by one that sinned [Adam], so is the gift [in Christ]." Or, more exactly, "Not as through one that sinned is the gift." The fifteenth verse shows the difference in the intensity of the two opposing powers; this shows a difference in extension, but not in the extension among men, for each force, the force for death and the force for life, reaches to all men. In the last verse the inference was from the contrasted sources. In this it is seen in a contrasted extension, not to men, but to their needs.

"The judgment, . . . the free gift." God's judgment, His judicial sentence to the condemnation of death, proceeded from "one" sin. Now that one sin measures the judgment in its breadth. There was one sin and its befitting judgment to match it; but, on the other hand, the free gift for justification, the free gift that issues in justification and saves, proceeded from "many offenses"; for every man is not only involved with Adam in sin, but he has committed innumerable offenses himself. To be saved there must be a free gift that will cover all these. The extent of the destructive power does not go beyond the one sin of Adam; the extent of the recovering power is as wide as the countless sins of any heart. The two forces, then, are measured by the difference in the number of sins to which each looks: the judgment to one sin, the free gift to many. How vastly more extensive, then, is the free gift! To take the two verses together, the contrasts are a shallow, narrow stream, and a deep, broad stream—the shallow stream from Adam no wider than his one sin, the deep stream from Christ as broad as the sum of all sins of men. And if the little stream sweeps the soul away to death, how surely the great volume of the other will carry one to the haven of life!

17. "For if by one man's offense death reigned by one." It is declared again that Adam's sin is the source of death among men, as was proved in verses 12-14. The verse before us bears on just one word in the preceding one, the word "justification," and is in the nature of a conclusion. That it begins with "for" may seem to lie against the idea of a conclusion; the word to be expected was "therefore" or "then." But "for" is appropriate too, for it can be used to reassert what has just been said, and as in 15:27, where it is translated in the Revised Version "yea" and in the King James "verily." The seventeenth verse serves to expand the word "justification" in the previous one, or to give the contents of that word. It brings in nothing new, only puts what we had before in new form. The first, the conditional clause of the verse, is given here for the third time; and the concluding part has been implied twice before in verses 15 and 16. These two showed the superiority of the saving energy in Christ. It remains now to say that those who "receive" this energy, this "abundance of grace," will surely be saved, or, what is the same thing, "reign in life by one, Jesus Christ." "Received" does not mean accepted, but made recipients of, as in 1:5; 4:11; 5:11; 8:15. The parallel between death and life is not preserved. Paul says death reigned; he does not follow this with the words "life reigned"; instead, "they . . . reigned in life." The latter is more expressive. The justified are kings in life.

Paul's argument has now reached its point: If the relation to Adam brought death, the relation to Christ formed in being made a recipient of the superabundant grace in Him will more surely issue in life. If death in Adam is certain, life in Christ is, if possible, more so.

18. The first word of this verse, "therefore," in the King James Version is too strong. The conclusion is already given

in verse 17, and now the writer steps back to take up anew and to finish the broken parallel begun, but dropped at verse 12. To have completed it there would have asserted an exactness which is seen now to exist only in the vital point, but not in the details. The statue in Christ has been shown to be much larger than the model in Adam. The verse should begin with the words "so then," which look back over everything that has been said from the twelfth verse on; and it should be rendered neither as the King James Version nor as the Revision presents it, but, "So then, as through one trespass it [the trespass] came to all men to condemnation, so also through one righteous act it [the righteous act] came to all men to justification of life."

The first "all" is as broad as the race and includes every one of mankind, even the babes. To deny for infants the condemnation of Adam's sin, and to say that penalty is impossible without personal transgression, is to deny too much. It is to deny salvation to the millions who die in infancy; for if they have no sin, how can they ever join in the salvation song, "Unto him that loved us, and washed us from our sins in his own blood"? (Rev. 1:5.)

The second "all," to whom Christ's one righteous act comes just as if it had been theirs, is limited by the words in the preceding verse, "they which receive [the] abundance of [the] grace." The first "all" indicates a natural and necessary relation with Adam; the second "all" indicates not a natural, but a spiritual and mystical relation with Christ instituted by the will of God. The first "all" refers to people of one character, the second to people of a wholly different character, and it is not universal.

19. "Disobedience, . . . obedience." This verse repeats in corroboration the statements of the last. The two verses are not primarily argumentative, but assertive of conclusions reached before. The paragraph as a whole is not argumentative, unless we expect verses 12-14. It must not be forgotten that from the beginning of the chapter Paul's topic is that justification by faith secures the final salvation of him who has it. This third point in proof does not rest on any fine-drawn argument, but on an exposition of facts. It is a fact that death comes through

Adam. It is equally a fact that those who are in the "last Adam" are saved. Paul has not one word in attestation of the parallel; he declares it.

The word "all" in the last verse is changed to "the many," as more suitable to the word "one." "For [just] as by the one man's disobedience the many [the rest, all] were made [rather "were set down in the class of"] sinners, so [also] by the obedience of the one [Christ] the many [who are in him] shall be made [shall be set down in the class of the] righteous." The word "made" is not causative, but declarative. Those in Adam were justly declared sinners, because thereby they were naturally such (Eph. 2:3): Those in Christ are declared righteous graciously, because they are so in Him. The future, "shall be made," looks back to the other future in the seventeenth verse, "shall reign," that explains it. The "obedience" does not refer to the whole sinless history of Christ, but to that culminating act on the cross in which He "became obedient unto death" (Phil. 2:8). The logic of this section as well as the uniform sentiment of the New Testament requires this (Eph. 2:13, 16; Heb. 10:12-14).

20, 21. These two verses have nothing to do with the argument now completed for the permanency of justification, except as they remove an objection sure to occur to the Jew. Paul has traced the origin of sin and of grace, or of death and of life, to two primal and ultimate sources, Adam and Christ. But the Mosaic law is a fact, and that law deals with death and life too. This point cannot be overlooked, and Paul now in few words shows the place which the law holds. Sin and death do have their origin in Adam, but long after his day the law was imposed to show sin's character. The law entered, or came in alongside, in order that "the offense [the fall] might abound." The law excited self-will and opposition, and the Jew's transgressions of it or falls before it showed them to be just what Adam was and worse. It did not solicit sin; it elicited. It was not intended gradually to remove sin, but to prepare the way for its removal in Christ.

Since the offense is a proof of sin, Paul at once drops back to this word to say, "Where sin abounded [a fact proved by the "offense" under law], grace [in Christ] did much more abound." This abundance of grace is the thing shown above, especially in verses 15-17.

The twenty-first verse draws the parallel once more, and finally, between Adam and Christ. Grace superabounded, "that [in order that] as sin hath reigned in [the sphere of] death [and by death—universal death, showing sin's universal sway], even so might grace [the grace that far exceeds sin in its power] reign through [by means of] righteousness [the righteousness in Christ] unto eternal life." This was the point to be shown: that this righteousness would not fail him who had it, but that it was forever. The matter concludes with the solemn words that this blessed, everlasting reign of righteousness is "by Jesus Christ our Lord."

CHAPTER 6

JUSTIFICATION BY FAITH DOES NOT FAVOR A SINFUL COURSE OF LIFE

THE CHAPTER has two main divisions: (1) continuance in sin is impossible to the justified man (verses 1-14), because he died to sin and is alive with the life of Christ; and (2) even sinning is unwarranted in justification of life, because it leads to enslavement to sin and to its appropriate wages, death (vv. 15-23).

1. "Shall we continue in sin, that grace may abound?" The question comes logically from the last two verses in the preceding chapter, where Paul virtually says, the more sin, the more grace. But it looks back also necessarily over the whole discussion of justification. That this question, involving such an answer as that which follows, should emerge at all shows clearly Paul's idea of justification. If the latter signifies "to make good," the question would be impossible. If justification means "to declare good," the question is pertinent. If the sinner is justified on the ground of any personal merit, for any good that he is doing with a view to justification, the question is inexplicable. But if God by His free grace in Christ Jesus justifies "the ungodly" (4:5), this question must come to the front and press earnestly for an answer.

And this answer is found wholly in the facts that go to make the Gospel story. It is not found in the obligation of the law that says "Thou shalt not"; it is not found in the gratitude which the justified man should feel toward Him who died for him; it is not found in good resolutions, in prayer, and in watchfulness; it is found in Christ.

104

2. "God forbid. How shall we, that are dead to sin, live any longer therein?" To live in sin is to be under its sway (vv. 1-14) and to practice it (vv. 15-23). Paul with vigorous language repels the thought that a justified man can remain in this enslaving service. The reason is that the justified are also dead to sin. This death belongs to their redemption, on the ground of which they were justified. "Dead to sin" is far from meaning the death of sin as a power or principle in the heart. (See under 8:11.) In the history of the Church many who have embraced this view have been driven from it by a sad experience, and those who have not been so driven have lived a life of self-deception. "Dead to sin" does not mean a resolution to imitate Christ; it is more than an act of will; it is death in and with Christ in the actual fact of His death. Christ's death was the believer's death also (II Cor. 5:14; I Pet. 2:24). Paul has virtually said this in the verses just above (5:18, 19). What the One did all did. He died not only for sins (I Cor. 15:3), but for sinners. He atoned not only for the acts, but for the actor. It is the consideration of the latter fact only that occupies this chapter—"We, that are dead," having died when he did. The blood shed at the cross washes the sinner as well as his sins. "If I wash thee not" (John 13:8).

To be saved is to be saved from sin first of all. After Paul has labored through five chapters to show that this salvation is a gratuitous gift to faith in Christ, how can he now refer it to something else, a subjective death in the heart of the sinner? He is not so illogical, but some of his interpreters are. When the apostle is asked whether his doctrine that grace covers every sin, the more sin, the more grace—"Let us do evil, that good may come" (3:8)—is not promotive of sin, his answer is just simply a further explication of grace, an opening up of a wider view of the work of the cross. The power against continuance in sin is faith in the cross.

Sin's power, its mastery over the soul, comes from its presence. The enlightened man soon sees that his guilt lies not so much in what he has done as in what he is. It is not his acts, it is himself, that is an offense against God. Sin dwells within him, tainting every fiber of his soul. He cannot escape it by anything within his own power any more than he can change the color of his eyes. It is ever present and is thereby master. But why seek to escape it? Why not continue in it if grace covers it? "How shall we, that are dead to sin, live any longer therein?" How can one on whom the sun has risen walk now in the dark? The believer died in Christ's death. The believer is dead, and that death answers for the guilt of what he is. Faith takes Christ for sinfulness as well as for sins; and indwelling sin has lost its power to vex the conscience and to cut off the light from God's countenance the moment that faith says, "He died for what I am as well as for what I did." Sin loses its power, because sin is gone from the heart by the death of Christ, in which the sinner dies.

Note three things: First, the question so far is not about continuing to sin, but about continuance in sin, in its power. Second, the only change that Paul contemplates in the justified man up to this point is a change in his attitude toward Christ; from being a nonbeliever he has become a believer. Third, this first verse makes but the first step in answering the question, "Shall we continue in sin?"

3. The question could not be asked if the Romans bethought themselves of what they assumed in their baptism. They were dead, as the verse above declares, for they were baptized into Christ's death. This third verse, then, is in the way of explication that the Romans died to sin, the hour of that death being the time when they entered the waters of baptism. The meaning of their baptism was death.

But how did they die by means of baptism? Paul answers, to quote the Revised Version: "Or are ye ignorant that all we who were baptized into Christ Jesus were baptized into his death?" They knew, of course, that they were baptized into Christ; but Paul insists on the one point that that baptism involved among other things oneness with Him in His death to sin. By the ordinance or in the ordinance they declared their acceptance of him as Saviour and so came "into" him. The nature of the union is not disclosed, but it is real. It is not effected by the baptism, but in it. In the baptism the believer virtually says, "I make Christ's death to sin my death to sin."

It is the symbolic response of the heart to the teaching of the Gospel that Christ's death is also the believer's.

But must it not be said now that Paul has abandoned his theme, salvation by faith, in substituting the word "baptism"? Why did he not say, "All we who believed into Christ," a common phrase in the New Testament (10:14; Gal. 2:16), "believed into his death"? The difficulty arises from the modern wrong conception of the New Testament meaning of the word "baptism," that it is a mere rite, an act to be done, at the best, because one believes in Christ. The New Testament writers never separate it from the faith which it embodies and expresses. It is the fixed sign for faith, just as any appropriate order of letters in a word is the sign of an idea. The sign stands for the thing and is constantly used for the thing. Hence Paul can say that Christ was "put on" in baptism (Gal. 3:27), and Peter does not hesitate to declare that "baptism doth also now save us" (I Pet. 3:21). It is referred to as the "laver of regeneration" (Titus 3:5), and said to "wash away sins" (Acts 22:16). To refuse to be baptized is to reject God, and the opposite is to accept Him (Luke 7:29, 30). Every one of these passages—and there are more like them—would teach salvation by a rite, salvation by water, but that the word for baptism is used as a symbol of faith. Faith so far is not one thing and baptism another; they are the same thing. The faith that accepted Christ in Paul's day was the faith that showed its acceptance in baptism. The water without the preceding faith was nothing. The faith without the water could not be allowed. Believers were baptized into Christ or they were not considered to be in Him.

The word being so used, it is easy to see that Paul has not departed from the gem doctrine of justification by faith; and by employing it he has gained definiteness of statement. Faith is a wide term and shows itself in many ways, each exhibition being exactly appropriate to the way in which faith is then exercised. The exhibition is an exponent of the faith. In faith of a coming flood, Noah appropriately built an ark. In faith that Israel would one day leave Egypt, Joseph gave commandment concerning his bones, that they be not left behind. In

faith that one dies with Jesus, he is buried with Him in baptism, the faith taking this fit form. The Romans had a broad
faith that ran out in many lines, and it was known far and
wide (1:8). Just one of these lines led to salvation—the one
that found its appropriate exhibition in baptism. When Paul
said they were baptized into Christ, they knew instantly to
what hour (see on 16:7) and to what line of their multiform
faith he referred—the faith that saw the man and not merely
his sins on the cross and in the tomb, so that to show itself
appropriately the whole man must be buried with Christ in
baptism. The act of baptism is an exponent, first of all, not of
the remission of sins, but of the death of the believer in Christ,
so that his sinfulness is atoned for. He himself has died to sin.

4. The second verse declares the fact of the believer's death
in Christ, a fact explained in the third. The two have just the
one thought—death. This fourth verse draws the natural conclusion: therefore we are buried with him by means of the
baptism into death. He does not say into "his" death this
time, because he is not now emphasizing the union with
Christ brought about in the ordinance, but the condition in
which it places the baptized man. He is dead. And this favors
the view that the phrase "into death" is to be joined with
"baptism." We are buried with Him by means of an into-
death baptism. To connect it with the verb "buried" gives an
unnatural figure, buried into death, but one that is supported
by some. The mention of the burial prepares the way for the
next step, the second in the question of continuance in sin.
It is only touched and then dropped to go on with the idea
of death until the end of the seventh verse.

We were buried with Him in order that, just as the Father
raised up Christ from the dead by means of that "glory" which
is the sum of the gracious excellence of His character, so we
also should walk in the newness of the principle of life. The
"should" does not express obligation, but the Father's intent
in the raising of the Saviour on our behalf. The mention of
the glory in connection with Christ's resurrection suggests that
the same glory will be exhibited in the walk springing from the
new life-principle.

5. This verse tells why there may be a new walk in pointing out the power of that walk. The reason is that, as we are one with Him in His death, so are we also in His resurrection, being endowed in the latter with the same life which He received in rising from the tomb. The reference is not to our future bodily-resurrection. "For if" (or "as"), a graft in a tree (John 15), "we became [not "planted," but] grown together [with him] in the likeness of his death [viz., our baptism], so shall we be also still grown together [with him] in the likeness of his resurrection [viz., our emergence from the watery grave]." To state this idea of union Paul has not abandoned his figure of baptism. Grafting, to be sure, is not done in water, but the union in the baptism is as vital as that between the graft and the tree. It must be noted that none can share in Christ's resurrection life except by first dying. We are buried in order to be raised (John 12:24).

Now for the first time Paul has clearly asserted union with Christ. For the thought is, If we went into the baptism in union, why should we not come out in union? The oneness in the immersion is proof of the oneness in the emersion.

6. He changes his figure, but holds in both the same point of view—the death of Christ. The connection is causal; we may say that we are grown together in the likeness of His resurrection because of our "knowing this," namely, the significance of the cross. It must not be said here, with Shedd, that "St. Paul adduces the personal experience of the believer in proof." Did any man ever experience that he died with Christ? The word does mean an experimental knowledge, but in this case, as in many others, it is the experience of faith (Gal. 3:7; II Tim. 3:1) and not of fact. It is by faith we know that "our old man," our former self before our acceptance of Christ, was (not "is") crucified with Him, in order that our body, the possession and slave of sin, might be (not "destroyed," but) annulled by dying with Christ to sin. By "body" is meant nearly the same as "old man." The latter is the man in his relations to life and to his own history. The former is the means of these. The intent of the annulling of this body by the cross was that we might no more do bond-service to sin, or, as the Revised Version," that so we should no longer be in bondage to sin."

7. That we are no longer debtors to sin, to render it any kind of service, is proved by the accepted maxim in human penalites that he who died (not "is dead") thereby stands acquitted (not "is freed") from sin. Death cancels everything.

So far, then, in the main Paul's answer to the question, "Shall we continue in sin?" is this: that every believer, and not merely a most devout man or two, is dead. It is not that he ought to die, but his death is an accomplished fact in Christ Jesus. Baptism means death and burial. In the crucifixion of Christ the believer sees himself crucified too. Not only were his sins there, but he himself was there, so that the "old man," the former self, was slain. How can he "continue" in sin when he and his sins are no more? The words "old man" suggest a new man, against whom there is nothing penal either for what he was or is, or for what he has done. These are objective facts of the Gospel, and the faith that has laid hold of them finds perfect liberty before a holy God and is certain of His love. This faith opens the heart for the incoming of that love mentioned in 5:5. When Christ is taken for no more than the forgiveness of sins, then baptism has wholly lost its significance, for it buries the man and not his sins, and the cross has been robbed of half its efficacy, for it crucifies the body of sin at the same time in which it puts away its guilt. The power subjectively against continuance in sin is belief in these objective facts of the Gospel.

8-10. Sanctification begins with this chapter with the question, "Shall we continue in sin?" Paul has securely laid the foundation of it in justification. There is no break with sin but by trust in the Gospel facts, and no one can have the power of the resurrection life in his heart until he dies with Christ in order to be raised with Him. To die is to be justified from sin, by which death comes union with Christ in life before God. Thus it is that God's righteousness is a righteousness by faith.

Spiritual power flows into the soul by union with Christ, but that fact is not developed until the eighth chapter. Here the eye is still turned upward, not inward.

At this point, therefore, Paul takes up the second means against continuance in sin; or rather it is the other side of what has already been given, and touched on just once in verse 5. "He was delivered for our offenses." This is verses 1-7. "He was raised again for our justification." (See on 4:25.) This is verses 8-14. The believer dead with Christ will surely "live" with Him, now in this present time, and then, of course, ever hereafter. It is only the present time that is here in view. Note that now for the first instance since 4:24 (q.v.) we have the word "believe," signifying, however, not faith in the Gospel directly, but persuasion or conviction of its efficacy. Since our present Christian life depends wholly on Christ's life, since we live only in His life (see v. 5 above), Paul need only prove that Christ, once raised, dies no more. That He died at all was because of sin, and for this He died "once" for all. Sin has no more dominion over Him, and in Him it has no more dominion over the believer. And now that he lives, he lives to God, or for God, for His pleasure and glory. This is said in proof that Christ can never again die, the suppressed premise being that he who lives for God must live forever. It is also suggested that we who live by the power of that life in Him, and which has become ours, will also live "to God," and so live both now and evermore.

11. With this verse an exhortation begins that is continued through the next two. To "reckon" is to account (2:26), to "conclude" (3:28), to think (2:3). They were asked to think of themselves ("yourselves"), just as God's Word here describes them in Christ, "dead unto sin" and "alive unto [or "for"] God." To conclude about ourselves what God has declared about us in the Gospel is faith (4:17). If the Gospel says we are dead to sin in Christ, we must say so too; if it says we are alive in Him, we must so reckon ourselves. This reckoning stands on the Gospel and not at all on experience. The very meaning and use of this word prove that Paul depended on a right estimation of the Gospel as the power against sin, and not on an inward experience of something, except as this

estimation is itself an experience. It is not be alive or become alive, but account yourself now alive in Christ. The happy rendering in the King James Version, "likewise," shows the correspondence between this verse and the tenth. As He died to sin once for all, reckon ye yourselves dead "likewise," and as He liveth unto God, so "likewise" do ye; for the last phrase, "in ["through" is not correct] Jesus Christ our Lord," in verse 11 joins with both "dead" and "alive."

12. And "therefore," now that you reckon yourselves alive in Christ and dead to sin—"therefore" looks back over the whole section—"let not sin reign in your mortal body." He says "mortal" to remind them of what they are in themselves, mortal because sinful (8:10). They must "reckon" themselves pure, and this reckoning is their chief power over sin, because God graciously so reckons them; but in themselves they are not so. See how clearly He implies that there is "sin" in this mortal body. But it is now "your" body; before accepting Christ it was "the body of sin." (For the meaning of "body" see on v. 6 above.)

"Let not sin reign." This is much more than an appeal to the exercise of will. It is an appeal to accept and make one's own by faith all that state which is brought about by union with Christ. The ideal Christian life is not a constant battle with sin, but a victory over it. Not until a man sees himself sinless in Christ by death and resurrection has he found the right way of approach toward sinlessness in life. He can attend to the present when he knows that he is absolved from all that he was and did in the past, as well as from all that he now is.

"That ye should obey it in the lusts thereof." The better reading is, "That ye should obey its [the body's] desires." The words "it in" are an unsupported addition to the true text. "Lusts" is obsolete English and should find no place in a modern revision. The sentence explains the word "reign." The persistent tendency of sin is to subject man to a gratifying of his own desires. James 1:14, 15, describes the steps by which sin dethroned in Christ regains its scepter. Note again how clearly Paul implies that the believer is still possessed of the desires of the body. As long as he has a body he has these desires. It is not their presence nor the presence of sin with its clamor to reign that is inconsistent with saving union with Christ. The Gospel is a means to save sinners (I Tim. 1:15). It can justify the "ungodly" (4:5). But what it cannot tolerate is obedience to sin. It is not the will of the sinful man that is to be done, but the will of God. Godet's rather vehement insistence that Paul here means only physical desires is wide of the mark. The body is the man. Psychology is as incompetent to explain Paul as geology is to explain Genesis. Moule is correct when he says they are "desires of every kind, whether sensual or not." (See Colossians 3:3, 5, 8, 9.) Even a desire after some particular service to God may be contrary to His will (I Thess. 2:17, 18). It must not be forgotten that when "our old man" was slain at the cross these "lusts" were crucified with him (Gal. 5:24).

13. Paul descends from the general to the particular. The "members" of the body, its various faculties and capabilities, physical and mental, must not be yielded at any time "unto sin" as weapons ("instruments") for unrighteousness, but (now he turns from the negative to the positive) "yield," by one decisive act, "yourselves to God." To "yield" means to present for service. This topic is taken up at length in chapter 12. It is in vain for one to present himself to God for service except in the Gospel fashion—present himself not merely as a forgiven sinner, but by faith in the Gospel, as one "alive from the dead," "a living sacrifice" (12:1); and present once for all to God the "members" of the body (same as above) as weapons for righteousness, practical holiness.

14. And you can make this holy warfare, "for" you have not only been set free from sin by dying to it, but it has also lost another means of hindering you, the law: "ye are not under law," a matter to be fully explained in the next chapter (see under 3:20); ye are "under grace." Grace and law are antagonistic and mutually exclusive. Sin and law go together, and yet, should the believer chance to go astray, he is still under grace. This raises the serious question of section (2)—whether sinning is not promoted by gratuitous justification.

15. "Shall we sin, because we are not under law?" This question was sure to arise, because human society and governments know of no way to restrain sin but by law and its penalites. The state's ruler is "the minister of God, a revenger to execute wrath upon him that doeth evil" (13:4) in breaking the law. The assertion "ye are not under law" was made to turn the justified man's gaze from Moses to Christ, from law to grace. That this can lead to an act of sin Paul denies with vehemence—"God forbid"; but he knew well that his simple, radical declaration "not under law" could not be accepted without defense. And even with his defense many are disposed to think that the obvious meaning cannot be the true one.

16. With this verse the answer begins. That answer is found in the nature of sin. Its immediate effect is slavery; its outcome is eternal death. To repeal the law against taking poison with suicidal intent would not affect the character of the drugs. Paul's readers know this—"Know ye not?" He only reminds them what the result must be if they sin. Faith in God is, first of all, faith in the ruinous power of sin (1:32). The compactness possible in the Greek of this sentence makes a literal translation somewhat difficult. It might be paraphrased slightly: Know ye not, to whom ye present yourselves as servants to the extent of obedience, his slaves ye are whom ye obey, whether sin's servants, whose end is death, or obedience's servants, whose end is practical righteousness? This states the universal law that a man becomes the moral subject of what he does. If he yields to sin that sin gets a grip upon him. If he lies once, not only is he likely to lie again, but that lie has him in its power. It has soiled his conscience and dimmed the light in his heart. This is also the teaching in Matthew 6:24; John 8:34; II Peter 2:19. No one knows this so well as the believer. To be sure, he may repent of his sin, but only Christ, and not the law, can restore him. It is also true that acts of obedience tend to a habit and enslave their doer in the comfortable bonds of righteousness. The two words "whether," "or," show that life has but two ways open, one or the other of which every man must choose; there is no middle course.

17. After stating this law that holds in all moral action, he speaks of the happy condition of the Romans, that, whereas they had been sin's slaves, thanks be to God, they had escaped bondage by obeying from the heart, sincerely and not in mere act of the flesh, that "form" or mold of teaching into which they were delivered. The King James translation is wrong here. It does indeed seem natural to say a form of teaching "which was delivered you," but this is not Paul's assertion. If it were, one shining point would be lost, that both they and God conjoined in the act of their salvation. They obeyed from the heart the type of teaching—the Gospel—into whose power His grace delivered them. The commentators debate the implication here, whether there were different types of doctrine among the apostles. There was a difference in presentation (see on 2:16), but none in form or mold. In this debate it is strangely overlooked that the implied antithesis is with that other "form of knowledge and of the truth in the law" (2:20). To be sure, in the passage here quoted there stands another word for "form," but practically synonymous with the one before us. The context, whether we shall be under law to be restrained from sin, or under the Gospel, settles the question of the antithesis and also explains Paul's earnest words.

"God be thanked." Paul had had no little trouble on this point (Gal. 5:1, 2).

It is impossible to think that in this phrase, "delivered into a mold of teaching," Paul did not refer to what he said in verse 4 above. Baptism is a symbolic mold or pattern of doctrine into which the Romans could be said to be delivered, and in accordance with which they are fashioned, for its idea is dead to sin and alive with Christ. He who called the same ordinance a "washing" or a laver "of regeneration" (Titus 3: 5) could consistently call it a mold of doctrine.

18. This verse continues the thought of the last, the happy condition into which the Romans were brought by their heart obedience to the Gospel; being set at liberty from sin by dying to it, they are now servants to righteousness. This word "servants," used all along, shows that now practical and not imputed righteousness is meant. At the very beginning of their

Christian course they were delivered from the guilt and from the power of sin in order to do acceptable works. They did not serve to be saved; they were saved to serve.

19. "I speak after the manner of men." For using the words "servants of righteousness," Paul explains, almost apologizes. This expression belongs not strictly to the believer's relation to Christ, but is human, "after the manner of men." The fact is, as stated in 5:17, that the saint is not a servant but a king. But in view of the "infirmity of the flesh," the feebleness of spiritual comprehension (Eph. 3:16) on the part of the Romans, he uses a phrase which they could understand. While it is far from expressing the whole truth, it is in the way toward it and cannot lead astray. This language of servitude, while it does not assert their lofty spiritual dignity, conveys the full measure of their duty—slaves to righteousness.

In a further use of this human metaphor, he exhorts them to a transfer of energy. Just as their powers and faculties had once been slaves to the monsters "uncleanness and iniquity," so that the issue was iniquity, they were to present these "even so" as slaves to righteousness, that the issue might be holiness. In yielding themselves as servants to do right, there issued at once a state of mind and heart called holiness. He does not say yet that this holiness comes from the Holy Spirit.

20, 21. Paul urges them ("for") to this holy enslavement by reminding them that the only freedom which they had in their former condition was freedom relative to righteousness. Such having been their condition, he asks, "What fruit had ye accordingly ["then" is ambiguous] in those things [those sinful deeds and habits] whereof ye are now ashamed?" (I Pet. 4:3.) They were "now" ashamed, which is to their credit and proves their enlightenment. They were not "then" ashamed, for this was impossible, because sin never sees its own hideous face until looks into the Gospel with believing eyes. The question all the time before the reader is, "Shall we sin, because we are not under law?" Men are not likely to repeat that for which they are "now" ashamed. "What fruit had ye?" I ask this painful question because ("for") ye know "the end of those things is [spiritual] death." There was no fruit. Note that Paul has quietly passed from the enslavement produced by sin to its legitimate result—death.

22. This verse describes their present blessed condition in contrast with their former one, pictured in verses 20 and 21. He does not now use the semi-figurative words "obedience," "righteousness," "mold of teaching" (see Moule, *in loc*), but that which comprehends them all—"servants to God." This service has immediate fruit issuing in holiness, whose end is eternal life. Here are two strange paradoxes: the end of sin is death that never dies, and the end of holiness is "eternal" life. The order and number of the terms must be noted—service to God, holiness, eternal life. The middle link of the three cannot be omitted (Heb. 12:14).

23. "Wages of sin; . . . gift of God." This verse gives the solemn proof for the last three. It lies in the fundamental law of the moral universe. Things are so constituted that sin ends only in death, and grace in eternal life. That which comes to sin is wages. Wages are what is due. The word means soldier's pay. Sin is warfare against God, and the appropriate pay is death. But that which comes to the servants of God is not wages; service is due Him and merits no reward (Luke 17:10). But that which comes to them is vastly more than any wages which they could earn—it is a gift of God, it is eternal life. The argument closes, as each one does, with the solemnly accumulated titles of the Redeemer: "The gift of God is eternal life through Jesus Christ our Lord."

In a word, then, the question, "Shall we continue in sin?" is answered. The answer is in the Gospel, the work of Christ. How can one continue in a state from which he is already delivered? Death was due as the wages of sin, and that death was paid in Christ. If it is, then, no longer service to sin, but service to God, life is needed—a dead man cannot serve God—and Christ's life is reckoned to the believer. Belief of the Gospel is the power against sin, and belief is to reckon one's self as God reckons. In Christ man is guiltless; this is his standing, which enables him to shun sinning because he now knows its destructive power. Believing acquaintance with Christ in His Gospel gives deliverance from sin and from sinning.

CHAPTER 7

THE LAW CANNOT SANCTIFY

IN 3:20 IT WAS SAID that "by the deeds of the law shall no flesh be justified in God's sight."

In 5:20 there is a second radical utterance about the law—it "entered, that the offense might abound."

In 6:14 there comes a third amazing statement—"Ye are not under law."

In this chapter these three points are taken up in the reverse order, and elaborated subsidiary to the leading idea that the law cannot save from indwelling sin. (1) How and why the justified are delivered from the law (vv. 1-6). (2) If the law makes sin to abound, is the law sinful (vv. 7-13)? (3) No man is saved by the law, for no man is delivered from the flesh by it (vv. 14-25).

There was a profound historical necessity for the discussion embraced in this chapter. Whether the composition of the Roman church was in the main Jewish or Gentile, its Bible, which it read and by which it knew God and Christ, was the Old Testament, the book of the law. The law was divine, given with most imposing sanctions on Sinai. For their own stability, as well as for a means of defense against acute and captious Jewish adversaries, Paul must make these Roman believers see why that law was not binding on them in their relation to God. The necessity was the more urgent from the fact that he defends justification by faith by these same Old Testament Scriptures.

In writing to the Hebrews, who were in danger of returning to the law, there was equal need of showing them not only its impotency to save, but that they were no longer under it. The latter came about by the radical change in the order of the priesthood (Heb. 7:12, 19).

In the well-nigh vehement Epistle to the Galatians Paul discusses this same question, but more in its relation to justification than to sanctification. Galatians is suggested in our fourth chapter rather than in this seventh.

This question of the law was the meeting-point of the enemies and friends of the Gospel. More than once his attitude toward it came well-nigh costing Paul his life (Acts 21:28, 31). It is not strange, then, that we meet it here and in almost every one of his epistles.

Paul's convincing teaching on the subject of law would bring a comfort and a relief to the believing Jew, and to the believing Gentile as well, that can hardly be appreciated. His instruction was their answer for abandoning an old and divinely established faith for a novel and untried one. The former was the trust of the fathers and the prophets; the latter, it could be said, was advocated by no one but heretics and renegades. But it has also intrinsic and permanent value. It is in the very blood of men everywhere to seek to set themselves right with God by doing good works. This chapter shows how futile all such efforts are.

1-4. "Or know ye not, brethren?" The chapter is linked by the word "or"—omitted in the King James Verison—with the fourteenth verse of the preceding one. He writes to them as "men who know the law." The Revised Version is preferable here. They knew the law, for it was constantly read and expounded in their hearing. They knew its permanent character, that it held dominion over man for life. In proof, he cites a single item from the code. A wife was held by the marriage bond as long as her husband lived; but if he died she was free, being no longer a wife, but the same as a virgin. She could marry again. Here is where this exceedingly simple illustration grows not only very profound, but at the first sight very perplexing. The point that Paul is after is that the law holds the man till he dies. But in the illustration it was the husband that died and the wife became free. And not a few commentators are puzzled and make dark what Paul intended to be plain. Moule says, "The metaphorical language is not strictly consistent." It is both consistent and scriptural. Sanday says, "In the working out of this illustration there is a certain amount of intricacy, due to an apparent shifting of the standpoint in the middle of the paragraph." But how strange that Paul should attempt to clarify a simple statement by an intricate illustration! He adds: "It is strange to speak of the same persons at one moment as 'killed' and the next as 'married again.'" But have we not had this "strange" thing several times in the previous chapter? "Our old man was crucified with him, . . . that we should not serve sin" (v. 6). "If we be dead with Christ, we believe that we shall also [now] live with him" (v. 8). (See Col. 3:3.) Shedd makes the amazing statement that the first husband stands for the law. Why, the woman was not married to the marriage law, but to a man, and now the law bound her. He adds, "If the figure had been regularly carried out." Its regularity is beautiful, but how is one to see it who makes the first husband the law? Meyer's explanation strikes the right note, but hardly goes far enough. When Paul begins, "I speak to you as those who know the law," this is not merely incidental or a compliment, but the key to the passage. The moment he mentioned marriage their thought would at once revert to Genesis 2:24: "And they shall be one flesh." And, therefore, when the husband dies the wife dies too; and the law, that binds while life lasts, binds her no longer, for she is dead. The wife is dead; the woman remains. The context, especially before, but also after, makes it inevitable that the first husband, though he is not mentioned, is none other than the crucified Christ. "Our old man is crucified *with him*." These Romans, from what Paul had already written, could not avoid believing that they died in His death, because in some way they were in union with Him. He was made under the law that He might redeem them that were under the law (Gal. 4:4, 5). He and they died together (II Cor. 5:14). Christ while under the law was the first husband.

The third verse serves to emphasize the rigor of the marriage law in its demand that husband and wife remain one, for if, "while her husband liveth, she be married to another man, she shall [by the divine law itself] be called [by the harsh name] an adulteress: but if her husband be dead, she is free from that law," because, being one flesh (Mark 10:8) with him, she died too. She is no more a wife than if she had never married. She is dead to the law of her husband, so that it has no longer a claim upon her. She can be "married to another man" if she chooses to marry.

The fourth verse brings in the conclusion. It significantly begins with the word "wherefore." It might be rendered "so that." It shows the exactness of the parallel between the woman's case and that of the believer in Christ. It is God's law that the woman should be considered dead in her husband's death, "so that ye," under a similar law, may be reckoned dead in Christ's death. Meyer denies this harmony, and makes the "wherefore" purely inferential. The sense is not materially affected; for the point reached is this: as the woman died to the marriage law in the death of her husband, so "ye also," like the woman, "my brethren," died by means of "the body of Christ" on the cross to the whole Mosaic law; "that ye should be married to another, even to him who is raised from the dead." In the case of the woman the husbands are two and distinct; in the case of the Romans the husband is the same, but in two different states, one, under the law, born of Mary, and the other the resurrection state. This duality in the relation of Christ to His own was taught first of all by Himself. (See John 14:18, 19; 16:16.) In II Corinthians 5:14-16, Paul, in speaking of living to the raised Christ, declares, "Yea, though we have known Christ after the flesh, yet now henceforth know we him no more." But our text itself looks at Christ in two conditions—"the body of Christ" and "him who is raised from the dead." These are identical in substance, but different in relation. The former was with men under the law; the latter belongs to the heavenly world. By death and resurrection Jesus passed from one to the other, so that when He met His disciples after rising from the tomb, He virtually said he was no longer with them (Luke 24:44).

The nature of that union which existed between Christ and

the race before the cross, so that His death was their death, is nowhere revealed; but to bring about such a union may be the chief reason for the incarnation.

The union with Christ is twofold, one in the incarnation, by which He stood for the race in such a way that when the One died they all died—"Ye were made dead to the law by the body of Christ." This is the union with the first husband. But now, second, the raised Christ is preached, and men may become united with Him in the Holy Spirit through faith. This is the second and the saving union, made possible by the first.

That men became dead to the law by the body of Christ does not make their salvation actual, because the intent of that death was not salvation, but that they might be married to another, to Him who is raised from the dead, in whom, and in no other way, the salvation is found.

But how did this question of the Mosaic law affect the Gentiles, who were not under it? In a very true sense they were under it. It was "against" them (Col. 2:14). When Moses shut up the Jew under law he shut the Gentile out, so that the Jew knew of no way of saving his uncircumcised neighbor but by proselytism (Acts 15:5). God's way was to remove the barrier of the law by breaking down this "middle wall of partition." Christ reconciled both (Jew and Gentile) unto God in one body by the cross, having slain the enmity by it, so that now "both have access by one Spirit unto the Father" (Eph. 2:13-18). In the matter of law the cross did as much for the Gentile as for the Jew, in that it brought about that primal relation of men to God when there was no law.

This fourth verse gives the heart of the epistle and of the Gospel. The Christian's life is not a memory, not an imitation of one who long ago lived, the former husband, but a wedlock union with Him who now lives in them and for them.

The object of the marriage with the risen Christ is that "we might bring forth fruit for God." The figure of the marriage is continued in the idea of fruitfulness. The fruit is love and joy and peace, a mind in harmony with God. The character of this fruit may be known in its origination from a heart in union with Christ to be its author. It is divine and spiritual, and so fit "for God." The very best that even the best man can produce outside of spiritual union with Christ is in God's sight but bastard fruit.

5. This verse shows why no fruit could be produced for God under the law. "When we were in the flesh," not in Christ, but under law, "the passions" (a better word than "motions") —the excitabilities and evil capabilities in the heart leading to their several "sins"—these passions, "which were [stirred to operate] by [means of] the law, did work [were active] in our members," mental and physical, to the extent of bringing forth fruit for death. This stirring of the passions to opposition Paul will elaborate in the next section.

6. This verse describes the present happy state of the Romans freed from the law and in Christ. "But now we are freed [the same word is translated "loosed" in v. 2 above] from the law"—Moses' moral and ceremonial law. How? Just as the wife was—by "having died to that in which we were held." The King James Version is quite faulty here. We were freed so as to (not "should") do service "in newness of [the] spirit, and not in the oldness of the letter." The newness is the new spiritual state or union with Christ; the oldness of the letter was their former state under the law. The letter means the law. This new service produced holy fruit; the service under law brought forth fruit for death.

7, 8. But if we had to be absolved from the law, just as we were absolved from the dominion of sin, in order to serve God, "is the law sin?" With this inquiry the second point in the chapter is introduced. (See remarks at the beginning of the chapter and (2) in analysis.) Paul replies in the negative with his usual vehemence—"God forbid." His sole and decisive proof for this negative answer is that that which reveals sin cannot itself be sin (Eph. 5:13). "I had not [experimentally] known sin, but by [means of] the law." He cites the tenth commandment to illustrate his meaning. For the words "lust," "covet," and "concupiscence" there is but one word, verb and noun, in the original—"to desire": "I had not known desire, except the law had said, Thou shalt not desire." But the moment that command came the sin in my heart took the command as an occasion to stir up within me every kind of desire. I thought of a thousand things which I wanted, and I longed for them now that they were forbidden. In quoting only a part of the command, omitting as he does the specifications under it in Deuteronomy, Paul shows that he understands it in its most sweeping extent. It forbids every strictly human desire. Understood thus, it has the same awful effect on men today that it had on Paul. It cannot be kept; it grinds to powder. The heart is nothing but a nest of selfish desires, to every one of which the command says No. The commentators take the sword out of the law's hand in saying it forbids only "irregular desire," "illicit desire" (Sanday): "desires after what is forbidden" (Meyer). This quenches the fierce blaze of the Sinaitic fire in the command and virtually reduces the ten laws to nine; for if the tenth forbids only what is irregular and illicit, it merely reiterates those which are given before it, and is a feeble summation instead of a burning climax. Moreover, how could Saul of Tarsus, with his blameless legal righteousness (Phil. 3:6) and his good conscience (Acts 23:1)— how could such a one as he "die" before a law which inhibited only the "irregular," the "illicit," and the "desires after what is forbidden"? In this sense he had kept the tenth law as every pious Pharisee did, and as every moral but unregenerate man does today. It was only when he came to see that it was desire itself that was forbidden, that the sin lay in the wish itself, not in the thing wished for—it was when he read the command just as he here gives it, "Thou shalt not *desire*"—that he died under its power. If it is said that this interpretation is impractical, that it dries up the springs of life, the answer is, just this is its intent, so that men may seek to escape "the corruption that is in the world by desire" (II Peter 1:4). The will absolutely subject to God, admitted by all to be the divine requirement, is practically impossible unless the desires are likewise subject. What God has given men—and He has given much—it is but gratitude to take; but every desire beyond is under the ban of the tenth law.

"For without the law sin was dead." It is not the law in its letter that stirs up sin, but the law in its deep spiritual meaning, as Jesus interpreted it in the Sermon on the Mount. Until this real meaning dawns on the heart and conscience, sin lies inactive and is dead.

9. "When the law came." It is not just clear what Paul means by these words. When did the law come to him? His history shows that the time could not possibly have been when at twelve years of age he, like other Jewish boys, was put under it and became a son of the law (Godet's view). Most likely he refers to his history on the Damascus road, when the light smote him. He learned then that instead of serving God he was obnoxious to Him, so that for three days he groped in darkness without eating and drinking. At length he prayed, and found life in professing faith in Christ (Acts 9:17, 18; 22: 16). Up to the time of this experience he was, in the Jewish sense, under the law, but really "without it." It had not yet "come" to his heart and understanding. He was "alive"; that is, every unregenerate actvity of his soul was in full exercise without restraint. But when the heart-searching law broke in upon his apprehension, he not only saw that he had broken it at every point, but the sin which he had not felt before arose in active rebellion against that law, and he died. The penalty for rebellion was death (Num. 27:13, 14). The language "alive" and "died" is metaphorical, like I Thessalonians 3:8 and I Corinthians 15:31.

10. "And the commandment, which [was intended for] life, I found [when it came to my sinful heart] to result in death [for I could not keep it]." Paul is not excusing himself, nor pitying himself; and he is at the farthest from saying in the words, "I had not known sin," "sin revived," that the law created sin. This is the point: the pool of his heart had looked like a spring of sweet water. The law was the staff that stirred it up and showed it to be nothing but mud at the bottom and full of all hideous reptiles. The question of guilt is not before him, but the revealing power of the law.

11. "For sin . . . slew me." This verse supports the last one in showing the process by which the law brought about "death." Sin, like the tempter before Eve (Gen. 3:1-13), taking the commandment for a starting-point, an "occasion,"

deceived him. Sin led him, as Eve was led, to think that the command was depriving him of some good; but in taking that which seemed good he gathered death with it. The law rose up against him and pronounced his doom.

12. The conclusion about the law follows not exactly as an inference from an argument, but as an exhibition of the law's holiness given on the dark background of sin. The question of verse 7 is answered. "Is the law sin?" No; "the law is holy, and the commandment [is] holy [for it discloses sin], and just [or "righteous," because it condemns sin to death], and good [or "beneficent," because its aim is "life"]." Bengel's exposition of these adjectives, followed in some commentaries, is lexical, but not logical.

13. This assertion about the goodness or beneficence of the law starts an acute objection: "Was then that which is good made death unto me?" Can wholesome bread prove poison to the hungry man who eats it? Does fresh, pure water start a fever instead of allaying thirst? How can that which is admitted to be "good," the law, prove to be "death to me"? This subtle objection is not only answered, but turned into an argument. It was not the law that brought death, "but sin." And sin wrought death, "that [in the purpose of God in giving the law] it might appear sin [inasmuch as it (sin)] worked death in me by that which is good." How desperate the disease that only grows worse under the appropriate remedy to heal it! But God had an additional purpose in giving the holy law to sinful man, namely, "that [in order that] sin by the commandment might become exceeding sinful." The coward is not known until he hears the command to march against the foe.

Paul, having now shown that the law was added "that the offense might abound" (5:20), takes up with this fourteenth verse point (3) above in the chapter, that salvation is impossible under the law, because it cannot deliver from the flesh (3:20). The law cannot give holiness, for the flesh is the seat of sin.

Two questions always confront the student on this passage: (a) Is this Paul's own experience? In the word "I," which was introduced at verse 7, does he contemplate no one but himself? The section is certainly autobiographic. Such a picture of the experience and despair of the heart in its contest with sin could not possibly be drawn but by one who had had the contest. It is because sin and law in their essence and power are learned only by experience that he now reasons from the latter. The law is not learned by hearing it; it must "come."

But, while this must be a page from Paul's own history, it is written in a way to be typical. He speaks not only for himself, but voices the agony of every man situated similarly. He has already more than once put his argument into dialogue form and introduced the words "I" and "you" (see 2:1, 17, ff; 3:7) with general and all-inclusive reference.

(b) The other question is much more serious: Do verses 14-25 depict the experience of a regenerate or an unregenerate man? Is this a normal Christian experience or a sinner's experience? The great names are found on both sides; for the former, Augustine, Luther, Calvin, Beza; and for the latter, Meyer, Godet, Stuart, Tholuck.

The first party claims, and with no little weight, that none but a regenerate man would make such a struggle against sin; that only such a one could say, "I delight in the law of God" (but see 2:17, 23); and that Galatians 5:17 gives in brief the contest between the flesh and the Spirit in the Christian, a contest like this detailed in the section before us. (But beware of the King James translation of Gal. 5:17.)

On the other hand, it is said, how can this be Paul's experience as a Christian, when he begins with the confession that he is "sold under sin"; when, after denying that the justified man "continues" in sin (6:1, 2), he admits that it holds him in its unbroken power; when, after proclaiming his freedom from law, and so from the "passions" of sins (7:5, 6; 6:18), he now sadly confesses himself their slave, incapable of doing one single good act? He "delights" in the law, but is in "captivity" to sin.

This division of interpretation ought to have suggested long ago that the understanding of this passage does not turn on the question of regeneracy or unregeneracy. An undivided decision in favor of one or the other would not shed a ray of light on the interpretation; it would estop interpretation by turning the course of argument away from its connection. For who is the man in this picture? A man under law; one who has discovered its heart-searching spirituality, but who in every attempt to keep it finds himself defeated by indwelling sin; one who says, "How beautiful to have no desires, to let God desire for me!" but finding at every turn that he wants everything in sight. Now this will be the experience of any man, regenerate or unregenerate, who attempts to keep the law. It might have been the experience of the sincere ruler (Mark 10:17-21), whom Jesus "loved." He came running and kneeled in his eager inquiry to know what to do. It might have been the experience of Paul during some part of his stay in Arabia (Gal. 1:17, 18), until he had wrought out in his heart and mind what the Christ in whom he had believed was to his soul. For, while this section is as unlike a normal Christian experience as early dawn is unlike broad daylight, there is no doubt that many Christians have it and have had it. The normal experiences given in 6:17, 18; in 7:4, 6; and especially in 8:1, 2, and I Peter 1:8, 9. The section before us, with its Laocoön contest, is the painful portrait of a man in deadly earnest to be just before God without Christ, either not knowing Him at all or knowing Him without understanding the Gospel. (See Gal. 4:9.) In Paul's day many sincere Jews, with reverence for their holy law, may have seen in this passage a picture of that agony with which their own hearts had once ached.

14. "The law is spiritual: . . . I am carnal." This verse is a proof of the last statement that not the law, but sin, proved death to him. As a natural law pertains alone to nature, as a mental law has no field but the intellect, so a spiritual law belongs only to the realm of spirit and can be kept only by holy beings. Between the law and one who is carnal there is a lack of moral adjustment. Peter, in his attempt to walk on the water, began to sink, because he was out of the sphere suited to mere doubting man. The priest could not carry the sacrificial coals in his hand in going from the altar into the holy place, and no more can a carnal man come before God carrying the fiery law in his heart; it would slay him.

If with this verse Paul drops the past tense for the present, it is not at all because he is giving his own condition at the time of writing. The change occurs in the verse before he resorts to the first person and while he is still speaking of the law. In verses 7-13 he expanded verse 5 above, showing in detail the operation of the law on the Romans, once under it, but not when he wrote (v. 6); hence the past tense. In this verse he speaks not of the operation, but of the permanent character of the law, which requires the present tense; and he continues with this tense to show what is always true of the "flesh" under law.

The "carnal" man is not only the man out of Christ (see v. 5 above), but also one presumably in Him, but ignorant of grace (cf. I Cor. 3:3 with 23). The condition of all such is given in the words "sold under sin," language borrowed from the slave market.

This little phrase, in which sin is personified, is the proposition whose proof follows to the end of the chapter. The unhappy slave chants his misery with monotonous repetition of the one idea—he would do good, but he cannot. The proof falls into three dirges, the last of which ends in the high key of a wail. The first dirge is verses 15-17; the second, verses 18-20; the third, verses 21-24. The last verse (25) sums all up. These three all go to show one who is a slave sold under sin.

15-17. The "for" with which this complaint begins introduces it as a proof of the proposition, "sold under sin." What the man does he knows ("allow" is incorrect) not. He is driven blindly. He hates what he does and does what he hates. This very conduct shows on both its sides that he "consents to the law that it is good." His failure, then, to lead a good life cannot be ascribed to his wrong attitude toward the law; that failure must be ascribed to indwelling sin. The "I" is just himself, body, soul, and spirit, that have been seized upon by the alien master which he calls sin. Note that

he does not yet hate his master; he does not know him; he
only hates his service.

18-20. This dirge does not advance the argument one step.
It comes to the same conclusion as the last one and in the same
terms—"sin that dwelleth in me." But, while it does not advance, it emphasizes by becoming more specific. There he
introduced the metaphor of a house: "sin dwells in me." He
now shows that sin occupies every room in the whole abode:
"there does not dwell in me a good thing." Sin lodges in
every chamber from the cellar to the roof. The law is doing
its work, "for by the law is the [full] knowledge of sin (3:20).
He thought there was some dust in the house, but now as the
white sunlight streams in at the windows, he sees the winged
motes everywhere, saturating the air, settling on the floor, de-
facing the furniture, and every motion he makes only sets
them flying. It is worse. For when he begins to beat around
to make things clean, it is as when Aaron smote the dust in
Egypt: it turned to lice (Exod. 8:16), and his house is possessed by them.

In a second point he is more specific than in the first dirge.
There he said in general terms, "what I would" and "what I
hate." Here he says "the good that I would" and "the evil
that I would not." The first did not show that it was good
that he could not do and evil that he could not shun.

The section begins with "for," leaning on the statement
that had just been made—"sin that dwelleth in me." "For" is
"explanatory rather than demonstrative" (Godet). The phrase
"that is, in my flesh," following "in me," is not restrictive; it
is appositional, serving to define the words "in me" and to
point out precisely what is meant by them. Every psychological exposition of this passage is wrong. To parcel out the
soul of this man and say some part consents to the law and
some other part commits sin, is to deny the principal proposition (v. 14) and every verse that follows. And this the psychological interpreters show by virtually saying that Paul
must not be understood at what he says: "I am carnal." It
is just one and the same "I" that is "carnal," that does "what
he allows not," that "hates what he does," that "consents unto

the law that it is good." It is precisely of his whole self that
he says "sin dwells in me." The carnal "I," thrilled by the
electric touch of the law, can consent to that law, can wish to
do the good, can hate the evil condemned by the law, can
"wish" and "hate" and "consent," yet never cease practicing
sin. The very proof that he gives that sin dwells in him is
"for to will [wish] is present with me, but how to perform
that which is good I find not." It is a carnal wish, for a spiritual wish is a spiritual deed (II Cor. 8:10, R. V.). That a
carnal man, as the one in this section is declared to be, could
have a spiritual wish or a spiritual consent to the law is a contradiction in terms. There can be no wish contrary to character.

21-24. The metaphor of a house is now dropped, and in
plain terms he repeats what was said in the two preceding
dirges, but in the form of result—"then." "I find then [in
my experience] the law [the unvarying principle (in reference)], to me who would do good, that evil is present with me
[to defeat the effort at good]." That "law" does not mean the
Mosaic law in this passage is the opinion of Alford, Godet,
Sanday, and many others. (For the meaning assigned above
see 8:2, "law of the Spirit.")

Verses 22 and 23, introduced by "for," unfold what Paul
means by verse 21. He delights in (with) the law—Moses' law
here, for he calls it the "law of God." He can "approve" it
as a Jew, being "instructed" by it (2:18). This delight is not
in that which is outward in doing it, but in the "inward man,"
in his "wish," in his "consent," in his "hate" of what the law
condemns. A proof of his delight in the law is his persistent
effort to keep it in spite of constant failure. The inner man
is not the new man (Eph. 2:10; 4:24). But along with this
delight he has an opposite experience; he sees "another," a
different law, a force in his members, his various capacities, a
force that does not fight a battle merely, but carries on a successful campaign against the law of his mind. The "law of
the mind" means the delight of the inward man in God's law.
This campaign is successful against him, because it leaves him
in captivity to the "law [power] of sin in his members," a

phrase defining what he had just called "another law." The argument has now come around to the point from which it started. What he deplores here is not his wrongdoing, but his slavery—"sold under sin" (v. 14). His pain is not the path of wickedness which he pursues, but in the chain that drags him along that destructive way—a chain that he cannot break. His sin is not an act; it is helpless subjection to the law of sin in his members. How can this be called a normal Christian experience? It is a legal experience, written to show that, whatever else the law can do, it can deliver no man, saint or sinner, from the flesh. Ye are "delivered from the law" by "being *dead*" (in Christ) to that in which ye "were held" (v. 6). It sometimes happens that a man long addicted to intoxicants wakes up to some appreciation of his degradation and of the ruin not far ahead of him in his course. In sober moments he reflects on the purity and liberty of the days before he touched the bowl, and he resolves to drink no more; but under the fierce clamor of his appetite his wish to do good breaks down. He resolves again, and again fails, and again and again. In this state he could read this section and make every word his own. To wish the good and at the same time to do the evil is not a normal condition. The struggling drunkard's case is a mild one compared with that of the awakened man under the law. The drunkard finds a master in one member, his appetite for drink; the man under God's law finds a master in every member. The drunkard does sometimes succeed in breaking his hateful bonds; the man standing under frowning Sinai never does. Christ must unshackle him.

This divided state, yearning to do good, but learning finally that the good is beyond his reach, wrings out the cry for deliverance from his wretchedness. This is the point to which Paul has been leading the argument. Experience shows that the law leaves a man, no matter how earnest to keep it, in a state of miserable slavery.

"The body of this death." Moule's statement that "this is that part of the regenerate man which yet has to die" shows to what limits even an otherwise fair exegete can be driven by a false assumption. His is that the man in this picture is regenerate. Why, the very next word declares that deliverance from the "body of death" comes not with physical death, but "through Jesus Christ." The "body of death" is just the man himself, the same that was mentioned in 6:6. By using the word "body" Paul indicates what he has all along said, that he was wholly sinful. His cry virtually is, "Who shall deliver me from myself?" He calls it "the body of this death," because it belongs to death and is under its power in being under the power of sin. Sin and death always go together.

25. "I thank God [that deliverance comes] through Jesus Christ our Lord." This sentence is brief and not complete in itself, because the method of the deliverance was fully described by Paul in verses 1-6 at the beginning of the chapter.

"So then . . . I myself . . ." These two antithetical propositions sum up all that has been said above—"a terse, compressed summary of the previous paragraph, verses 7-24, describing in two strokes the state of things prior to the intervention of Christ." There is a similar condensation in 1:32. "I myself," apart from Christ, "with the mind," that "wishes to do good" and "delights in the law," thus "serve" it—"serve in the oldness of the letter" (v. 6 above); "but [I myself] with the flesh [the enslaved man] [serve] the law of sin ["in my members"]." (See 15:14, where the same words mean "apart from other information.")

CHAPTER 8

IN CHRIST JESUS A GODLY LIFE IS
INSURED BY THE HOLY SPIRIT

G ODET, in his introduction to this chapter that begins with
no condemnation and ends with no separation, quotes
Spener as saying, "If Holy Scripture was a ring, and the Epistle to the Romans its precious stone, chapter 8 would be the
sparkling point of the jewel." It takes up the little phrase in
chapter 7, "serve in newness of [the] spirit," and develops it.
The opposite service mentioned there, "in the oldness of the
letter," the law, is the theme of chapter 7.

This chapter is the counterpart of the fifth. The fifth shows
that justification by faith in Christ is once and forever—it is
permanent; here we have the same thing—a godly life, the
fruit of justification is insured. There the argument for permanence of justification is based on its ground, the love of God
in Christ Jesus; here it is based on the power of the Spirit
in Christ Jesus. There the justified man was looked at only
in his relation to God; here he is also considered in the midst
of his conflict with the flesh and the world, over which he
triumphs by the aid of the Spirit. Hence some points just
touched on there are developed here. The Holy Spirit is only
once mentioned there (5:5), said to be given, but nothing
more; here His office is completely unfolded. Two short verses
there (3, 4) speak of "tribulations"; here they occupy attention almost wholly from verse 17 to the end. There the conclusion is briefly given—"Grace reigns through righteousness
unto eternal life;" here it is presented at length in a most
powerful and poetic strain (vv. 31-39).

There are four topics in the chapter: (1) deliverance from

the flesh by the power of the Spirit (vv. 1-11); (2) realization
of sonship by the same Spirit (vv. 12-17a); (3) preservation in
sufferings (vv. 17b-30); (4) a pæan of triumph (vv. 31-39).
Furthermore, the chapter brings all the lines of argument together and shows them in their happy issue in salvation, the
eternal sequence of grace.

1. "There is therefore now no condemnation." The connection by the word "therefore" is with the first clause of the
preceding verse, and through it with that to which the clause
refers. "Now"—as the argument at present stands. The "no"
is emphatic—no condemnation from the law, and none on
account of inherent sinfulness; none from any source or for
any cause. Those who make the "now" temporal miss the
shining point that "no condemnation" means none possible,
none forever. This happy condition belongs only to those
"in Christ Jesus." The rest of the verse is not genuine and
is omitted by all modern editors of the text.

2. This verse tells not why, but how, the deliverance came
about. It gives not the ground, but the agent, of the freedom.
It is the seventh chapter condensed to one sentence. When
a man by faith comes into Christ Jesus he finds there the
Spirit's law or controlling force effecting life in the soul. This
law is neither the moral nor the Mosaic law; it is not the "law
of the mind," not the "law of faith" (3:27), but the operative
force of the Holy Spirit, whose presence awakens spiritual life
and sustains it. He that has the Son has life (I John 5:12),
because in the Son he finds the life-giving Spirit. By faith in
Christ a man finds not only acquittal from sins, but also the
power by which he no longer commits them; for this law of
the Spirit sets him at liberty ("free") from the "law of sin
and death," fully described in verse 23 above as an enslaving
force in his members. The spiritual law is set against the
carnal and overcomes it. The law of gravity ever keeps the
serpent crawling on the earth, and he cannot rise above it; but
give him wings and now he has a power superior to gravity by
which he can fly. A man cannot rise above the clouds; his
own dead weight holds him down until he steps "in" the car
suspended beneath the balloon and cuts loose, when he finds

another force dominating the force of gravity and carrying him aloft in spite of it. "In Christ Jesus" there is a power that sets one at liberty from the sinful force in his members. Gravity never ceases, but it may be overcome. The law of sin in the members exists as long as they do, but "in Christ" it cannot operate.

3, 4. These two verses tell, first, how it comes to pass that the man in Christ Jesus is "free from the law of sin" in his members, and second, why. The "law [of Moses] could not" condemn sin in the flesh, because it was weaker than the flesh. It was weak through the flesh. The anchor of the law was strong in itself, but it would not hold in the mud bottom of the heart. It could and did condemn the acts of the flesh and punished some of them even with death, but the sin in the flesh it could not condemn; it only excited it to rebellion. "When the commandment came, sin revived" (7:5, 9). To condemn is to pronounce sentence against and to inflict due penalty. Christ died not only for acts of sin, but for sinners, sin in the heart. (For the former see 3:23-26; 4:25; for the latter, 6:6-10.) If "he that is dead is justified from sin," it is because the sinfulness in him was condemned in Christ. The verses before us are the counterpart of 6:6-10.

"God sending his own Son in the likeness of sinful flesh." Here is both the deity and the humanity of Christ (I Tim. 3: 16). He is called His "own" Son to distinguish Him from others (v. 16 below), and He was such before He was "sent." He did not come in the likeness of flesh, or He would have been no proper man, and He did not come in sinful flesh, or He would have been a sinner; but he came "in the likeness of sinful flesh." He was neither a phantom nor a sinner, but a perfect man. He must be such a man, that God might condemn sin in the flesh.

God sent Him (an offering) "for sin." Godet's "wholly different explanation," denying that Paul had the "condemnation on the cross" in view, is unscriptural. In leaving out the cross Godet has left out the Gospel. The phrase "for sin," equivalent to "concerning" or "about sin," is all-comprehensive. He was sent not merely about the guilt of sin, but about its existence as well. He came not only to condemn its guilt, but its presence in the heart even when passive. If the cross is not mentioned, but, on the other hand, the sending and the manner of it ("in the likeness of sinful flesh") are made prominent, this is just to confine our attention to that on which the condemnation fell. The cross is plainly implied in the word "condemn." Christ stood for men in His person in the flesh, and so the condemnation which fell on His flesh is equally theirs who are in Him. And therefore the text does not say "his," because it is theirs also. Had he not been sinless, He could have been condemned, to be sure, but He could not have risen again so that men might come to be in Him. And "there is therefore now no condemnation to them that are in Christ Jesus," because their sinfulness was condemned in Him together with their sins.

God's purpose in thus sending His Son was that the "righteousness" demanded by the law, namely, a holy heart, might be "fulfilled in [not "by"] us, who walk not after [in accordance with the promptings of] the flesh, but after [the promptings of] the spirit." To "walk" means to live and act. The last two phrases, beginning with "who walk," do not tell why or on what ground the righteosuness of the law is fulfilled in believers, but who are such. They give a description and not a reason. Those who are in Christ find there the Spirit that not only begets a new life, but gives direction to its impulses. The third verse gives the ground of regeneration; the fourth, its realization.

Why did not Paul, instead of the phrase, "who walk not after the flesh, but after the spirit," say "who believe"? For believing involves such a walk and is not genuine unless it exhibits such a walk. The answer is that he has the regulating method of the Mosaic law to combat, and he wishes to show that believing contains a real and effective energy for life which is not in the law—a walk in the spirit.

5-8. This brief section shows the contrast between the man described in 7:14-25 and the man "in Christ." The fifth verse in its first sentence shows why the righteousness of the law is not produced in the man not in Christ, that is, in the man who walks after the flesh and so under law: he "minds [likes, cares for, aspires after] the things of the flesh." Even his religious notions spring from his own unregenerate conceptions. On the other hand, "they that are after [according to] the spirit [mind (care for, like)] the things of the spirit." "They that are." The "are" asserts their character. They that are after the flesh are natural, carnal men (John 3:3, 6).

6. This verse gives the nature of the carnal mind as the reason why it cares only for the things of the flesh. "To be carnally minded is death." Death is absence of life and of all power to do the things belonging to life. On the other hand, "to be spiritually minded [as he is who is in Christ] is life and peace." Such a one is endowed with the life and peace of the Holy Spirit and can attend to the Spirit's things.

7. The first sentence defines the "death" of the last verse. It is "enmity against God." In the seventh chapter the inability to do God's will, the death, was merely bewailed; here its moral character is given—it is guilt. As surely as God is love, so surely the natural dislike to follow Him is hostility and hatred.

The natural mind is enmity to God, because it does not subject itself to His law; it is in a state of rebellion. The brief sentence, "neither indeed can be," is a diluted translation, lacking the climactic force of the original, which contains another "for." The carnal mind does not subject itself to the law of God, for, indeed, it cannot. Here is 7:14-25 in a nutshell. Paul says there, "I am carnal, sold under sin," and I cannot do the things that I delight in, contained in the law. But an additional fact must now be given that this inability is an impotency of enmity and guilt. A man may not be conscious of a feeling of enmity; he may even claim to love God; but the very fiber of the man out of Christ is here declared to be in opposition to Him. (See on 5:6, "without strength.")

8. "So then." Another fault in the King James Version; it ought to be simply "and." This eighth verse is not a logical conclusion, but a solemn assertion: "And they that are in the flesh [not in Christ] cannot please God." What is said of the carnal mind, that it is impotent for good, is now asserted of

all the unregenerate. Out of Christ, a man may be religious and serve in "the oldness of the letter," but he neither pleases God nor is he God's friend.

This section (vv. 5-8), then, gives a very substantial reason, in the character of the unrenewed or carnal mind, why only those who walk after the spirit (v. 4) found in Christ (v. 2) can fulfill the righteousness of the law. It shows at the same time that being in the flesh and being under law, the two states occurring together as they do, is a union in helpless guilt.

9. In happy contrast with those who "cannot please God," because they are in the flesh, that is, under its power, Paul addresses the Romans directly to assure them of four great results from the possession of the Spirit: "not in the flesh"; Christ's own (1:6); their own spirit alive; certainty of the future life of the body. "Ye [emphatic] are not in the flesh, but in [the control of] the Spirit, if indeed [no doubt expressed; it is on the supposition that] the Spirit of God dwells in [makes his home with] you." The supposition is that the Spirit is not a fitful influence, but an abiding guest or, rather, host. Note how he says, Ye are in the Spirit if the Spirit is in you.

On the other hand, "if anyone [how delicately he avoids saying "ye" when it comes to this painful statement!] has not the Spirit of Christ," he does not belong to Christ. The Spirit of God and the Spirit of Christ are one and the same Holy Spirit. None but the reader who neglects the logic will take the phrase "Spirit of Christ" for the temper or disposition of Christ. The Spirit proceeds from both God and Christ.

10. "And if Christ be in you." Here are three different phrases meaning one thing: "the Spirit of God," "the Spirit of Christ," and "Christ." He comes from God the Father (Acts 1:4); He is given in Christ the Son (8:2); and does not speak of himself (John 16:13), but manifests "Christ" (John 14:21). The threefold mention shows the work of the Trinity in the sanctification of the believer.

When Christ dwells in a man "the body is dead because of sin." Paul does not say "flesh," because he means the literal body. The saints are subject to physical death and die, because of Adam's sin (5:12). But the spirit, the saint's own personal spirit, is not alive, but "life." It has the life of Christ, because of His righteousness imparted through faith. The righteousness here mentioned is comprehensive, including justification and sanctification. He says the Spirit is "life," but He does not say the body is death, for, while the spirit of the man in Christ is already redeemed from death, his body in due time, at Christ's coming, will be.

11. "Raised up Jesus, . . . raised up Christ." The indwelling of "the Spirit of him [God] that raised up Jesus [the historic person] from [among] the dead" is a pledge that He who raised up Christ, the covenant head, will also make alive "your mortal bodies." He was raised not only as Jesus the man, but as Jesus the Christ, who stands for all who are in Him. This quickening of the mortal body takes place either because of or through (the reading is in doubt) the Spirit that dwells in you. And thus the Trinity is connected with the resurrection.

This closes the first section of the chapter—deliverance from the flesh by the power of the Spirit. His help is threefold: He delivers in Christ from the condemnation of the flesh (vv. 1, 2); from the power of the flesh (vv. 3-8); the whole man, spirit and body, from the power of death (vv. 9-11).

It is now plain to be seen that the elucidation of the sixth chapter by the objective view has everything in its favor. To make that chapter subjective is to anticipate this section. Paul takes one step at at time. There he gives the things to be believed, without which there is no sanctification; here the things to be experienced. Until faith takes Christ for the Saviour from the flesh, it cannot find that He is also the inward sanctifier.

12, 13. (See (2) in analysis above.) Some (Moule, Lipsius) would join these two verses with the last section and begin the new one with verse 14. But with his intention to speak of sonship Paul wishes to show that, first of all, it is realized in a right life; and so Jesus taught (Matt. 5:44, 45). And in such a life is found the best starting point for the discussion—the best for without it there is no proof of the lofty relation (I John 2:4).

The section begins as a deduction ("therefore") from verses
9-11. Because the Spirit has given life to our soul and will give
life to our mortal body, therefore "we are debtors not to the
flesh," which could not bring us any deliverance to live after it.
Mark how Paul implies not only that the flesh still exists, but
also that there is danger from it. He discriminates. Our only
obligation is not to live after it; otherwise we may owe it much.
But it is to be the slave, not the master. In the warfare of life
it is to be the soldier, sent into any dangerous situation, and
not the captain, who directs the siege. If this order is reversed,
if a man yields to the desires of his heart and follows his own
likes and dislikes, "if ye live after [according to] the flesh," ye
are going to die. The flesh belongs to the world, and the man
who is yielding to its promptings is in the world, living like
the world, and must perish with the world. He is a child of
"this world" (Luke 16:8), but not a child of God; he is not
living like His only Son (I John 2:6).

On the other hand, "if ye by [not "through"] the Spirit put
to death the deeds of the body." The emphatic words are "by
the Spirit." His presence is instant death to the evil deeds of
the body. To subdue these by other means is deceptive as-
ceticism. By the force of will they may be chained, but, as the
section above shows, only God's Spirit can destroy them. Observe he does not say destroy the flesh, nor destroy the body,
but the deeds of the body—its aspirations, impulses, desires,
and works (Gal. 5:19-21). To destroy the body, the seat of the
flesh, would be to destroy one's self. Paul uses the word
"body" here as objective of the flesh. (See 6:6 and Col. 3:5-9.)
The flesh is one's constant and most intimate associate. The
man in Christ is not in the flesh, but it is in him, and the problem of salvation is not how to transmute the flesh into something good, but how to live with this devilish thing every day
without being overcome by it. The presence of the Spirit
solves the problem. "If ye by the Spirit put to death [at one
stroke] the deeds of the body, ye shall live"—live the life of
sons.

14. "For." The sequence appears as soon as it is noticed
that putting to death the deeds of the body by the Spirit, the

theme of the last verse, is exactly equivalent to being "led by
the Spirit" in this verse, and that the little sentence "ye shall
live" means live as sons. To be led by the Spirit is to put to
put to death the deeds of the body, and to be a son in consequence of such leading is to live. Life by the Spirit gives sonship.

15. After having argued their sonship on the ground of their
pious walk in the Spirit, he supports the argument now by the
testimony of their experience. They are sons, "for" they did
not, on becoming followers of Christ, receive a "spirit of bondage again unto [into a state of] fear" (II Tim. 1:7). "Spirit"
in this verse seems to mean disposition or temper (Num.
5:14), such as men had under the law. The Romans were not
conscious of such a slavish spirit, for on becoming followers of
Christ they received a "spirit of adoption," which awakened
the feeling of sonship and by which they "cried" (out, confidently, Gal. 4:6), "Abba, Father," an endearing repetition of
words used by Jesus himself (Mark 14:36).

16, 17a. The Holy Spirit testifies to the same fact. Note
how Paul distinguishes between the divine Spirit and the
human in which he dwells. "The Spirit himself bears witness
along with our spirit [and two witnesses establish the truth],
that we are children of God." The relation of the human and
the divine cannot be explained in the work of salvation, but
they are distinct, and the Holy Spirit destroys neither the voli-
tion nor the personality of the human.

For the word "sons" in verse 14 Paul now uses the tenderer
term "children," begotten ones, which goes to show that the
word "adoption" is not to be pressed. They are not merely
legally adopted, but really born sons (I John 5:1), spiritually
begotten. They have all the rights and prospects of children:
"if [since] children, then heirs"; and not heirs to a lesser, but
to an equal ("joint heirs" gives point to the assertion) portion
with Christ, the first-born. They do not inherit a secondary
share, not a share through Him, but with Him. "Thou hast
loved them as thou hast loved me" (John 17:23). (See also
Matt. 19:28; I Cor. 6:2, 3; Col. 3:4; Rev. 3:21.)

This second section of the chapter teaches then, first, that

the Spirit, who puts to death the deeds of the body, gives life
to the man; second, that this life is the life of sonship; and,
third, that this sonship involves the fullest meaning of the
word, assuring an equal inheritance with Christ.

17b. Paul turns abruptly to the subject of suffering. (See
(3) in analysis above.) And yet not so abruptly, for the suffering of real Christians at all times is, and especially at that
time was, a constant daily experience. We are joint heirs with
Christ "if [since, as the fact is] indeed we suffer with him" in
order to share His glory. This suffering is not penal and not
in the contest with our own flesh, but comes to His followers
because, like Him, they live in opposition to the world that
hates them (I John 3:13), and, like Him, reprove the world's
works (John 7:7). To suffer like Him is to suffer with Him,
for He makes His followers' pains His own (Acts 9:4, 5). It is
almost an axiom of the Gospel that the path to glory is the
path of pain (Mark 10:38; Phil 2:9). Therefore the intelligent believer does not hesitate to undergo sorrow in his service
to Christ; he rather covets it in order that he may be glorified
with Him; for the joint heirs are those who suffer that they
may be glorified. Suffering is the seed that ripens in fruit of
glory.

The discussion of this topic is concerned with that which
gives sustaining power and comfort in suffering. The points
are three: (a) the vastness of the future glory, an expansion
of verses 3, 4 (vv. 18-25); (b) the Holy Spirit's aid (vv. 26,
27); and (c) God's general control of all things to bring about
His people's ultimate good (vv. 28-30).

18. Paul had weighed the sufferings of the present time
against the future glory. This verse gives the estimate—they
are not worthy, are no account in the comparison. In themselves the present tribulations for Christ are vast and painful
(II Cor. 11:23-28). If then before the glory they are nothing,
what must the glory be? (II Cor. 4:17.) It is not "in us," but
toward us, "to usward," for Paul is contemplating much more
than that which affects the person directly.

19. So vast is this glory that the very (irrational) creation,
or "creature" (Isa. 11:9; II Pet. 3:13), is awaiting it with eager

expectancy, longing for the "manifestation," the unveiling, of the sons (v. 14 above) of God at His advent (Col. 3:4).

20, 21. As God's sons look with longing to the future, first, because their present condition is painful and is not the ideal condition, and, second, because the future will bring them redemption, just so the creation, personified all through this passage, looks to the same future; first, because it is now under the curse, and, second, in the future, in the glorification of the faithful, it will find deliverance. The twentieth verse gives a reason for the "earnest expectation" drawn from the present condition of creation, and the next verse a reason (when we read "because") drawn from the future. "Was made subject to vanity" is ambiguous. Creation was not *made* so, for originally creation was "good," and it was subjected to vanity, that is, to attain to no good end permanently. Any good that comes from creation must be evoked by man's hard toil. This condition did not come about by its own will ("willingly"), but because of Him (God) who subjected it to vanity, not finally, but upon a basis of some provision for the future, called "hope." This verse clearly implies that creation ("all nature") is neither in its original condition nor in its final condition. It fell when man fell (Gen. 3:17-19); it shall be restored when he is, and shall be no longer subject to vanity, but to him (Heb. 2:5-9). It is eagerly awaiting the revelation of God's sons, because that is the time when it "also shall be delivered from the bondage of corruption [the subjection, v. 20] into the liberty of the glory ["glorious liberty" is wrong] of the children of God." The creation is promised the liberty of the glory, not the glory.

22. This verse explains the "liberty" of the last in showing the need of it in creation. The language is highly poetic; creation is personified. "We know," says Paul, from observation of the patent fact, "that the whole creation groans" together in all its parts, and travails in birth pangs to bring forth that which is new and fair. Cold winds moan and earthquakes shake. "All the voices of nature are in the minor key." All things sigh before God, as Bonar sang:

> Come and make all things new;
> Build up this ruined earth;
> Restore our faded paradise,
> Creation's second birth.

23. This verse puts the sons of God in a different category from creation. "They" in italics in the King James Version should be "it," creation. Not only creation, "but ourselves also," who, even though we have the first-fruits of salvation, the Spirit, "ourselves groan within ourselves, [because or while] waiting for the adoption, to wit, the redemption of our body." The right of sons believers have already (see v. 15 above), but not the realization; and the body is dead because of sin. The "redemption of the body" is more than resurrection and more than the change that will come to that generation which shall not die (I Cor. 15:51). It is this and more: the instating of redeemed man in his original position in creation and his relation to it—a redeemed man in a redeemed world. The conception is Jewish (Ruth 4; Eph. 1:14; Rev. 5:9, 10). Verses 22 and 23 are placed logically side by side. Creation groans and God's sons groan, for both are looking for things which will bring each in right relation to the other.

24, 25. "For we are saved by hope." A much better translation is that of Moule, Liddon, and others: "We were saved in hope." When by faith the salvation from sin occurred, the believer found himself in a condition of hope. From this condition Paul argues in these two verses for the "redemption" just mentioned. "The attitude of hope, so distinctive of the Christian, implies that there is more in store for him than anything that is his already" (Sanday). Hope suggests something unseen, unrealized; for what a man sees, what he already has, he does not hope for. "But if we hope [the Christian's condition] for that we see not, then [as he said in v. 23] do we with patience wait for it." The hope of the exceeding glory gives the holy patience that persists in good work (2:7) amid suffering.

26, 27. The Spirit's aid. (See (*b*) under 17*b* above.) "Likewise the Spirit also [just like hope] helpeth our infirmi-

ties." "Weakness" is a better reading. Without the Spirit the
saint has no strength to attain to that for which he hopes. Paul
illustrates this in one single item belonging to Christian walk.
Prayer is the simplest and easiest of all activities, and yet "we
know not what we should pray for as we ought." Whether
this refers to the words (the manner) of the prayer or the subject makes little difference. The two views come to the same
thing. The Spirit helps in every way. The weakness is not
only in prayer, but general. He helps by taking hold with the
saint against the opposition. The only other instance of the
word (Luke 10:40) is instructive. How He helps in general is
not told, but in the matter of prayer He does in the heart what
Christ does before God (see v. 34 below): He intercedes in
our behalf. The earnest manner of His intercession is shown
in the words, "with groanings which cannot be uttered," yearn-
ings whose depth is beyond the power of words to convey.
But, while the utterances are not intelligible," he [God] that
searcheth the hearts [of the saints] knoweth what is the mind
of the Spirit." God knows the meaning of the Spirit's groan
and interprets the inarticulated aspiration of the heart, "because he [the Spirit] maketh intercession for the saints [in the
groans proceeding from their hearts] according to God." That
wordless prayer is born of the Spirit in accordance with God's
purpose.

28. Here Paul abandons particulars to show generally that
the whole activity of God is directed toward the ultimate good
of those that love Him. (See (c) under 17b above.) While
the details of this verse and the next one present some difficulties, the line of argument is clear. The present verse asserts
the fact that God is making all things work together for the
good of His people; the next verse gives the reason for the fact
in His predestinating them from the beginning to be like His
Son. What He has determined at the beginning to accomplish
nothing along the way can thwart. His predetermination con-
trols everying affecting those who love Him.

"We know"—from God's dealing with the Old Testament
saints and from personal experience. "That all things"—to
be taken in its most comprehensive sense; some of the things

are named in verse 35 and verses 38 and 39 below. "Work to-gether"—in concert with us, because they are under God's con-trol. The means are various, the purpose one. How Jacob was pained for long years by the loss of Joseph! And how Joseph was "hurt with fetters" when "laid in iron" (Ps. 105:17-22)! But God took this means to make him ruler of Egypt and savior of his sorrowing father and his household. "All things work"—they are not accidents or blind chance; God is working through them. This is true only of "them that love God," now further described as those "who are called according to his purpose," to show that their love to God was not a mere natural love, but the fruit of His special love toward them. "Called" does not mean invited, but effectually called (1:6), almost equivalent to chosen. This call was in harmony, in accordance, with His "purpose" or free decree to bring them to glory in Christ. Those who love Him are those whom He has called.

29. Now it is not allowed to any vicissitude in the life of such to harm them. "For whom he did foreknow [that is, his called ones who love him] he also did predestinate" for likeness to Christ. To predestinate is to determine from the start what shall be the outcome. It is this active, living, ever-present, and controlling predestination that shields the lover of God from harm and turns "all things" to his good. To "foreknow" does not mean to approve on the ground of character; it does not mean that God foreknew who would believe and there-fore predestinated them. God's appointment to eternal life is chronologically before faith (Acts 13:48). The natural man does not "seek after God" (3:11); his mind is "enmity against God"; it is not subject to the law of God, "for indeed it cannot be" (8:7). How can those "dead in trespasses and sins" (Eph. 2:1) believe in God? How could God foreknow some men as believers, when belief was impossible to them? What His prescience saw in all men was enmity and helpless-ness in sin because of a love of it. Even when they knew Him they deliberately chose to dishonor Him (1:21-23). Candor must admit that these plain Scriptures teach the helplessness of man in his sin. But it is said that by the preaching of the

Gospel and the aid of the accompanying Spirit men are brought into a condition where they can believe, and God foresaw who in this condition would believe and predestinated them. This is an invention outside of Scripture to meet a difficulty, an invention that will not bear scrutiny. For this condition, to be effective, must be one in which the death in sin is removed and the enmity is overcome, which is nothing less than regeneration. And thus we should have regeneration as a condition of faith, and, worse yet, that in this condition God would only see *some* who believed and whom He might predestinate. Other regenerate ones who failed to believe would perish.

Foreknowledge would better be left where Paul leaves it—without any of these additions. It differs from prescience, by which God knows all things. It does not in itself include the idea of selection, but when Paul says, "whom he did foreknow," we see it is closely connected with this idea. He foreknew certain persons ("whom"), knew them before they had an existence, took note of them (Amos 3:2; Matt. 7:23), and these He destined to glory. His purpose included their faith, of course, but this is just the word that Paul has not used since 5:2 and does not use until we are well-nigh through the next chapter. Where he does not use it we would best not. And we would best leave the suggested difficulty of responsibility and free will where he leaves it. He places the salvation of God's people wholly in God's hands, and surely there it is secure, secure only because it is there.

A sculptor would make a beautiful image in marble. He knows among many the huge rough stone which he will use for his purpose. He destines this block for the end which he has in view. That determination on his part preserves it. He will chisel and rasp and file on the block, but he will not do anything to hurt it, and he will see to it that no one else mars it. God's foreknowledge and predestination are the preservation of His people, making all things work for good.

"Conformed" means made like, not outwardly, but inwardly, in character. God predestinates men not for Heaven, but for holiness. He makes "all things work together" toward this end. Trials and crosses under His control are sanctifying. "Tribulation works out patience" (5:3). The ultimate purpose of God's predestination is to surround His Son with a multitude like Him, that by this likeness they may be His brethren. The likeness will be completed at the resurrection. Since no one as yet, save Jesus, has experienced this (I Cor. 15:23), He is called the "first-born."

30. This verse gives the steps by which the likeness to Christ, the glory, is reached: "foreknew," "predestinated," "called," "justified," "glorified," five golden links connecting God's gracious purpose in the eternity past with its consummation in the eternity to come. The last word, "glorified," in the past tense, indicates the certainty of His purpose. (See on 4:25, last paragraph.) But this verse does more than to analyze what precedes; it presents an argument by means of the recurring words "whom" and "them." These are also links in the chain, forged in with it. "Whom" He did foreknow, "them," all of them, He did "predestinate." The next "whom" takes up the same persons and carries them to the next stage, and so on to the end. The argument, when condensed, comes to this: that the very ones He foreknew, these, without the loss of one, He glorified.

These verses give an intelligent view of Heaven. God did not predestinate and call His people to a place, but to a likeness and a relation, to be conformed to the image of His Son and to be His brethren, that is, to be God's sons. Heaven is not where His people shall be, but what they shall be.

31. Here the hymn of triumph sounds its first exultant note (see (4) above.) "What shall we then say to these things," the things considered in the last few verses? Many timid and unintelligent and even unbelieving things are said; how one may yield to temptation, may lose the Spirit, or his faith may fail. The one overwhelming answer is, "If [since] God is for us, who can be against us?" Why does Paul not say, "what can be against us" rather than "who"? The hostile force is mainly personal (see the immediate context below and Eph. 6:11-13), but not wholly so. In all conflicts and trials "God is for us." In temptations He rescues (I Cor. 10:13);

the Spirit may be grieved by our waywardness, but He will abide (John 14:16); and as for faith, will God care for everything except that which is vital? Is He "for us" in everything but faith? He cares for this first of all (I Tim. 1:14; Luke 22:32).

32. How can anything be added to this verse? God, who is "rich in mercy," in undertaking to save men spared nothing. Heaven was emptied to enrich God's called ones. Everything was given (Eph. 1:3) that His people might be saved. The verse contemplates none but His own. The "all" is in contrast with the One delivered up for them. Paul does not assert that with Christ God will give all things. He rather asks, "How shall he not with him also freely give us all things?" The Father, after bestowing the Son, knows of no way to withhold the rest. And to give the rest is small in comparison after He has given the Son. He who could part with the costly jewel could readily give the little case in which it is preserved. The mother who could give away her babe would wish its raiment to go with it.

33. "Who [personal again] shall lay anything to the charge of God's elect?" To "lay to charge" is a legal term, meaning to bring to account, bring a charge against. Paul returns in this word to the forensic language of the earlier chapters (and see Acts 26:7). God's "elect" are His own chosen people. The word recalls the "whom" and "them" above. The answer might be put interrogatively. "Is it God that justifieth" who will accuse? But it is more forceful to read it as an assertion, almost an exclamation: It is God that justifieth His own elect; can wicked men or lost spirits or Satan himself call again to account those whose case has been favorably decided in the highest place of judicature? Even to speak against God's people impeaches the Judge and is contempt of court—Heaven's court. His decision of justification in favor of him who believes is final and irreversible.

34. "Who is he that condemneth?" As no one can open the case again and bring a charge before the court, so no one can condemn, for Christ is a fourfold protection. Are there offenses? He "died" for them. Is there need of life? He is

"risen again," and we are "saved by his life" (5:10). Do we
need representation and influence at the court? He is in the
chief place of authority—"even at the right hand of God." Do
we in hours of transgression and weakness need an Advocate?
(I John 2:1.) He "ever liveth to make intercession for us"
(John 17).

35, 36. "Who shall separate us from the love of Christ?"
It is Christ's love toward us. Again we have "who," for the
impersonal conditions which Paul goes on to mention do not
come of themselves. Paul is no doubt writing here from his
own experience, and all his troubles came from wicked men.
Why does he ask whether troubles shall separate us from
Christ's love toward us? Because they seem to hang like a
heavy cloud over the head, shutting out the light of His countenance. If He is loving His people, why do these miseries
overtake them? The proof of His unchanging love is His
Word, not our experience. Experience would often disprove
His love. But He never loves His people more than when He
allows them the honor to suffer for Him (Acts 5:41 and v. 17
above). God's love for Jesus did not cease when He was hang-
ing in agony on the cross.

The word "sword" suggests the words of Psalm 54:22, which
teach that His people now suffer no more than those of former
days, and surely they were loved.

37. "More than conquerors." Who can be "more" than
a conqueror? He that cannot be conquered. A little waste will
soon exhaust a cistern, but a living fountain with sources deep
under the hills, though it may for a time be choked up, cannot
be dried up (John 4:14). In all these adverse things His true
followers "are more than conquerors," not in their own
strength, but "through him that loved" them. Note, it is not
"loves"—not present tense. He does love them through all
trials, but their unconquerable strength lies in that one act
of love when He died for them and by rising gained for them
imperishableness (Gal. 2:20).

38, 39. "For I am persuaded." It means "I have been and
am persuaded; I stand persuaded." He has an unalterable
conviction in the matter. The verses support the last one, "we

are more than conquerors through him that loved us." The apostle's eye looks through all time, through all space, and through all worlds, and in the most sweeping language he asserts his persuasion that there is nothing "able" to break the golden chain that binds the heart of God to His people. They may be put to death in His cause, or in the course of nature die in it. He loves them in "death." Life is more trying and has more dangers than death. He loves them in their "life." There are bad angels and organized principalities for evil. He has already made a spoil of them (Col. 2:15). Against secret "powers" of satanic malignity we can stand in the "power of his might" (Eph. 6:10-12). The "things present" are very pressing, but love unclasps their grip. The "things to come," the future, may be ominous, but "the Lord is my Shepherd; I shall not want. . . . Surely goodness and mercy shall follow me all the days of my life" (Ps. 23). And nothing in space above, nor depth beneath, nor "any other created thing"—this language embraces every conceivable adversary in the universe —shall be able to separate us from God's love toward us in Christ Jesus. When He gave us Christ Jesus He gave us in Him all the love He felt toward the Son.

This is the climax. The preceding sections have been dry and doctrinal; but there is here demonstrated the vital connection between doctrine and love. It is out of these hard sayings of predestination and election that there flows this hymn of adoring confidence. The love of the Spirit is found in the teaching of the Spirit.

THE THEODICY—GOD'S PRESENT
DEALING WITH THE JEWS

THIS IS THE THIRD GRAND DIVISION of the epistle. It takes up the little section in 3:1-8, "What advantage then hath the Jew?" and carries the answer to its utmost limit. This must be borne in mind, for however far Paul may digress in the discussion, this question is always before him and to it he continually returns.

This matter about the Jew's relation to Christianity was a vital one in Paul's day. The current interpretation of the Old Testament was radically affected by it, and the Messiahship of Jesus hung upon it.

The apostle found his chief defense of the doctrine of justification by faith in the Old Testament; it is witnessed by the law and the prophets. His argument in the fourth chapter is unanswerable; but even such an argument does not carry conviction if in itself it starts legitimate and serious objections and creates more difficulties than it removes. Faith did just this. It appeared to array the rest of the Bible against Paul. For faith blotted out before God all distinctions among men, religious and national (Gal. 3:28), and reduced all to the same level. God's people, whose mark had been circumcision, were henceforth to be found only in the select band of the faithful. Faith usurped the divine sign given to Abraham. The Jew with his "oracles" must give way and give place to an elect Church. And there were still other difficulties stirred up by the doctrine of faith.

It has been tacitly assumed in Christian interpretation that

153

Judaism's day is over; that an elect, leveling Church built on faith in Christ was the intent of the law and the prophets; and that it was the duty of all Jews to drop their peculiarities and come into the Church. Such an assumption the Jew ascribed to Paul. It is strangely forgotten that the mother church in Jerusalem and Judea never had a Gentile within its fold, that none could have been admitted, and that every member of that primitive body of tens of thousands was zealous of the law (Acts 21:20). They accepted Jesus as the Messiah, but abandoned none of their Old Testament customs and hopes. Christianity has suffered not a little in the continuous attempt to interpret it not from the Jewish, but from the Gentile point of view. The church in Jerusalem, and not the church in Antioch or Ephesus or Rome, furnishes the only sufficient historic outlook.

When the devout but unbelieving Jew opened his Bible almost anywhere he found promised to the seed of Abraham a universal kingdom of righteousness. Now he might be willing to accept faith as a condition of righteousness, but the Church into which it would lead him was neither a kingdom nor was it universal. Its doctrine of election precluded universalism with one stroke. Augustine laid the foundation to make the Church so, and the result is sadly known. The honey of the Church was not only lost in the vinegar of the world, but made the whole mass sevenfold more acid. The promise of the kingdom was world-wide (Dan. 2:44; 7:14, 27; Zech. 14:16-19; Ps. 2:8; Isa. 2:1-5; 11:1-9, et al.). The Church has no such promise. To make it the interpretation of these and many similar Scriptures is to make an end both of the Scriptures and of interpretation. Paul did not attempt this method.

Again, these and other passages promised that the Jew, with his Messiah as King, should have universal supremacy in the world, and all other nations were to be in subordination. Faith knew no supremacy. It created a body of believers following a rejected Saviour, with no promise that it was ever to be treated in any other way than He was (Matt. 10:22-25; John 15:20).

Again, if the Old Testament knew a suffering Messiah, it

also knew a triumphing one. The Second Psalm is Scripture as well as Isaiah 53.

Again, universal reign, supremacy of the Jew, a world King, were all promised to the people whose distinctive national mark was circumcision, and this mark was forever (Gen. 17: 13, 14).

Now the Jew was grieved and angered that righteousness by faith warred against these hopes. It went to all nations, but sought none, sought only believing individuals. It claimed God as its own, and in its onward progress left the Jew behind. Unless Paul can answer these objections, Jesus is not the Messiah and the Church is not God's people.

And Paul does answer. As a national sign circumcision stands with much advantage every way; but to make it the ground of righteousness is as unscriptural as it would be if the Ethiopian, who has a promise of salvation (Ps. 68:31), should expect it on account of the color of his skin. The Jew remains a Jew and has his inviolable promises, and the Ethiopian has his, but neither realizes them by anything but faith. Here was the Jew's failure.

Paul's course of thought is that for the present Judaism is sidetracked; but God's Word has not failed, nor is He unjust in leaving Israel to fall. What He is doing meanwhile in gathering an elect body of believers which has none of Israel's promises, this, though not revealed in the Old Testament, can be abundantly defended by it (9:24-29), just as righteousness by faith was buttressed by these same Scriptures. In God's own time He will return to Israel (Isa. 11:10-12; Acts 15:16, 17), when they shall "all" be saved and come into their promises and privileges. Their present rejection, to be received by and by, is God's purpose for the saving of the world and to enhance His own glory.

The topic of this section must not be confounded with that in the Epistle to the Hebrews. The two are quite different. Hebrews is dealing with the question of approach to God, the question of worship and acceptance. Once the Jew drew near by means of divers sacrifices and ceremonies prescribed by Moses. These were superseded in Christ, and while they remain instructive, they are no longer mediatorial. Hebrews teaches just what Romans teaches up to the point now reached in the latter, that without faith it is impossible to please God. Hebrews is absolutely silent on the theme of this theodicy, but declares how God now and forevermore is to be served—in faith. It says nothing about the Jew nationally, and nothing about the Church.

The question before us is not one concerning ceremonies. It is deeper and broader. It embraces God's whole plan to bring the world to Christ. That plan is outlined in the Old Testament, that contemplates the salvation of all nations as nations, with the Jew's individuality preserved and himself far in the van.

The Church does not usurp the special promises made to Israel; whose unbelief shall not "make the faith of God without effect" (3:3), and the world will not be converted till Israel is, for the Church has no promise of this, and Israel has.

CHAPTER 9

ISRAEL'S REJECTION CONSIDERED

(1) Israel's rejection of Christ is a great sorrow of heart to the apostle of the Gentiles (vv. 1-5); (2) it is not inconsistent with God's Word (vv. 6-13); (3) it is not inconsistent with His justice (vv. 14-29); (4) present state of the case (vv. 30-33).

1-3. "I say the truth in Christ, I lie not." The transition from the eighth chapter is abrupt. The sudden change may be accounted for psychologically. The apostle had just been contemplating the certainty of the glory of the sons of God; his heart goes now to the other extreme, the failure and misery of his own countrymen.

This vehement language was necessary, because in giving the Gospel to the heathen Paul was looked upon by the Jew as an enemy of his own nation. Some of the Roman church, knowing as they did the exclusiveness of the Jews, might be persuaded that Paul was an apostate rather than an apostle of God. He must defend himself. He is about to outline Israel's shame. Let it be seen that the picture is drawn not by an enemy, but by a loving friend, whose heart is breaking as he paints.

"Accursed from Christ." This language is startling and has troubled many; but it is in the very spirit of Israel's great leader, Moses (Exod. 32:32), and may we not say, though the word is different, in the spirit of Christ? (Gal. 3:13). Besides, this is not the language of deliberation, but of heart-breaking passion, in which he says, " I could [were it permitted or were it possible] wish myself accursed [away] from [not "by"] Christ." It is this grief at the loss of men, this intense

157

yearning for their salvation, that made Paul the preacher he was.

4, 5. "Who are Israelites," or being such as are Israelites, a term of the highest honor, God's princes (Gen. 32:28). He enumerates seven particulars which belong especially to them: (a) they were adopted as God's people; (b) they alone had the Shekinah "glory"; (c) the "covenants," made with the fathers (Gen. 6:18; 15:18; Exod. 2:24) and renewed from time to time (hence the plural), were theirs alone; (d) the "law" amid imposing splendors was given to them; (e) the temple "service" was divinely prescribed for them; no other nation had an authorized worship; (f) they were the only people who had "promises" of the Messiah and of direct blessings through him; the other nations received them through Israel; (g) the "fathers"—Abraham, the head of many nations, Issac, and Jacob—were theirs; other nations had great ancestors, but Abraham, Isaac, and Jacob have the honor of being not merely natural, but divinely chosen chiefs.

Besides these seven all their own, the Israelites had one other honor in which they shared, an honor that overtops all the rest. The "whose" changes now to "of whom." The fathers are theirs, but the Christ, though He came from them in His human relation, belongs to the world. To show the greatness of this honor Christ is declared to be God over all, blessed forever. Sanday (*Commentary, in loc.*), after an exhaustive examination of all the arguments bearing on the punctuation of this passage, "with some slight, but only slight, hesitation," admits that Paul here applies the name God to Christ. No other view gives the passage its climactic point.

Paul mentions all these things not only to set forth the Israelites' pre-eminence, but to show the painfulness and difficulty of the problem now in hand. They had the promises and the Christ sprang from them, and yet these covenant people were reaping nothing from these advantages. Jesus belonged to them, but they did not belong to Jesus. Could Paul's doctrine of an elective justification for all nations be true? Israel is rejected.

6. Paul abruptly lays hold of the question. The Jews have failed, but God's Word has not. (See (2) above.) The emphasis is on the phrase "the Word of God." The proof of no failure is that the promises were made to Israel, but they were not made to them on the ground of their natural descent from Abraham. The real Israel is within the limits of the natural Israel. For Paul is not now contemplating the Church composed of men from Jews and Gentiles alike. These, though called "Abraham's seed" (Gal. 3:29) and "children of Abraham" (Gal. 3:7), are never called Israel or Israelites. Galatians 6:16 is not an exception to this statement, but a proof. (See Ellicott, *Commentary, in loc.*) Paul is defending God's Word in view of the claim that Jesus is the Messiah with a true people following Him, and in view of the fact that Israel is not saved. His answer is that "they are not all [true] Israel, which are of [from] Israel." The latter may mean the patriarch (Jacob) or it may mean the nation natural. What Paul denies in either case is that the real Israel, contemplated in the Old Testament promise, is not identical in number with the nation of Israel.

7. That the real Israel should not be as wide numerically as the natural Israel is supported by the further statement that even Abraham's natural seed were not all of them children of the covenant. The promise was limited to Isaac, and Ishmael was left out, although he also is called Abraham's "seed" (Gen. 21:13). Paul thus keeps the all-important point foremost, that the promise to Israel was a vital promise, still holding, but not on the condition of mere natural descent. God did not surrender His prerogatives in the case to nature. Note that to reach clearness in this and similar Scripture the phrase "seed of Abraham" must be properly referred. It has three meanings, two of which occur in this verse, the natural seed (John 8:37) and the real seed. Its third, quite distinct from these, is the Church (Gal. 3:29).

8. This verse shows the significance of the promise, "In Isaac shall thy seed be called." If God limited the promise to one of Abraham's children, excluding Ishmael and the sons of Keturah, it follows that "they which are the children of the

flesh are not the children of God." God's children are not
the product of nature; they are not begotten by man, but by
Him. Who, then, are His own, to whom the promises were
spoken? Not even the natural descendants of Isaac; for the
principle already given, that the children of the flesh as such
are excluded, excludes Isaac's fleshly descent, excludes Esau.
God's children are those of whom Isaac is a type. He was
born not by the energy of nature, but was a supernatural
creation in accordance with a divine promise. Hence "the
children of the promise are counted [are reckoned, equal to
"called" in v. 7] for the seed [or "as seed"]" (John 1:13).
"Children of promise" is not equivalent to promised children.
The word is almost personified. God's promise is a potent
energy, quickening those to whom His covenant pertains.
Thus the seed is found "in Isaac," in his line. They are all
his offspring, but not all the offspring are "counted for the
seed."

9. If the children of the promise are the only ones
"counted," of whom Isaac is the apt type, it is necessary to
show that he was a child of promise, as this verse does. The
original order brings out the force better: "For of promise is
this word," the quotation which follows. The emphatic word
is "promise." Accordingly, as Meyer strikingly observes, "We
see that not the bodily descent, but the divine promise, constitutes the relation of belonging to Abraham's fatherhood."
But he fails to observe a subtle point in the quotation. The
child was to be not only the gift of God's power, "will I come,"
but given in His own time: "At this time will I come." The
happy season for the realization of the promise was not yet.
He selected the time as well as the child, and the time was
when he should come with quickening power. Paul intimates
that Israel's hour has not yet dawned.

10-12. "And not only this [or, fully expressed, "And not
only Sarah received a divine promise concerning her son"];
but when Rebecca . . ." In Rebecca's case the divine action
is still more pointed. In saying that she was with child "by
one," Paul is not calling attention to the unity of the fatherhood, which would be absurd. It does not mean by one man

(Meyer), as though there might be two. The "one" focuses the attention on him in whom the seed was called, "even our father Isaac." He is significantly called "our," that is, Israel's, "father." The promise was in Isaac's line of descent, and yet even here there is a selection and a limitation.

The "for" (v. 11) bears on this clearly implied limitation, and brings in the statements that illustrate it. The children were not yet born; they had done neither good nor evil; the selection, then, was not made either on the ground of their character or on the ground of their works. To say that God foresaw the good character and good works of Jacob is to import an idea that is repugnant to the logic of the statement here made by Paul and contradicted by the subsequent facts. Jacob's history does not show him to be a better man morally than his brother; his very name indicates his character. (See below on v. 14.) Human merit, present or foreseen, does not enter into God's choice. Again, if God chose Isaac and rejected Ishmael it might be said mistakenly that the selection was made because of the latter's irregular parentage. That mistake is not possible in the case of Jacob and Esau. Isaac and Ishmael had only one parent in common; Jacob and Esau had both and the children were twins.

We are next told the reason for dealing thus with the twins: "that the purpose of God according to election might stand." It is an according-to-election purpose. Paul finds the source of salvation in God alone. He had a "purpose" to save. This purpose cannot be of "none effect," but must "stand," because, first, it is not universal, but is limited to an "election," a selection, as in the case of Isaac against Ishmael. The one elected was the one He promised. The idea of promise, with which Paul began, is the same as that in the word "election." And, second, God's elective purpose will "stand" because it is determined "not by [or "of"] works, but by [or "of"] him that calleth," that is, God himself. Now, in order that God might show this purpose, a purpose that was elective and based on His own will, He said before the twins were born, "The elder shall serve the younger." By His own will He reversed the order of nature and took but one of the twin sons of Isaac, in whom the seed was promised.

If Paul began this chain of reasoning under the proposition (v. 6) that the Word of God has not failed in the case of the Jew, and now concludes it with the proposition that His purpose has not failed, but must "stand," there is only an apparent shifting of terms. It is the Word of God that embodies the purpose, and in speaking of the latter Paul means no other purpose but the one disclosed in the "Word." The propositions are logically identical. The Jews erred, not knowing the Scripture. They stuck to their baseless notion that because they were the natural descent of Abraham they were heirs of salvation, a notion against which Jesus solemnly warned them. He admitted that they were Abraham's natural "seed," but denied that they were His promised "children" (John 8:37, 39).

13. "As it is written, Jacob [have] I loved, but Esau [have] I hated." Omit "have" in both cases. This scripture, which looks only logically at the original two, but directly at their descendants (Mal. 1:1-4), is quoted to corroborate the original choice. God's motive in it was neither love of the one nor hate of the other, but simply "of him that calleth." But, the choice once made, God's love followed Jacob's seed, showing the reality of His election, and His hate followed Esau's, showing the reality of His rejection. The word "hated" need not be softened.

Paul has now so far vindicated God's Word despite the failure of Israel. Jesus is the Messiah, even if they as a nation have not participated in His blessings; for when Paul closely scans the source of the nation he finds it has no promise on the ground of lineal descent from Abraham. That promise belongs only to chosen elect ones among the nation, chosen for nothing whatever pertaining to them, but solely after God's own will. This starts a serious objection about the divine justice, which Paul proceeds to answer. (See (3) above.)

14. "Is there unrighteousness with God?" This question could not arise unless Paul wished himself to be understood as teaching that God chose Jacob and rejected Esau for no assignable reason outside His own will. If God chose Jacob because He foresaw his faith or his virtue, and rejected Esau for an opposite character, reason would approve and the question of this verse could not be asked. But when it is taught that God chose Jacob for no good in him, and rejected ("hated") Esau for no bad in him, man's narrow heart feels that an injustice has been done. This sentiment Paul repels: "God forbid."

15, 16. Paul finds the argument for his vehement denial of injustice in God not by abstract reasoning about the idea of justice, but in the Scriptures. The quotation is from Exodus 33:19. The great Jewish captain is earnestly seeking grace from God. It might be supposed that he could attain it on the ground of his office and merit; but even "to Moses," God saith, He gives mercy not because he is Moses, or because he seeks it, but just because it is God's "will" to do so. It is a bold, crisp assertion of the divine freedom in bestowing grace. "In any case through human history wherein I shall be seen to have mercy, the one account I give of the radical cause is this—*I have mercy*" (Moule). Mercy is the outward manifestation of the feeling of compassion.

The conclusion follows. God's mercy is not the response to human desire nor to human effort. It is not of him that "willeth" or wishes it, as Moses did, and not of him who "runneth" in the path of right. Willing and running may indicate the possession of grace, but they are not the originating cause. They may be the channel, but they are not the fountain. The source of grace is God's own will, that goes out to whom He will. Mercy is "of God, that showeth mercy" independent of any motive in man.

17. "For the Scripture saith unto Pharaoh." Moses' history bears on the election of Jacob; Pharaoh's on the rejection of Esau. The latter is cited for the same purpose as the former—to show God's freedom and sovereignty in dealing with men. As He grants mercy after His own will, so also He withholds it, and hardens whom He will. Ten times in the Scripture about Pharaoh it is said he hardened himself; but

Paul makes no account of this, for his clear intention is to account for Pharaoh's overthrow by the free purpose of God. And yet God did not harden him for the sake of the hardening, but that the divine power might have a field of display and that the divine name might become known. If Pharaoh had willingly and sweetly allowed the people to depart, there could have been no miracles "in Egypt and in the Red Sea" (Acts 7:36), and the children of Israel would have had no fame as God's own chosen, a fame that endured for centuries (I Sam. 4:8). God's glory is promoted in the overthrow of a sinner as much as in saving one. God wished men to know Him and His power, and for this purpose "raised up" Pharaoh, which means neither that God created nor preserved him for His purpose, but that God brought about everything that belongs to the history of the king.

In selecting Pharaoh as an example of God's hardening Paul shows his skill. Pharaoh was a detestable heathen oppressor, and undue prejudice would not be excited against the doctrine in illustrating it by his case.

18. This gives the solemn and awful conclusion of the section beginning at verse 14, or even as far back as verse 7. The word "whom" is singular. The subject is not one about nations, but about individuals, not one about ethnic supremacy or leadership, but about personal salvation. "Therefore hath he mercy on what man he will, and what man he will he hardeneth." God is absolute sovereign, allowing nothing to direct His activity but His own will. His Word is true, as true as He is, but He has never uttered a word to abridge His freedom, nor can His Word, like a promissory note, be pleaded against His freedom. This hardening process is going on today; it can be read as clearly in current history as in God's Word. And yet man is also free in choosing God and free in refusing Him. The reconciliation of these two is a question of philosophy, and philosophy fails in the effort. The Bible does not attempt it, but stops with asserting that both are realities.

19. "Why doth he yet find fault?" This puts the query of verse 14 in a more aggravated form. There it is a question

about the justice of God; here it is virtually a charge of injustice. He hardened Pharaoh; He willed to harden him. Pharaoh did just what God willed; he did not resist His will; no one does whom He hardens. "Why doth he yet find fault" and visit dire punishment upon sinners?

20. "Nay but, O man." Paul has already answered this question as far as possibly it ever can be answered. The answer is to the point and practical. It is that God is free to do as He will; He is a sovereign; and what is the idea of absolute sovereignty but that He who has it is under no obligation to give a reason for anything which He does? If He must give a reason for His actions He is no longer sovereign, but the reason given enjoys that distinction, not to say the persons to whom it must be given. This matter is not peculiar to the Gospel; it belongs to every religion that owns a personal God. A God is one whose will is free, whose will is law.

The question, then, "Why doth he yet find fault?" is not only impious, but blasphemous. The man sets himself up to condemn not only the decree of God, but to claim a higher justice for himself; he replies not merely against God's judgment, but against the only possible conception given in the word "God." In complaining against God for hardening a man to do a wicked thing and then finding fault with that man for doing it, the complainant says, "There ought not to be such a God; that is, there ought to be what is really no God, one with such notions of justice toward men as I have!" The man exalts himself above God in sitting in judgment upon the divine acts. The fallacy is in his idea of what constitutes a God. Godet weakens Paul's rejoinder, "Who art thou that repliest?" by saying that he means "a reply to a reply." No; Paul's whole argument is drawn from the nature of God. His opponent is more than a debater; he is well-nigh atheistic. Shedd's exposition here is better than Godet's: "An irreverent equalizing of man with God."

It must not be forgotten that whatever God does is necessarily just; because, if there is anything outside His own will by which to measure the actions of that will, that thing is higher than God. For human reason or human sense of right to sit in judgment on God's acts is as foolish as it is wicked.

Again, he who replies against God must mean, if he means anything, that it is God's hardening that deprives a soul of salvation; that if God did not interpose with an election, and take some and leave others to be hardened, all men would at least have an equal opportunity of salvation. This is false. If God did not elect, none would be saved, for there is "none that seeketh after God" (3:11). And men are not lost because they are hardened; they are hardened because they are lost; they are lost because they are sinners (1:21).

God is not responsible for sin. He is under no obligation to save anyone. Obligation and sovereignty cannot both be predicated of God. If He saves anyone it is a sovereign act of mercy, and for that very reason His justification is tantamount to salvation.

It must not be supposed (with Sanday, apparently) that Paul's argument through this section is an ad hominem drawn from the Jew's Old Testament conception of God. It is drawn from the nature of sovereignty, the necessary conception of God. Neither does Paul lay his hand on the mouth of the objector and cry, "Stop!" He confutes him with one single logical shaft: God is God.

"Shall the thing formed say." Note that Paul does not say, "Shall the thing created say to him that created it." It is not a question of original creation, but of subsequent destination. What would the ability to fashion be worth if it were under the dictation of that which is to be fashioned?

21. "Hath not the potter power over the clay," from the same lump to make one part a vessel to honor and another to dishonor? (Isa. 45:9; 64:8; Jer. 18:1-10.) This illustration enforces the idea of God's sovereignty. To be sure, men are not senseless clay but beings of feeling and will; and yet, with all feeling and will and intelligence, they are as helpless, being sinners, to fit themselves to please God as clay left to itself is helpless to become an ornamental vase. The potter does not make the clay. He takes it as he finds it and fashions out of the same lump—the "clay" and the "lump" are identical in

character and quantity—one part a vessel to ornament the house and another part a vessel for some base use. Originally the two were the same thing—clay; the potter determined their destination. Pharaoh and Moses originally belonged to the same guilty lump of humanity. Moses was inherently no better than the Egyptian king. God had mercy on one and fashioned him into a glorious instrument of deliverance for His people; the other He hardened, and to deny God's justice in so doing is as absurd as to deny that the potter has a right to turn base clay into a slop jar. Why it is that men are sinners neither Paul nor the Bible anywhere teaches; but sinners under God's wrath they are, and He is not responsible that they are sinners, and from the lump of sinful humanity may choose for His service whom He will and may harden at His pleasure. To confess this is the very highest exercise of reason.

22. Now, after Paul has vindicated the idea of God in vindicating His sovereignty—for a God who is not absolutely free to do as He will is no God—he shows next and in addition how graciously He exercised his freedom. Though "willing to show his wrath [today], and to make his power known," as in Pharaoh's case, He, after all, endured in much longsuffering the vessels of wrath fitted to destruction. Paul does not now say that God fitted them. He bore with them. Jerusalem, that crucified His Son and slew His followers, was still standing after more than a quarter of a century. God tempered His sovereign wrath with long-suffering.

This sentence, embracing verses 22-24, is not complete. It is almost a worshipful exclamation, but may be read as in the King James Version, "What if," or "What shall we say if."

23. Closely connected with the last verse by means of the word "endured." The "vessels of mercy" called also for endurance. The writer of the epistle could not forget that, had God's just wrath fallen upon the Jews at the time that they earned it, he himself would have been lost. But God with much long-suffering restrains His wrath against sinners, "and [he does so] that he might make known [by calling and justification] the riches of his glory on the vessels of mercy [the elect], which he had afore prepared unto [eternal] glory." They are not vessels of favor, but of "mercy," in that He showed them mercy. These, it is said, "he prepared afore." Paul is doubtless referring to 8:29 in the word "afore."

Men, being sinners, have no rights remaining before God; in His justice He might destroy them all. But He chooses to save some sinners in the exercise of mercy, and for the time restrains His wrath toward the rest. These two verses bear on the idea of His sovereignty in showing how He exercises it; the next one with the quotations following shows toward whom He exercises it.

24. "Even us [the "vessels of mercy"], whom he hath called." This is His own sovereign call. The rest heard the Gospel, but were not called by Him. Unless the word has this special meaning here and in 1:6; 8:28, 30, it has no meaning. The "called" were found not among the Jews only, but also among the Gentiles. This is by no means the ultimate, but only the present, exhibition of His sovereignty. Paul keeps the two classes separate here, for he still has God's dealing with the Jew in mind, to whom the thought returns exclusively at verse 31 below. The promise of salvation was not conditioned on nationality, but is "of him that calleth" (v. 11 above) and may extend to all nations: "Even us, . . . not of the Jews only, but also of the Gentiles." He supports this statement chiastically* from the Scriptures.

25, 26. These quotations from Hosea 2:23 and 1:10 are combined, and predict the call of Gentiles. The phrase "and it shall come to pass" (v. 26) is not Paul's, but the prophet's. "Call" and "called" do not mean invited or named, but called with the call (v. 11 above and 8:30). The "place" is indefinite, and means any place in the world. The prophecy originally seems to refer to the ten tribes, but as they had been excluded from the nation and were practically heathen, Paul refers to them as a type of the call of the Gentiles.

---

*Chiasmus: an inversion of the order of words in two corresponding parallel phrases or clauses, or of words when repeated.—Editor's note.

27-29. These verses look at the case of Israel as predicted in Isaiah to show that the mass would be reprobated and only a "remnant" saved. The first quotation is from Isaiah 10:22, 23, on which Paul puts a gloss, representing the prophet as "crying" in alarm and wonder, thus softening the stern prediction that, while Israel may be countless in number, only the elect few will be subjects of grace. "For," continues Isaiah, the Lord "will finish the work, and cut it short in righteousness." The righteousness is that of Jehovah's judgment or wrath upon Israel's waywardness. The Revised Version makes some large changes in this verse: "For the Lord will execute his word upon the earth, finishing it and cutting it short." With either reading the meaning is clear. Summary and severe judgments were to fall on Israel, and of such a character that only a remnant would be left to know God's grace. The original reference in Isaiah was to the return from the captivity; but Paul sees the applicability of the prophecy to his own time; it may come in force again in the future.

The apostle makes one more quotation (Isa. 1:9), that brings his teaching about God's sovereign and electing grace to a startling climax. But for the divine interference Israel would have become as Sodom and been made like unto Gomorrah. Depravity would have run its course to this tragic end. But God "left unto us a very small remnant," which "small remnant" Paul calls a "seed" in quoting from the Septuagint. The cities of the plain were obliterated for their sin, and none were left to revive them; and so it would have been in Israel's case had not God "left" (spared) some. Israel has nothing of which to complain. God's election destroyed none; it is the sole reason why any were spared. The covenant name Jehovah is not used here, but "Lord of Sabaoth," or of hosts or armies, which suggests His sovereignty.

30-33. "What shall we say then?" (See (4) above.) What are the facts so far as this discussion is concerned, the facts as seen wherever the Gospel has gone? Not that the Word of God has failed, but that the prophecy has now become history, to be seen in history. First, some Gentiles, who were making no effort (reminding the reader of verse 16 above, "it is not of him that runneth") after righteousness, reached it. They did not will, but God did. Since these Gentiles had no works, God bestowed righteousness upon them, that is, they had a righteousness of faith. The article "the" before "Gentiles" in the King James Version is an error, strangely repeated in the Revised Version. Paul, with the fact of election in his mind, could not and he did not write this illogical "the." That some Gentiles, those who believed, were righteous, was attested by their living. They had abandoned idolatry, worshiped God, and claimed no merit for themselves (Phil. 3:3).

A second fact in accord with the argument above was (and is) that Israel as a whole, though following the (Mosaic) law of righteousness, the law that is connected with righteousness, did not attain to that law. Omit "of righteousness" in the second instance. Israel attained to the letter of the law, but not to the acquittal from sin. Gentiles, who willed not, attained; Israel, who willed for themselves, failed, for salvation is not of man's will. Some take "law" here in the sense of rule, a rule of moral and religious life that would win righteousness.

That Israel had not become righteous was plain to everyone, and thus facts in both directions testify to the correctness of Paul's logic and the aptness of his quotations from the Scriptures. It was said that Gentiles would be saved, and Gentiles are saved. It was said that the mass of Israel would be rejected, and so it is, and God is just in it all and His Word has not failed.

"Wherefore?" Why did Israel not reach righteousness? Paul does not say they failed because they were nonelect. Election accounts for the saved, but nonelection does not account for the lost. The comprehensive reason for the latter is sin, and the essence of sin is self-will, self-will even in seeking God. These Jews took their own way of being reconciled to God. They did not even seek Him by the works of the law, but "as it were" by works of the law. They decided for themselves what the works should be and so had flesh works. In their self-will they practically denied God.

It is at this point that Paul passes from the sovereignty of God to the responsibility of man. The two cannot be harmonized in the human understanding, except as the Scriptures harmonize them; that is, by insisting on and holding to both. The Scriptures and reason assert the absolute sovereignty of God, and Scripture and the human conscience assert with equal force the responsibility of man; so that the practical error arises when either one of these is denied or when one is explained in a way to exclude the other. It must also be remembered that, while man cannot save himself, moral inability does not relieve from responsibility. Man's inability lies in his sinful nature (8:7), and God cannot be made responsible for sin. The sinner's inability to do right, to do God's will, is the acme of his sin.

A world of sin is a world of confusion. Sin introduced confusion between God and man, and confusion cannot be explained. The real difficulty between God's absolute sovereignty and man's responsibility is metaphysical and not Biblical. How can there be one sovereign free will and other free wills? And when Fritzsche says that Paul's view is "absolutely contradictory," he is virtually demanding that Paul cease preaching and turn philosopher to solve the insoluble. But Paul leaves the question where he found it, and goes on now in this and the next chapter to show that Israel's failure was their own fault.

"They stumbled at that stumbling stone." The "for" is probably not genuine, but it shows the correct relation of the sentences. They failed to believe because the Christ came in a way which their works disqualified them to approve (I Pet. 2:7, 8).

"As it is written." The quotation is a combination of Isaiah 8:14 and 28:16. That which was applicable in the prophet's time Paul sees to be applicable also in his time. God's enemies stumbled then because of Him; they stumble now at His gift of Christ. At the same time Christ is a security for him that believeth on Him. The "whosoever" in the King James Version is not genuine and mars the sense. Paul is quoting this Scripture not to show the universality of salvation, which the word "whosoever" would suggest, but in proof that the Jews failed by lack of faith. The word "believeth" carries the main idea. He that believeth shall not make haste to some other refuge for salvation, or, what is the same, he shall not be put to shame by trusting in this stone.

The substance of the chapter is that, in spite of Israel's rejection, in spite of the present mixed following of Jews and Gentiles as the Lord's people, God's Word has not failed, for God never pledged away His sovereignty in it, but, on the other hand, predicted that salvation turned on His will and call.

CHAPTER 10

ISRAEL'S FAILURE THEIR OWN FAULT

THOUGH GOD DID NOT ELECT the mass of Israel for salvation at this time, their present rejection is not to be explained by His withholding grace, which was freely offered them, but by their sinful lack of discernment (Luke 12:56; 19:44; 21:24).

The chapter contains four topics: (1) Israel failed to see that Christ was the end of the law (vv. 1-4); (2) the free character of salvation (vv. 5-11); (3) its universal character (vv. 12-18); and (4) they failed to see that all this, as well as their own rejection, was the prediction of their own Scriptures (vv. 19-21).

1. "Brethren, my heart's desire . . ." "Good pleasure" is preferable to the word "desire." It will be noticed that each one of the three chapters in this theodicy begins with a warm expression of the apostle's own feeling. He will not let it be forgotten, in bringing these heavy charges against those of his own blood, that he is writing in pity and not in anger. He is not an enemy of Israel. Moreover, this prayer, as well as the sentiment beginning the ninth chapter, could not have been entertained by the apostle if he at the same time considered Israel's case hopeless. As Bengel says on this verse, "Paul would not have prayed had they been altogether reprobate." If he prayed "that they might be saved" he must have believed the possibility of their salvation (II Cor. 3:16). In the next chapter he confidently predicts it (11:26).

2. It was because Paul saw Israel's zeal for God that he was so solicitous for them. And yet zeal does not imply a right heart nor acceptance with God. Their zeal was not directed by "knowledge," not regulated by spiritual discernment. They had the means of knowledge, but not the knowl-

edge. This little phrase, "not according to knowledge," is the key to the chapter.

3. "For they, being ignorant." Here are given the contents of their ignorance: "ignorant of God's righteousness [by faith in Christ], and going about [seeking] to establish their own righteousness [by works of law, in zeal for the latter, they] have not submitted themselves" to the former. Here the two kinds of righteousness are set in contrast. These two are the sum of all on earth, and they are mutually exclusive in the human heart. The Jews at this time were not unacquainted with the righteousness of God, but they were "ignorant" of it.

4. "For Christ is the end of the law." The Revised Version retains both articles. "End" means termination. It is true that he is also the aim and the fulfillment of the law. Tholuck combines the two ideas of termination and aim; Alford stands for the latter. But the sharp contrast here, as well as the (original) word, requires the meaning termination. The law is no longer a means of righteousness.

Sanday surely errs in saying that this verse is a proof that the Jews were "wrong" in not submitting themselves to the righteousness of God. It is not a question of right or wrong, but of fact. The Jews claimed that in following the law they were submitting to God, for He gave the law. No, says Paul; in so doing you are not submitting to the righteousness of God. "For Christ [whom God gave and you reject] is the end of the law for [with a view to] righteousness to every one that believeth." The Jew's system was one of doing; but God's was one of believing, one of grace. Law and grace are mutually exclusive and antagonistic systems (4:4, 5; 11:6). Because the Jew held to law he was not in subjection to God. The proof that he was not is this great principle of grace recorded in this fourth verse.

5. That Christ ends the law in making nothing but faith necessary to righteousness is confirmed in the further contrast of the two systems. (See (2) above.) Moses describes the righteousness of the law as one of doing—"the man that doeth those things." The point made here is not that no man can do those things prescribed by Moses, but that, in case he did

do them, it would be his "own righteousness" and not God's, which is next described at length.

6, 7. "But the righteousness which is of faith speaketh on this wise." Paul does not say that Moses describes this righteousness; he does not set Moses against Moses. He says the righteousness itself speaks; it is self-descriptive.

It must be carefully noted what Paul is after. The points are just two: first, that the Jew's intense religious zeal in devotion to the law, a zeal that touches the apostle's heart, is, after all, not God's righteousness, but in flat contradiction to it. This is seen in the nature or character of the two. A faith-righteousness in Christ must end law-righteousness, for Moses describes the latter as one of doing. But now arises just at this point a second question. Admitting, as the Jew would, that the two are antagonistic, he would not admit that the righteousness in Christ was genuine; he would make that claim for his own. Hence, beginning at this sixth verse, Paul not only completes his contrast between the righteousness by law and the righteousness by faith, but to the end of the section at verse 11 adds the other argument, that nothing but righteousness by faith is God's.

"Say not in thy heart." This is a quotation from Deuteronomy 30:11-14, with Paul's interjected explanations by means of the equating phrase "that is." The difficulty that stands here is that Paul takes words that Moses seems to use of the law, and makes them descriptive of the righteousness of faith.

Two considerations relieve the difficulty. First, the contrast is not between the law and faith, but between the righteousness proceeding from the two. The law bears testimony to both kinds. The righteousness of faith is witnessed by the law and the prophets (3:21, 22).

The second consideration is that Paul interprets this passage in the original Mosaic intent of it. This intent after the Gospel came was not difficult to see. The thirtieth chapter of Deuteronomy refers to the ultimate gathering of all Israel. Moses promises that in the future God will circumcise the "heart" of Israel. He further says, "If thou turn unto the Lord thy God with all thine heart, and with all thy soul" (Deut. 30:

10). The very next verse introduces our quotation: "For this commandment which I command thee this day, it is not hidden from thee, neither is it far off. It is not in heaven . . ." The chapter itself speaks of both kinds of righteousness; it mentions not only the "commandments," but "this commandment."

This difference between singular and plural must not be overlooked. It speaks both of keeping the commandments and also of turning to the Lord with the heart. The Gospel gave Paul the key to the latter, and he quotes the passage as not applicable to the righteousness of the law, but descriptive only of the Gospel. When, therefore, Sanday implies that "words used by Moses of the law" are applied by Paul to the Gospel "as against the law" (Commentary on Romans, p. 288), and denies to Paul a "true interpretation" of this and similar passages (p. 306, id.), the only question is, Which is the safer expositor of the Old Testament, the professor or the apostle?

The righteousness of the law is defined in terms that imply doing. The passage quoted here by Paul defines the righteousness of faith in terms which shut out all doing. No man need attempt the impossible thing of ascending to Heaven, which means to bring Christ down; He has already come. And no one need go over the sea or, what is the same thing, descend to its depths, the abyss, to bring Christ again from the dead; He is already raised. God's "command" (Deut. 30:11), His work, is not "hidden from thee"; it is already done (John 6:29).

8. "But what saith it?" This little question belongs not to the quotation, but is Paul's, and serves both to pass from the negative to the positive side of the description of true righteousness and to call attention a second time to it. It declares that God's righteousness is not distant and difficult, but "the word [Moses did not say "commandments"] is nigh thee [like the air of heaven], in thy mouth, and in thy heart: that is, the word of faith [referred to in Moses], which we [apostles] preach." It is a word or command not for doing, but for believing.

9, 10. These two verses give the contents of the "word of faith." "That" is equivalent neither to "in order that" nor to "because." The first is forbidden by the original word (*hote*), and the second in that there is no need to prove the express assertion that "the word is nigh thee." Paul would not attempt to prove Scripture by his own assertion; but he may tell what it means. This "word" by the preaching of it is brought to the mouth and the heart of the sinner as the atmosphere comes to the lungs. Man does not make it; he breathes it and lives.

Since Christ has already come down from above, has died, and has been raised from the dead, nothing remains for the Jew or for anyone else to do but to confess it with his mouth and believe it in his heart. Paul specifies the vital element in Christian faith, "that God hath raised him from the dead." He was raised for our justification (4:25). The faith that leaves this out, although it may accept everything else in the Christian's creed, is not Christian and is not saving. The Jew's "doing" denied it. The "for" of the tenth verse does not introduce a proof, but an analytic explanation, of the salvation just mentioned—"thou shalt be saved." If one believes with the heart, that belief brings him into righteousness, right standing before God, and if now he confesses openly in his life his adherence to Jesus, that confession leads on to the final salvation. Thus salvation is resolved into its two elements, a heart trust that provokes a true confession of His name. And yet the two are one; for confession without belief is either self-deception or hypocrisy, while trust without confession may be cowardice (John 19:38).

It sounds a little odd, in view of Paul's words, "with the mouth confession is made," to hear Sanday say the confession "is made in baptism." Paul links baptism with faith (Col. 2:12).

If the order of the words "mouth" and "heart" in verse 9 is reversed to "heart" and "mouth" in verse 10, this occurs because in the former Paul is following Moses' order, who presents the "word" rather as a creed and climactically, not only in thy mouth, but in thy very heart. The tenth verse presents the words in the order of experience.

11. This quotation from Isaiah 28:16, with the expansion of "he" into "whosoever," clearly implied in the original, is in proof of the last verse that salvation is by faith. The two words about believing and confessing in the last verse are here reduced to one, "believeth." (For "ashamed" see on 9:33.) Perhaps none but an apostle's eyes could see salvation by faith in the quotation above from Deuteronomy 30. But we must think the zealous Jews either obstinate or blind that could not see it in this verse in Isaiah, were it not for the same lack of perception attending men still. Salvation by works, even in evangelical circles, is pursued today by all such as cannot unquestioningly, like a little child (Mark 10:15), accept this same word in its sublime simplicity.

12. "For there is no difference." As Israel failed to perceive the character of the righteousness offered by God, but excluded by their own righteousness of works, so they necessarily failed to see the universality of God's righteousness. Works are not suited to sinful men (4:14, 15). It is with this failure that Paul now deals. (See (3) at the head of the chapter.) He moves off at the word "whosoever" in the last verse, and explains it in this one. As there is "no difference" among men, Jew or Gentile, in their sinfulness (3:22, 23), so there is no difference in God's mercy toward all, Jew or Gentile. The "call" of faith from the heart of any man is not merely answered, but richly answered.

13. "For, whosoever . . ." This, from Joel 2:32, is the scriptural proof of the universality of God's mercy. The quotation is very much like that in verse 11 above, but there is a difference in use: there it confirms the believing, here the universality. Hence here in the original it is not simply whosoever, but everyone whosoever. The apostle seems fond of repeating the noble Gospel sentiment that believing prayer from any heart of man receives an answer rich in righteousness.

14. "How then shall they call?" With these verses begins an argument extending through several verses, to prove from another point of view the universality of the Gospel. If this Gospel is general and designed for all, if its language is that "whosoever shall call upon the name of the Lord shall be saved" (v. 13), it is then inevitable from the word "call" that the Gospel must be preached everywhere. If such general preaching is predicted (v. 15) and has been accomplished, there is thereby evidence of the Gospel's universal character; and if it is found that Israel has heard this world-wide Gospel and has not believed it, the responsibility of their rejection is upon themselves. Says Gifford, "From the nature of the salvation just described (v. 13), it follows that the Gospel must be preached to all without distinction" (*Speaker's Com., in loc.*). If the universal condition of salvation is to call on the Lord, only the general spread of the Gospel can make such a call possible.

By successive steps Paul argues from Joel's cardinal words, "Whosoever shall call," to the sending out of the preachers. Men cannot call on Him in whom they have not believed, and, to be sure, they cannot believe in Him of whom they never heard. And how can they ever hear without a preacher? The spread of the Gospel is dependent on the living messenger. The sending forth of Bibles is not sufficient; Israel had them, but did not profit by them. The Ethiopian eunuch, earnest man though he was, did not understand even the luminous fifty-third chapter of Isaiah until the preacher sent to him opened the Scripture for him (Acts 8:26-40).

15. "And how shall they preach, except they be sent," sent by God? The first heralds who formally and definitely went out either to the Jews or to the Gentiles were commissioned by the Holy Spirit (Acts 2; 10; 8:2-4). There is no clearer passage for the call into the ministry than this: "How shall they preach, except they be sent?" (Gal. 1:15, 16). No matter how well a man be qualified otherwise, if he is not divinely "sent" he is a profane intruder. No matter how humble and lacking in brilliance, if he has this credential he need not be discouraged. The Father sends the Son, and the Son sends the preachers (John 17:18).

Paul has now argued backward from the nature of the Gospel, which demands that men call on the name of the Lord, to that which this call implies, a general sending forth of min-

isters. That such would be sent forth is confirmed by a passage
from Isaiah 52:7 (see Nahum 1:15): "How beautiful are the
feet of them [how welcome is their coming] that preach . . .
peace, that [not "and"] bring glad tidings of good things!"
There was a partial fulfillment of Isaiah's words in the return
from the captivity which the prophet foresaw. Paul sees a
deeper meaning, which points to the mission of the Gospel
messengers, and now his argument so far is complete. A Gospel intended for all requires ministers sent to all, and this
harmonizes with the prediction that they would be sent.

16. "But they have not all obeyed the gospel"—the "glad
tidings" mentioned above. Paul restrains himself, as in 3:3.
He might have said, "How few believed!" This general disbelief, however, does not disprove that the "sent" messengers
were God's. It actually confirms their authority. For Isaiah
foresaw this unbelief and predicted it in the sad words, "Lord,
who hath believed our report?" or, "Who hath believed thy
message heard from us?" The prophet (Isa. 53:1) is now
speaking of the Messianic times, as the connection shows clearly. Paul says "they" have not obeyed. The word is general,
but he has Israel in mind, whom he soon mentions. Israel's
rejection of the Gospel is a proof of its truthfulness. Not only
the few who in all time have believed revelation, but the many
who reject it are a confirmation of its divinity. A Gospel
universally believed would not be God's. Jesus said, " I am
come in my Father's name, and ye receive me not: if another
shall come in his own name, him ye will receive" (John 5:43).
And ever so God's messenger is known by his general rejection.

17. "So then faith cometh by hearing, and hearing by the
Word of God." Paul is not referring to the act of listening
as the source of faith. Listening is itself faith, and all men
listen to something. Saving faith, of which he is speaking,
comes from heeding saving doctrine; this is his vital point.
This verse can be paraphrased thus: Genuine faith comes by
a message heard (from us), and the message heard (is) by
means of the Word of God, the Word given the messenger,
the Gospel. The "Word of God," or, as some read here, "of
Christ," does not mean His command to preach.

But why does Paul utter the words of this verse? It is the logical conclusion of everything from verse 13 above. The "call" that brings salvation demands faith, and this faith comes from the Word of God sent through His messengers. But, while this conclusion looks back to the beginning of this little section, it is drawn directly from the quotation immediately preceding, which itself comprehends what has gone before.

18. It being now shown that the Gospel which is necessary to faith has been universally given, could it be that they who have not obeyed (v. 16) did not hear? "But I say, Have they not heard?" The answer to this is a quotation from Psalm 19: 4. The quotation refers to the silent but effective message of the stars: "Their sound went into all the earth, and their words unto the ends of the [inhabited] world." Paul is not quoting these words in proof that men have heard. In the verses immediately preceding there is already sufficient proof of the opporunity to hear. By quoting the Psalmist it is beautifully suggested how vain would be the excuse that men have not heard. The very stars declare God's glory the world around (1:20), and how much more must the preachers mentioned in verse 15 above! Paul in using the Psalmist's words does not mention him, and uses no formula of quotation. If men have not believed it is not because they have not heard. The opportunity of hearing was as wide as the star-studded heavens. The believing was limited to a "few" (Matt. 7:14).

19. "But I say, Did not Israel know?" For emphasis Paul repeats the words "but I say" of verse 18. "Israel" is not in contrast with others intended in the preceding verse, for Paul has had Israel in mind all along. The whole chapter, as is shown at its beginning, refers primarily to nobody else. He names them now because the very word "Israel" ought to answer the question in which it occurs. Know what? The Gospel or its universality? Both; for he who knows the Gospel at all very soon comes to know that it is for all. In the third verse he denied that Israel knew: "For they, being ignorant of God's righteousness." If he here affirms that they did know

he merely pronounces the former a willful, guilty ignorance. (Cf. John 7:28 with 8:19). The contradiction is only in form.

He answers the question, "Did not Israel know?" by three Scripture quotations. "First Moses," away back in his day, predicted the faith of the Gentiles, who were "no people," and the guilty ignorance of Israel; because a "foolish" nation, one void of understanding, would see the truth of the Gospel to which Israel was blind, and embrace it, and thus "anger" Israel (Deut. 32:21). If the Gentile perceived, it is the Jew's own fault that he did not.

20. "But Isaiah is very bold" in what he utters against Israel (Isa. 45:1). Where Israel was groping and failing to find the Messiah, those who sought Him not clearly discerned Him. How can Israel be excused for ignorance of a world-wide Gospel, when even the heathen discovered it?

21. The third quotation, immediately following the one above from Isaiah, brings the matter of their guilt to a climax. God never ceased to plead with them; but they were "disobedient and gainsaying." But even in this rebellious state he calls them "people," a hopeful word with which to begin the next chapter.

CHAPTER 11

ISRAEL'S FAILURE NOT COMPLETE

THIS CHAPTER from the historical point of view is logically
necessary. The Old Testament clearly promises Israel
headship or leadership in the world's worship. This primacy
they had held from the days of Moses until the days of Paul,
when the latter became the chief instrument in transferring it
to "another nation" (Matt. 21:43), composed of elect persons
called from all peoples (I Pet. 2:9, 10). This promise of headship was made to Israel not on the ground of their national
descent, as the ninth chapter above shows, but, after all, it was
a national promise. It belonged to the natural descent, and
constituted their "advantage." It could not possibly be realized in the Church, because the latter knew no racial distinctions. The essence of Judaism was separation from other people. Two facts stood out prominently in Paul's day: first, that
the Church for the present had displaced Israel in the leadership of God's worship in the world; second, that Israel had a
promise in their "oracles" that was not realized in the Church
and could not be; for the aim of the latter was not national
separation, but diffusion, or, more exactly, election from all
nations. The first question Paul has already considered in the
ninth and tenth chapters. Israel was justly displaced, and by
their own fault. With the second fact the present chapter
deals. Israel as a separate people is to be restored and to realize the promises made to them in the Old Testament. God's
far-reaching plans in the riches of His wisdom for the salvation
of the world are here disclosed, provoking the exultant hymn
in verses 33-36. Israel's present failure proves to be the world's
wealth now and their own finally.

Paul's thought in this chapter moves around two points:

(1) that the present rejection of Israel is not total (vv. 1-10), and (2) it is not final (vv. 11-36). Under (1) he shows that as it was in the days of Elijah (vv. 2-4), so now there is an election of grace (v. 5), but not of works (v. 6), and that the rest, as the Scripture declares, were hardened (vv. 7-10).

Under (2) there are four items: (i) the rejection of Israel had a twofold aim, (a) to turn the stream of the Gospel to the Gentiles, and (b) by this means to provoke Israel to emulation (vv. 11-15); (ii) the likelihood of Israel's restoration should move the Gentiles to humility and maintenance of faith (vv. 16-24); (iii) the apostle's prediction of Israel's restoration (vv. 25-32); and (iv) the worshipful doxology (vv. 33-36).

1. "I say then, Hath God cast away his people?" The preceding verse shows to whom Paul refers. It is "gainsaying" and rejected Israel that is God's "people." "For I also am an Israelite [of the purest blood, being] of the seed of Abraham, of [through] the tribe of Benjamin." Paul was an Israelite not by proselytism but by blood. He asserts his pure Jewish descent not as evidence that Israel is not wholly rejected, for the proof of this proposition does not begin before the next verse is reached. He has asked the question, "Hath God cast away his people?" in a negative, deprecating spirit, and his being an Israelite accounts for the manner of the question. He is in full sympathy with his race and may be expected to answer the inquiry about Israel fairly. (See on 10:1).

2. "God hath not cast off his people whom he foreknew." In the word "his" and the phrase "whom he foreknew" there is a double proof that Israel, though for the present rejected, is not cast off. Among the nations of the world the Jews were the only one chosen by God for His own, with whom also He entered into covenant relations. A king may be rejected by his subjects, but he does not reject them. Moreover, God "foreknew" Israel. For the meaning of this word see on 8:29. In this present Christian age God foreknows individuals in every nation, but Israel is the only nation He ever foreknew. He elected it as a whole to obtain the salvation in Christ when the appointed time for the blessing shall come (Matt. 23:39). This constitutes Israel's "advantage" and makes it to be "much every way," for no other nation has as a nation the promise of salvation before theirs.

3, 4. And even for the present the case of Israel is not as bad as human observation would declare it to be. By the phrase "of Elias," or literally "in Elias" (I Kings 19:10-18), Paul resorts to the method of citation used before the Bible was divided into chapters and verses. (See Mark 12:26; Luke 20:37.) The prophet thought the nation ruined in his day; but the divine response assured him of thousands whom God had "reserved," or left to Himself, from the flood of unbelief that had come upon the land. The prophet saw the overwhelming, devouring tide, but he could not see the secret influence of the divine Spirit, who was leaving to God, and preserving from Baal, seven thousand faithful ones.

5. "Even so then at this present time." Paul was better acquainted with his days than the prophet had been with the period to which he belonged; for the apostle had the prophet's experience to guide him and better means of observation. He knew that in every church from Jerusalem to Rome there were always some Jews who accepted Jesus as the Messiah, "a remnant according to the election of grace." They had not bowed the knee to the Baal of unbelief, because God's Spirit now, as in the prophet's day, had rescued them from the faithless sentiment of the nation against Jesus of Nazareth. This remnant, this reserve from the unbelieving mass, has come to be and exists in accord with God's electing grace, the phrase being added to show in what manner the remnant obtained salvation.

While the nation lies fallen and faithless, elect individuals are being brought into the Church, where, if they lose the national "advantage," they get sweet access to God in the forgiveness of sins.

6. "And if by grace, then it is no more of works." The "no more" is not temporal, but logical. Grace and works are mutually exclusive methods. If the remnant was selected on the ground of grace, their legal works had no part whatever in the selection, else (the) grace would have lost its character as grace. In this second mention of grace there is no article in the original.

This verse expands the phrase "election of grace." It serves also to show that the election, fully vindicated in chapter 9, is by means of grace. This, which was implied before, is now clearly stated. The Old Testament promised a remnant; it is shown now that nothing but grace secures it. The latter half of this verse, "but if of works . . ." is rejected by all modern editors.

7. "What then?" How does the case now stand? "Israel [the nation] hath not obtained that which he seeketh for [viz., righteousness (9:31, 32)]; but the election [the elect remnant] hath obtained it." Paul uses the abstract "election" rather than the concrete "elect," to throw the emphasis on the means and not on the result. "And the rest [the mass of natural Israel] were [not "blinded," but] hardened." Since the remnant was saved by grace, there was no injustice done to the "rest." For who can complain if salvation came to some where none deserved it? And if the undeserving remnant was saved because God would and when He would, why may not the "rest" be saved in His own time and by the same free grace?

8-10. Scripture is quoted not only in confirmation of the hardening of the "rest" of Israel, but also as descriptive of their sad spiritual condition during the time of their rejection (Isa. 29:10; Deut. 29:4; Ps. 69:22, 23). The parentheses in the King James Version in verse 8 must be removed. The words "unto this day" are not Paul's, but a part of the quotation. What was true in their author's day remained so in Paul's, and is yet sadly true. In the word "table" there is a picture of men feasting, eating and drinking, unconscious that their enemies are just upon them. The Jew's carnal security while trusting in the law proved his spiritual ruin. But the quotation is poetic, and need not be rigidly defined. "And bow [thou] down their back alway" under the heavy legal yoke (Acts 15:10). The "alway" does not mean forever, or the whole discussion concerning Israel must end here. "Alway," converted in a few cases by some editors into a phrase, occurs about seven times, and means continuously or without interruption

(Luke 24:53; Heb. 13:15). It is not an indefinite, but a limited term, limited by the circumstances of which it speaks.

11. From this verse to the end of the discussion Paul considers the case of the great fallen mass of Israel. (See under (2) above.) He has already shown the cause of the fall (9:31-10:21) in their own sin, the result of which was their hardening. It remains to speak of the divine purpose in their present moral condition and the outcome of the whole.

"I say then, Have they stumbled that they should fall?" The question is put negatively and deprecatingly, as in the first verse above. They did not stumble that they might fall, did they? Was this the whole and only purpose? They are fallen, but is this the intended outcome of their history? "God forbid." There was a gracious, far-reaching aim in their rejection. The early preachers of the Gospel were so full of the Spirit that they must preach; the Gospel was like a fire in their bones; and since the Jews would not receive it, they turned elsewhere (Acts 11:20; 13:46, 47). Through the Jews' fall salvation went to the Gentiles, to provoke the former to emulation. "Jealousy" is not the best word. In time Israel will see that the world has gained what they lost by their obstinacy, and the salvation of the Gentiles will teach Israel what they did not learn before they saw that salvation. Two happy results, then, flow from their fall: a world diffusion of the stream of life, a stream in which the fallen Jew may in time wash himself from the uncleanness of his own self-righteousness (Isa. 64:6).

12. "Now if the [sinful] fall of them is the riches of the world [in that by the fall the world got the gospel], and [to repeat the same question in another form, if] the diminishing of them [is] the riches of the Gentiles; how much more their fullness?" Three words here demand attention. Twice Paul calls the Gospel sent to the Gentiles their "riches." It was not their territory, not their armies, not their culture, not their treasures, that constituted their wealth (Rev. 2:9; 3:17). Again, the word "diminishing" has had various renderings, "loss," "diminution," "defeat." It occurs in only one other instance in the New Testament (I Cor. 6:7), where it is translated "fault." Furthermore, has the word a moral or a numerical sense? Sanday stands for the meaning "defeat," which Godet says is impossible. On the whole, the word seems to be numerical, and signifies diminution. Israel was reduced to the small number of the elect. And it must be noted, though it is but a shade, that it is not the elect that Paul has in mind, but the nation thus reduced. It was the diminishing of the nation, and not the elect, that brought riches to the Gentiles.

Again, the meaning of this word determines that of the last one, "fullness." The latter is also numerical. It denotes that which fills out or fills full an empty space. Israel by their fall created a great void in their ranks. The "fullness" looks to the future reoccupation of this present vacancy. Note how the salvation of the world turns on God's dealing with Israel. Their fall sent the Gospel to the Gentiles; their fullness is to issue in something vastly greater than the present riches; ultimate redemption is relative to them. In a very wide sense "salvation is of the Jews" (John 4:22).

13, 14. "I am the apostle of the Gentiles," or, as the Revised Version, "I am an apostle of Gentiles." Paul has shown such an ardent desire for the welfare of the Jews, and has now, beginning at chapter 9, devoted so much of his epistle to them, that an explanation is due to the Roman church, which, as this passage implies, was Gentile. Whatever Jews were in it had lost Jewish caste. "I speak to you" (the whole Roman church), you, the "Gentiles," about Israel, for their welfare mightily affects yours. (At this point in the King James text insert a colon.) But while I speak to you and am an apostle of Gentiles, this apostleship looks also toward Israel (Acts 9: 15; Rom. 1:5). "Inasmuch then as I am an apostle of Gentiles, I glorify my [Gentile] ministry [I endeavor to give it a resplendent success]: if by any means I may provoke to emulation my flesh [the Jews], and might save some of them."

The "for" introducing these two verses is not genuine; the approved reading is "but." The verses are not a parenthesis, but a logical part of Paul's argument, answering an objection that might arise in the minds of his Gentile readers because he says so much about the Jews. He is laboring for the Gentiles, glorifying his office to them, but with the salvation of at least "some" Jews in view. For Gentile salvation cannot be accomplished directly, cannot be reached, without the "fullness" of the Jews. Therefore he is interested in the Jews for the Gentiles' sake, and the Romans ought to be interested in them for the same reason. If Paul can in laboring for the Gentiles save "some" Jews, he has accomplished so much toward the "fullness" necessary to the completion of Gentile or world salvation.

15. "For if the casting away of them . . ." This verse gives the grand reason ("for") for Paul's laboring to reach the Jew through his Gentile ministry. It is a kind of ministry little thought of today. The condition of Gentile Christianity is not such now as to impress the Jew with its superiority.

The verse repeats the idea of the twelfth and brings this section of the argument to its climax. The "casting away" is equivalent to "their fall" or "diminution"; the "reconciling of the world" is equivalent to the "riches of the world" or "of the Gentiles"; the "receiving of them" is tantamount to "their fullness"; and the "life from the dead" to the "how much more." For the significance of the phrase "reconciling of the world" see II Corinthians 5:19. In the verse before us it means that on the Jews' rejection God was pleased to send the Gospel to the Gentiles. This reconciliation on God's part became the "riches of the Gentiles." The difficult point in the verse is in the words "life from the dead." The question is twofold: Who receives this life, and what is it?

On the surface the answer to the first question seems plain. In the first member of the sentence the clause "reconciling of the world" must mean the Gentiles. The parallel demands the same meaning for this second clause. The casting away of the Jews was the "reconciling of the world"; the receiving of the Jews into favor again will be "life from the dead" extending over the world. Of course the phrase in question must mean something vastly more than the action contained in the words "reconciling of the world," or there is no climax. But what is that "how much more"? Meyer contends that the words must have their literal meaning and that they refer to actual bodily resurrection. If Paul says "life from the dead" instead of "resurrection from the dead," it is because his eye is fixed upon the permanent and blessed state beyond the act which leads to it. This answers Alford's objection based on this word "life." Meyer's view is favored by Sanday, and "so many have understood it" (Boise). It has the advantage of preserving the literalness of the words and of being in harmony with that expectation of the Jews—an expectation of resurrection warranted, as they thought, by their own Scriptures. If Paul, as above, makes his argument point toward the resurrection of the Gentiles, it was because it was necessary to assure them also of this "hope" (Eph. 2:12), without which they had lived in all time past. But the resurrection of the Jew must occur at the same time. He looked for it. Paul says the Jew instantly served God day and night in hope of attaining to this promise (Acts 26: 6-8). Jesus constantly held out this hope (Matt. 8:11; Luke 13:28-30; John 11:25). He showed Himself again and again the master of death. The Jew looked for resurrection at the coming of the Messiah (Dan. 12:1, 2), but he failed to see that Jesus was the Messiah and so failed of the resurrection. When Israel shall be received again, then comes their own resurrection as well as that belonging to the world. And so Paul has adroitly but powerfully turned the attention of his Gentile readers to the Jews. Until the latter are received the Gentile cannot hope for resurrection.

16. "For if the first-fruit be holy." The "for" is not in the original. It ought to be "now" or "but." (See 2 under (2) above.) Paul has not yet asserted that Israel will be restored, but he has shown what blessed results would follow if they were restored. It is their fall that is still before him, and on this he bases an exhortation to his Gentile readers.

"First fruit." For the figure see Numbers 15:21. The handful of dough offered to the Lord was evidence of the worthiness of the whole mass from which it was taken. The patriarchs Abraham, Isaac, and Jacob are the first fruits, and neither Christ nor the first Jewish Christians at Pentecost, for branches could not be said to be broken off from these. "Holy," not in the moral sense, but as consecrated to God for His own purpose. For this technical sense see Deuteronomy 7:6 and I Corinthians 7:14. The "lump" is the whole lineal descent from the patriarchs. The "root." He changes his figure from a lump of dough to that of a tree, because the latter is easier of expansion in argument. The root, again, is Abraham not merely as a man, but as one having the promises; and the branches are his descendants, the fleshly Israel, called "holy" in the sense given above.

What Paul is after in this discussion under the figure of the olive tree must be clearly kept in mind, or his parable dazzles without helping sight. (a) He is not considering Abraham as the ground or root of salvation, for this is Christ. The failure to understand Paul here has led some (Origen, Theodoret) to call Christ the "root." (b) It is not a question of fruit-bearing, but of dependence, or his figure would not be true to nature. Fruit is in accord with the engrafted scion, and not with the nature of the root. (c) It is not a question of the continuity of the Church. Sanday's statement, "The olive tree, the church of God looked at as one continuous body," is confusing. The olive tree is the Jewish nation as a whole, which was anything but a church. Moreover, the continuity of ancient Israel in the Church is both inconsistent with the character of Israel's restoration and contradictory of the declared relation of the two. The Church is not a branch sprung from the root, but a graft brought to it. Israel is the basis of the Church, but not the source. Israel is a development, the Church a creation (Eph. 2:12; 3:9). (d) The only question considered is from what national sources and in what chronological order and relation God called men to be His own spiritual people. He did call some Jews to be His, but they were not made His because they were Jews. The olive tree had the promise of salvation first, and Paul here shows why that promise was not realized now, and that, while there remains a possibility of its future realization, meantime the branch from the wild olive, the Gentiles, came into relations with the good olive.

17. "And if some of the branches [the "rest" in verse 7 above] be broken off [denied the covenant salvation of Abraham], and thou [the Gentile believer, addressed directly for emphasis], being a wild olive [not "tree," but branch, a mem-

ber of an alien race having no direct promise of salvation (cf.
Eph. 2:12 with 19)], wert grafted in among them [made by
faith a child of the covenant and of God], and with them [the
believing Jews, the branches left standing] partakest [didst become a partaker] of the root and fatness of the olive tree."
Some by rejecting the "and" read "partaker of the root of the
fatness." The root is Abraham, not as a mere physical pro-
genitor of Israel, but as the covenant father (Gal. 3:16, 29;
Rom. 4:11, 12), and the root of the fatness is the covenant
with Him which supplies the fatness, the salvation. The Gentile was grafted in by means of his faith to which he was
elected (Acts 13:48).

18. The "if" (since) beginning the last verse extends over
the first part of this one. If some (a miosis) were broken off
and thou wast grafted in, "boast not against the branches" that
were broken off and are fallen. The boasting of the Gentile
in this case would be most painful to him who could wish himself accursed for his brethren, his kinsmen according to the
flesh. "But if thou boast" thou art absurd, for "thou bearest
not the root, but the root thee." The covenant of salvation
made with Abraham is not sustained by the Gentile; he is
sustained and saved by the covenant. It was clearly promised
that the nations should be blessed, but blessed in Abraham
(Gen. 22:18).

19, 20. From Paul's admonition the Gentile believer would
deduce ("then") a reply: "Branches [omit "the"] were broken
off, that I [emphatic] might be grafted in." Paul admits the
fact ("well"), but warningly directs the proud Gentile's attention to another side of it: by want of faith they were broken
off, and only by faith do you stand as a wild branch on the
good stock. You stand not because they fell and not because
you are a Gentile, but solely by faith, having no direct covenant. It might be well for Gentile Christianity to lay this to
heart today. When simple trust in God fails, what better is
a Gentile church member than the wrongly despised Jew? The
admonition suits every age: "Be not high-minded, but fear."

21. Why fear? Because "if God spared not the natural
branches," to whose ancestors the promises were made and

who were "his people" (v. 1 above)—if He spared not them because of their unbelief, why should He spare you, a wild branch, if you become faithless, as they are? Why should God have any more regard for a faithless Gentile Christianity than for faithless Judaism? The italic words in the King James Version add nothing to the sense, rather hinder. (See the Revised Version.)

22. "Behold therefore." Because the Gentile stands solely by his faith, let him "therefore" avoid boasting, and cease from high-mindedness, and stop saying "I," to look rather at the action of God. "Severity" and "goodness." On them which fell came severity, and on "thee, goodness [the Gentile merited nothing], if thou continue in his goodness." The contingency must not be overlooked. This continuance depended largely on God's favor toward the Gentile believer, but also upon his own conduct. The relation of the two here, as elsewhere, is not given. The Gentile is responsible for his conduct, and if he fails to honor God he will fall as did the Jew. (See the letters addressed to the churches in Rev. 2:3.) "Otherwise thou also shalt be cut off." For why should God spare a hollow, faithless Church that fails to appreciate its ineffable mercy (Eph. 2:4, 5), when He spared not "his people"?

23, 24. "And they also, if they abide not still in unbelief." When God's purpose in breaking them off is served their blindness will be removed (II Cor. 3:14-16), and they will come into the blessed "advantage" mentioned in 3:2. Here again there is a contingency. God does all, but He acts also on the human conscience and will mediately. He would influence the Gentile by fear lest he be broken off; He would move Israel by hope, the hope of regaining his lost standing. His rejection is not absolute and final. "God is able to graft them [the fallen branches] in again." Paul's reference to God's power is not to His abstract ability, which would be commonplace, but He is able, stubborn as Israel seems, to remove his unbelief, the real hindrance. The twenty-fourth verse elucidates ("for") what Paul means in appealing to God's concrete power as the means of Israel's restoration. He is able to graft them in again, because in love He can shape their

194   THE EPISTLE TO THE ROMANS

circumstances, their religious education, and their history in a
form to lead them to Christ. The figure of the olive tree in
this verse is not to be pressed, else his "how much more" becomes "how much less." For certainly it would be easier to
graft in a living wild branch than a dead natural branch. Israel
lies sapless and withered. The inherent condition of the
branches, whether dead or alive, is just what does not come
into view. The point is the usual course taken in grafting. The
gardener for some purpose might graft a wild shoot on a good
stock, but "how much more" likely is it that he will graft in
good branches! A man might leave by will a large portion of
his estate to the son of a stranger, but how much more will he
devise for his own children! Divested of the figurative language, Paul's thought is this: if God could wean some Gentiles
from their idol-worship and their gross immorality and lead
them to adopt the religion of another nation, can he not
"much more" lead Israel to adopt their own ancestral worship
when they are once brought to see what it is, and that it is their
own, and that their ignorant works have been perverting it?
God's ability is in His unfailing love toward Israel.

What is gained in the figure lies in its suggestion. "Nature"
seems to mean here the established course of things in the
kingdom. Its course lay through Israel. Gentile salvation is
contrary to "nature," and Jewish rejection is also contrary to
"nature." The course of things, that is, nature, will in due
time assert itself. Therefore let the Gentile fear; let the Jew
hope. The wild branch may be broken off, the fallen one
grafted in again.

25. With this verse begins (see (2) iii above) the direct prediction of fallen Israel's restoration. Paul has been speaking
of the possibility of it. Here he justifies ("for") his assertion
of the possibility by declaring that there is a temporal limit
to Israel's rejection. It only lasts "until the fullness of the
Gentiles be come in." This is revealed for moral purposes,
that the brethren of the Roman church, being Gentiles, may
not be "wise in their own conceits" and arrogate to themselves a religious supremacy that can never end. How completely this very Roman church does this very thing today,

and how fully Protestantism imitates her so far! To the religious world this section of this chapter is a dead letter and is made "of none effect" (Mark 7:13) by the current tradition. This Jewish blindness with its limit in time is called a "mystery," that is, a fact which could not be known except by revelation. Religious history is not a natural development; its source is in the divine will and its explanation is in His Word. History may throw some light on the Bible, but the Bible sheds much more on history. It is not because the Jew is morally worse and the Gentile morally better that religious supremacy passed from one to the other; it came about because this was God's plan to save both Jew and Gentile. And the transfer having been made, human ken could not have dreamed that it is ever to be reversed; it is a "mystery" which the Gentile is slow to believe.

"That blindness [hardness] in part has happened to Israel." It is not a total, but a partial hardness; it exists not for all time, but only "until the fullness of the Gentiles be come in." This phrase, "fullness of the Gentiles," is obscure. It certainly does not mean that all the Gentiles are first to be saved. The Scriptures nowhere promise this for the present age, for which Paul knows of nothing but an election, the idea of which excludes that of general and complete salvation. Furthermore, Paul (in v. 15 above) puts the conversion of the world not before, but after, the "receiving" of Israel, their restoration being the chief condition in the salvation of the Gentiles.

The phrase may mean (so Govett) that the void made in Israel by the hardening and fall of a part is filled up from the Gentiles. In this case the "of" would, as it might, mean "from," and the words "come in" would get a fair meaning— come into the vacancy. In the parable in Luke 14:16-24 the bidden guests refuse to come, after which the servant is sent into the highways and hedges (among the Gentiles), "that," as the host said, "my house may be filled." He got the fullness for his house from these strange places. In Matthew 22:1-14, after the king has destroyed the city in which his first invitation was rejected, he finds a supply of guests by going beyond and bringing together as many as he found, "both bad and good," a part only of whom were accepted, "for many are called, but few chosen." This view is not worthy of the harsh condemnation of Godet, that it "tortures at will" the words of the apostle. It is plausible, but lacks support from anything in the context.

The explanation of the phrase is not to be found in any numerical, but in the temporal view. "Until" suggests time. The whole context brings up the notion of time. Jerusalem is to be "trodden down until the times of the Gentiles be fulfilled" (Luke 21:24). This view has so much in its favor that it overbalances the difficulty left by it in the words "be come in." The phrase may be used metaphorically.

26. "And so all Israel shall be saved." "So" looks to the removal of the circumstances just mentioned, the partial blindness and the limit. The illogical notion that "Israel" here is the spiritual Israel is no longer held. It is the fallen, rejected, natural Israel, the only nation in this age that has the promise of salvation as a whole. It will not be merely Christianized, but Christian. He gives a Scripture proof that Israel shall be saved: "It is written [in Isa 59:20 after the Septuagint, and in other places substantially, Isa. 27:9; Ps. 14:7], There shall come out of Zion [Ps. 110:2] [the place of God's glory] the Deliverer [the Goel, a strong kinsman who avenges his weaker friends], and shall turn away ungodliness [Ps. 99] [impieties] from Jacob." The word "Jacob," the fleshly name, found in the quotation, gives the meaning of the word "Israel." Whether the reference is to the first or to the second coming of the Messiah is not indicated. The promise of deliverance for Jacob is connected with a coming of the Christ. He has come; He will surely make good that for which He came.

27. A second Scripture proof of Israel's restoration. "And [not "for"] this [which follows] is my covenant unto them, when I shall take away their sins." The word "Jacob" looks at them in the mass; the word "their" looks at them individually. The sense of the verse is, "When I shall take away their sins, this taking away of sins is my side of the covenant with them." God's covenant promises the taking away of sins,

and it cannot be broken. The verse seems to be a condensation of Jeremiah 31:31-34.

28, 29. Paul now reviews and sums up the previous discussion. Israel in their relation to the Gospel are "enemies [regarded as such by God] for your sakes." He withheld the Gospel from them that you might have it. But Israel in relation to their own election by God as His people are "beloved for the fathers' sakes," Abraham, Isaac, and Jacob. The election here does not refer to the elect remnant now in the Church, but to God's choice of the Jewish nation as His own (Deut. 7:6). That Israel is beloved for the fathers' sakes sounds strange in view of what John the Baptist said: "Think not to say within yourselves, We have Abraham to our father." But John was only denying salvation on the ground of natural descent, which Paul also denies. The covenant descent, which requires the faith of him with whom the covenant is made, is everywhere allowed (Luke 13:16; 19:9; Acts 3:25). "If the first fruit be holy, the lump is also holy: and if the root be holy, so are the branches." Israel is beloved not as the natural, but as the covenant descent. God loved the fathers not alone as men, but as those who believed His promise about an innumerable progeny. That love is a guaranty that God will make the descent like the fathers and worthy of them. He will not mock the fathers' faith about their progeny. He will take away ungodliness from Jacob, and see to it (v. 23) that they "abide not still in unbelief." For while beloved for the fathers' sakes, they will be saved by faith. They are an intensely religious race, strangely preserved. Their zeal will in due time be according to knowledge.

That Israel is still beloved is proved by the general principle of the kingdom, based on the divine character, that the "gifts and calling of God are without repentance." The "gifts" are not the "moral and intellectual aptitudes" with which God has endowed the Jews (Godet), but their own peculiar possessions, already enumerated (9:4,5). The "calling" is that act of God in which He chose them for His people. These gifts and this calling are "without repentance" on God's part; He will never recall them. Having once given them to Israel, He makes them theirs forever; He does not change (3:3; Mal. 3:6).

30, 31. "For" introduces these two verses not as a proof, but as indicating how the general principle just mentioned will be realized by Israel. "For as ye in times past . . ." The contrast between the "ye," the Romans, and the "their" shows that the Roman church was in the main Gentile. These Gentiles once disbelieved God and were dead in sins; but they obtained mercy by the unbelief of the Jews, as described in verses 11 and 12 above. And just so "these" have not believed, "that through your mercy [the same mercy shown to you] they also may obtain mercy." As the Gentile's disobedience brought him the mercy of God, so the Jew's disobedience will bring him the same mercy, in which he will realize that God's gifts and calling are changeless.

32. The "for" introducing this verse is hardly argumentative; it confirms nothing. Verses 30 and 31 practically restate everything from verse 11 in a single sentence. The verse before us puts these two verses, especially the thirty-first, in another form, almost that of a general principle of God's dealing with men. His whole action with both Jew and Gentile comes to this, that he "hath concluded [locked up as in a prison] them all in unbelief [with this grand purpose], that he might have mercy upon all." There is nothing richer than His mercy. If the Jews, for instance, had obeyed Him they could have experienced only His fidelity. Mercy, which wholly excludes privilege or merit, is the grand idea (Eph. 2:4, 5). The Jew will find His gifts and calling, but them come to Him as a matter of mercy—mercy that excludes "boasting" (3:27). Authorities are divided on the meaning of "all." It certainly does not refer to the elect; the whole context forbids that. But does it mean all men, all individuals (Meyer, Alford), or all nations, the Jews and the Gentiles about whom Paul has been speaking? The context is decisive for the latter.

This general principle, as some have failed to notice, describes God's attitude toward men, and not the outcome of that attitude. It does not contradict other plain Scriptures by teaching universal salvation, or salvation without faith. "The

Scripture hath concluded all under sin, that the promise by
faith of Jesus Christ might be given to them that *believe*"
(Gal. 3:22). The principle says nothing about the outcome
of the divine mercy toward all. It simply declares that God has
actively and directly locked up all in sin so that He may have
mercy toward all; that if they are saved they are saved by mercy.

This is the final and complete explanation of the Jew's fall.
He was by nature a sinner; God hedged that nature about with
a rigid law to show him what his real character was. He tried
to find liberty within its iron bars, but gets only slavery. Mercy
alone can deliver him. The Gentile in Paul's day had no law,
but sought liberty in wisdom, his own wisdom (1:21,22), and
in his quest became a fool and a slave to his lust.

God knows that man cannot save himself, that no form of
civil government and no system of ethics, even though it be
that of the Old or of the New Testament, can attain to liberty.
But man does not know it; he is in the rough prison, shut up
under sin to learn it, to learn that salvation cannot be reached
by human effort, that it comes down from God, the absolute
gift of His mercy.

This divine purpose of mercy is not only the explanation of
the Jew's fall, but of the continuance of the world in sin. It
is the key to those terrible first chapters of the epistle. Universal condemnation leads to the universal principle of mercy.
And what Paul saw in his world-wide view in his day is still
sadly true. The nations are in sin; Israel still refuses the Christ.
The lesson of sin's prison-house is not yet learned; but what
the elect have found out all along—that there is no hope in
themselves—the nations will learn in due time, and man's
works will cease, and God's principle of mercy toward all will
bring salvation. God now elects men from both Jew and Gentile; Jew and Gentile will then elect God. Verse 32 is the
climax of the epistle.

33-36. Having completed his argument, Paul, in reviewing
God's plans and purposes as they were unfolded to him, breaks
forth in a lofty strain of adoration to Him who is guiding the
nations and the world to salvation. "We have learned Paul's
meaning only when we can join in this ascription of praise"

(M. B. Riddle). It is a hymn of faith not in man, but in God. To be sure, there was a chain of churches reaching from Jerusalem to Rome, but the world around was sunk in heathenish darkness; Satan was god of the world (II Cor. 4:4), "the spirit that now worketh in the children of disobedience" (Eph. 2:2); false professors were many (Phil. 3:18) and false teachers were arising (Acts 20:29,30), while bonds and afflictions awaited the apostle himself (Acts 20:23); but he saw the meaning of it all in seeing that God had an ultimate merciful purpose for all, and hence this optimistic worship. (See iv above under (2).)

"O the depth!" With most commentators, this should probably be translated, "O the depth of the riches and of the wisdom and of the knowledge of God!" He unfolds these chiastically, treating of the wisdom and knowledge to the end of verse 34, and of the riches in the remaining two verses. The word "depth," as Chrysostom suggests, is the language of wondering admiration when one cannot see all. "Riches" is to be taken absolutely. It is not the riches of His grace, nor of any one thing, but of all. God is inexpressibly rich. "Wisdom" adapts means to ends, and "knowledge" sees both in all their relations. Paul, from the mountain height attained in his argument, beholds in one view the history of man from the beginning in Adam to the triumphant end in Christ as King of kings. This history is not man's, but God's in His dealing with man, a history of God's own wisdom and knowledge. Paul is the true historian of the race as well as the true philosopher. No man can be either who leaves God out. Hence man's history of himself is one of blood and failure. The Bible teaches more real knowledge about mankind than is to be found in all other books.

"How unsearchable his judgments, and his ways past finding out!" Mere human wisdom cannot understand them and so pronounces them folly (I Cor. 2:14). His "judgments" are the product of His wisdom; His "ways" the mode of His procedure (Meyer) in making His decrees effective. Here is the secret of profound reverence and devout worship. This swelling doxology, this burst of praise, comes forth as Paul scans the "ways" of God and sees something of His wide purposes for men. It comes not from a contemplation of God's infinitely tender heart, but of His infinitely wise mind. Men know God's acts; the masters know His ways (Ps. 103:7).

History and prophecy! Without these, true reverence cannot be reached. A mystery remains, for His judgments are unsearchable and His riches have a depth that is lost in darkness. But it is the mystery of intelligence and not of superstition, a mystery that swathes reverence with a celestial glory. Paul could not have worshiped here had he been able to see all; but he saw enough to console him for the present rejection of his kinsmen according to the flesh; enough to satisfy him that the Word of God had not failed, though Israel was not saved; enough to be sure that, while only a meager elect number from both Jew and Gentile was as yet accepted, this was God's way that ultimately He might have mercy on all. Therefore, standing in the midst of a world full of idolatry and woe, Paul adored.

34. "For who hath known the mind of the Lord?" A proof ("for") from the Septuagint Scriptures (Isa. 40:13) that God's judgments and decrees are such as they are declared to be in the last verse. It is well-nigh a challenge to produce the man outside the circle of the inspired prophets and apostles— the wise man that understood God or that could give Him advice. The religious element in uninspired history and philosophy is folly, and Paul has already (1:22) in this epistle called its authors fools (I Cor. 2:8; 3:19, 20). This verse again looks chiastically at what precedes, "the mind of the Lord" corresponding to the mention of "knowledge" above, and the word "counselor" to "wisdom." God's love explains God's gifts, but His mind and wisdom alone explain His providence or the manner in which He makes the gifts of love effective.

Modern thought of the advanced sort fails here. It attempts to explain everything by love, with an inadequate notion even of what that is, and so belittles the Book of divine history and prophecy by denying it any proper inspiration. Who has known the mind of the Lord, except as it was divinely revealed to him? "Thou shalt love the Lord thy God with all thy mind" —study His ways.

35. With this verse Paul enlarges on the word "riches" above. The reference is to Job 35:7 or 51:11. No one ever gave to God. Salvation and the whole plan of its administration are of grace. No one ever receives God's favor as a recompense for something done. The "Lord over all is rich unto all that call upon him" (10:12). They call not to give, but as beggars (Matt. 5:3) to receive out of His store.

36. "For of . . . through . . . to him, are all things." This verse is the proof that no one gives to God and therefore receives a recompense. For "of him" are all things; He is their source, the Creator. And "through him" are all things; He is the mediator of their existence; He upholds, rules, and directs. And "to him are all things"; He is their final cause; they serve ultimately not man's, but God's, ends. To Paul this was not a dry statement of theologic fact, as a matter of course, but a reason for worship. All things, all events, are full of God. To Him be the befitting glory to the ages. Amen.

(1) It is to be noticed in this momentous discussion that Paul regards God's covenant with Abraham as one embracing his natural seed and perpetually valid; that he uses the words "Jacob" and "Israel" not in reference to the Church, but to designate this natural seed. In the Old Testament he must have read these words in the same way, so that he did not apply what concerns Jacob and Israel to the Church. Much of the Old Testament remains unfulfilled.

(2) Again, he keeps up the sharp distinction between Jew and Gentile; but the ultimate salvation of both is vitally linked together, so that neither party can be saved without the other. Paul, though an apostle to the Gentiles, labored also to save the Jews on this very account. Missions to the Jews are eminently scriptural. His own conception of the matter was "to the Jew first." (See on 1:16.)

(3) Again, neither the unbelief of Israel nor of the nations is estopping the current of God's rich grace. What the nations are losing, the "election" from all nations is gaining. The Gospel disbelieved by races is saving individuals.

(4) While Paul does not predict the breaking off of the en-grafted wild olive branch, the Church, he warns it ominously. It has no guaranty in a covenant, as has even fallen Israel. It stands alone by faith. The individuals of the Church, the elect, have the most comforting assurance of eternal salvation, but God has not promised to continue to elect. Indeed, it is impossible to see how individual election, the source of the Church, is consistent with God's ultimate "mercy upon all." Election is a means to an end in God's wide dealing with men. When the end is reached, election will cease.

(5) And finally, Paul contents himself with predicting the fact of Israel's restoration. He has not one word to say about the details, whether the Jews will revive their ancient liturgy, rebuild Jerusalem, and possess their land; of these and similar questions he is instructively silent.

CHAPTER 12

RELIGIOUS DUTIES

THE CHAPTER HAS TWO MAIN DIVISIONS: (1) special duties (vv. 1-8), based on specific endowments of faith, and (2) general duties (vv. 9-21); or the first might be called official, because they were to be discharged toward the Church as a whole, and the second personal, because they regulated the conduct of each member with the other.

1. Paul does not command like Moses; he beseeches. His entreaty gets its point and strength through the mercies or compassions of God. These mercies, as the "therefore" shows, are the ones mentioned above (11:30-36), a paragraph that condenses the whole theodicy (9—11). These solemn facts of election and hardening, of breaking off of some branches and grafting in others, are called "mercies," because the end of all is "mercy upon all" (11:32).

"That ye present your bodies." "Present" is a temple term for the bringing thither of anything to God. So Jesus was presented (Luke 2:22), and so Paul would present each believer (Col. 1:28). He entreats the Romans to make themselves a sacrificial offering to God. This word "present" occurs first in the epistle at 6:13, a verse which this chapter now unfolds. It is there translated "yield." (See note there.) "Bodies" is the comprehensive term for the whole man, body, soul, and spirit (I Thess. 5:23). It is equivalent to "yourselves," but better suited than the latter word to Paul's sacrificial idea.

"A living sacrifice, holy, acceptable." They had all this in Christ. They were alive from the dead in Him, they were consecrated or holy in Him, they were acceptable to God in Him. These were not qualities to be sought by them in addition to justification; they came with it and belong to it. These three words analyze or give the contents of their righteousness in Christ. They were to present themselves such as they already were. "Your reasonable service." It was not to be a literal presentation of their bodies, but a rational service. The idea is that of spiritual worship in contrast with the tangible carnal sort in Judaism. They presented themselves by heart worship of God (John 4:23, 24).

2. "Be not conformed to this world." The world, or age, is looked at in its moral features. It is "this" world in contrast with one which is coming. What makes this world is its spirit, its pursuits, and its domination. Its spirit is selfishness and not love; its pursuits are the pleasing of self and not God; and its domination is from the evil one and not from Christ, whose rule it rejects (Eph. 2:2; Gal 1:4; John 14:30). To be conformed to it is to be world-like, or age-like, selfish, self-seeking, and devoid of the Holy Spirit. It is to have the same moral fashion.

"Be ye transformed [not by mere outward means in modes of dress and of eating and drinking, but] by the renewing of your mind." The two words "conform" and "transform" are widely different. The former looks to the outward mold, the latter to the inward substance. The Romans were not simply to shun the fashion of the world, but its character, to have not only a different way of living, but a different heart. The word "renewing" occurs in but one other place in the New Testament (Titus 3:5), and there in connection with "regeneration." The latter is the divine act in which the religious life begins. The "renewing" is the "following up, the consequence, the consummation" (Trench, Syn.) of regeneration. In regeneration the believer is passive; in the renewing he is in active co-operation with the Holy Spirit, the agent of the renewing process. The renewing continues what the single act of regeneration, done once for all, begins (II Cor. 4:16).

The "mind" is the organ of moral thinking and knowing. The word has been used thrice before in the epistle: 1:28, where the organ was judicially perverted that men might not think right in moral matters; 7:23, 25, where its action was normal, but, in attempting to realize its perceptions, always defeated by enslavement to the flesh; 11:34, where it means God's infinite ability to know. Since men are transformed by the action of the mind, transformed by what they think, how important to have the organ of thought renewed! (Eph. 4:23.)

"That [in order that] ye may prove [recognize by the right action of the renewed mind as worthy] the will of God," the thing willed by Him, which is "good" in its aim, "acceptable" or well-pleasing to Him, and because of these two "perfect" in itself. The margin of the Revised Version is the preferable translation here.

Beware of the chapter mark which cuts off these two verses from what precedes, as if an entirely new thought were taken up with chapter 12. These two verses are intimately connected with the summing up at the close of chapter 11. That summary led Paul to adoring worship as he viewed God's wide-reaching plans. And the idea of these two verses is worship evoked and provoked by the same view. The Romans are to present themselves for a rational service, a worship in which the spiritual reason leads. This worship is impossible except by men dissevered from conformity to the world. He who is ruled by the world's spirit and pursuits, to whom the world is the only great thing, cannot worship. The spring of the worship, as well as its power, is just what it was in Paul, a mind that discerns God's will in the dispensational ordering of the world to bring about its ultimate salvation (see Eph. 3:14-21), a mind that sees that will as good and acceptable and perfect. When the cornerstone of creation was laid, all the sons of God shouted for joy (Job 38:6, 7); and he, too, will worship who sees the cornerstone laid by God in Christ for the new creation. It takes mind (v. 2) to know mind (11:34). These two mentions of the word look each other in the face across the chapter bar, and man's mind in its moral activity never acts normally except in adoring worship. "Present your bodies" is the first step. "That ye may prove the will" is then, first of all, His will in Christ for the redeeming of the nations, Jew and Gentile. And only as this will is known can anyone see how he is himself to act. The renewed mind dwelling on the sublime purposes of God gains an increasing delicacy of discernment of its own moral action, and is prepared for personal guidance in all questions of duty and living, and to occupy spiritual offices acceptably. It is at this point that Paul branches off on duties. The qualification to discharge them is a knowledge of God's ways.

3. "For." What Paul has said in verse 2 is confirmed by the demand upon the Romans for self-estimation. This request comes from his own apostolic "grace." It is addressed not to the body, but pointedly to each individual member in it, for one proud, wrong-headed man in the Roman assembly could disturb all. Piety promotes thinking, but let no man judge that his thought is so superior that it can embrace all. In view of the fact that the plan of salvation is the product of the divine mind, let him think "soberly," and not go beyond what God has given him to believe ("faith") about these things. The opinions of the head, the opinions demanded by one's theological views, are mischievous unless they are also the opinions of that faith given by the Holy Ghost. Paul shows his estimate of the importance of the sentiment of this verse in that it is framed by a play on the word "think" to fix attention and remembrance upon it, and in that it is introduced by a reference to his apostolic authority. The Revised Version brings out the meaning a little better. Who saw more of God's will than Paul, and where is there a humbler man? The secret of it is that he knew.

4, 5. This likening of the Roman church to the human body is a condensation of I Corinthians 12:12-27, written less than a year earlier, and both for the same purpose. Each member of the human frame has its own character and office, but no one is sufficient of itself, no one can do anything apart from the whole. And so let no one "think" of himself as if he were not dependent on all the rest. There is a wisdom in some far superior to that in the rest, and it shows that it is wisdom in humbly serving those that do not have it (John 13:13, 14). When a man thinks too "highly" of himself to walk in union with God's lowly people, his estimation of himself far surpasses God's. The head cannot say to the feet, made only for the earth, "I have no need of you" (I Cor. 12:21).

6-8. The King James Version, along with the Revised Version and some commentators, separates the section embraced in these verses from the one immediately preceding; but a semicolon is better than a period. The connection: "Every one members one of another; and [or "but"] having gifts differing according to the grace that is given to us." Of these gifts seven are mentioned (Eph. 4:8-12; I Cor. 12:28): four semi-official, prophecy, ministry, teaching, and exhortation, and three general, giving, ruling, showing mercy. These gifts get their character and their measure in the divine grace that bestowed them. Prophecy is the gift of uttering God's will under the direct impulse of the Spirit, but in the Church it did not amount to authoritative inspiration (I Cor. 14:29-33; I Thess. 5:20, 21). Ministry is not so specific. It embraced the preaching of the Gospel (11:13, rendered "office"), the service in money (II Cor. 9:1), and general help rendered to the saints (Col. 4:17; Heb. 1:14). The teacher set forth principles of the kingdom, its fundamental truths, learned from the Bible (II Tim. 3:10, 16; 4:3), and built up the hearer to distinguish between the true and the false (Eph. 4:14). He that exhorted encouraged and entreated. In I Timothy 4:13 two of these words come together.

"He that giveth." This was some special function in giving, private and personal, a gift of faith, and not general giving which belonged to all. "He that ruleth." This is a faulty rendering; the apostolic churches had no rulers. It ought to be "He that presides" or "superintends." Paul may have referred in this term to their elders (I Thess. 5:12; I Tim. 5:17). "He that showeth mercy." Such a man had a gift to aid those overtaken by misfortune of any sort. (See story of good Samaritan.) The word "mercy" here has no reference to sin.

The italic words in the King James Version fairly represent the best interpretation of this passage. Paul says if we have the gift of prophecy, let us prophesy in this manner: "according to the proportion [measure] of the [our] faith." Faith does not mean here body of doctrine. It is the prophet's own per-

sonal trust. There was dealt to him a measure of faith (v. 3 above) for this work. God gave him an insight into the Gospel of Christ. Let his prophecy not go beyond that and become vainglorious and arrogant. Men who have an office are under strong temptation to go beyond what they know in it. Thus they greatly injure themselves in coming to believe the utterances of their own ignorance, and they mislead others, who believe them because they are accredited teachers. Let the prophet rigidly limit his gift by the faith of his gift.

If one has a gift of "ministry," let him wait on his ministering, give himself to it, and be content with that, while not attempting something for which he is not gifted. And so of the "teacher," let him stick to his teaching, and the "exhorter" to exhortation.

The man of means who has the blessed gift of giving, let him exercise it not ostentatiously, not to create obligation, but in simplicity. The "ruler" must not be slothful, but diligent, and the man who looks after the unfortunate must do it with a bright and cheerful aspect.

This section on the gifts is plainly a reminiscence of what Paul had written to the Corinthians (I Cor. 12). He introduces it with the same figure about the body and lays special stress on the matter of prophecy. He had learned by the shameful misuse of these gifts at Corinth the temptation which they afforded carnal men. There was no abuse at Rome, but he would forestall it. The notice of seven gifts lends the discussion the idea of comprehensiveness of all others.

9. "Let love be without dissimulation," without hypocrisy. Feigned love is nothing but disguised hate. The little sentence implies more than it says. Love was so prevalent, and so strongly characterized the Church, that he who had it not was tempted to simulate it. This caution about love is virtually the theme of the rest of the chapter, the second section (see (2) above) beginning here. To the close of verse 13 the original contains no verb, but is made up of participles showing continuous action, or of adjectives of the same character.

"Be [continue] abhorring the evil [especially in conduct]; be cleaving to the good." This is intended to regulate moral sentiment.

10. "In [not "with"] [the matter of "brotherly love" or] love to the brethren be kindly [kind-like] affectioned one to another." Let it not be a mere church love, but such a love as parents have for children, or husbands for wives.

In the matter of "honor," without which sentiment a church could not exist, do not claim it, but fail not to show it. The church is the "noblest school of courtesy."

11. "Not slothful in business." A much-misunderstood and oft misquoted text. It has no reference to secular business as such. The word means zeal. "In zeal [the outward] not slothful; in spirit [the inward, the human spirit] fervent; serving [doing bond-service to] the Lord." The church life was to be characterized by energy, by warmth, and as being a service to the Lord. For "serving the Lord" some read "serving the time"; but this has little support.

12. "Hope...tribulation...prayer." These three make up the bulk of many a Christian life. The hope of the better things at the end (8:17-25) is not to be calmly held as a mere article of belief, but as the inspiration of continual joy (I Peter 1:3-13).

As to tribulation—a better word is "affliction"—it is sure to attend the life of faith. The shield against it is not fretfulness or complaint, but quiet endurance. When the "hope" dawns the affliction will be forever over, gone like a painful dream.

"Prayer," both Church and individual, is not to cease because no answer seems to come, but is to be a continual and persistent ("instant") habit. If Paul does not commend faith in prayer, it is because persistence is one of the largest elements of faith.

13. As to one's possessions or incoming wages (Eph. 4:28), they are to be divided with those who have neither. "Saints" is the New Testament term for believers in Christ, and does not suggest eminence in piety. (Compare I Cor. 1:2 with 3:3 in the same epistle.) And every house is also to be a Christian inn, where believers, apostles, teachers, and others may find gladly given entertainment without cost. Note that this verse enjoins a giving different from that in verse 8 above.

14. The repetition of the word "bless" enforces the duty. The Roman church, for more than two hundred years under a succession of heathen emperors, had abundant occasion to recall this injunction (Luke 23:34).

15. "Rejoice...weep." The mother enters into the innocent joys of her children and is grieved in their sorrows, for she is one with them and loves them. And believers are "members one of another." Jesus did not mourn at Cana, nor did He exult at the tomb of Lazarus. He wept with Mary and Martha, even though He knew that in another moment all cause for tears would be gone. And may we not say that today, enthroned with the Father, He is glad in what gladdens His and grieved in what grieves them? As it is much easier to bewail another's woe, in that it does not excite envy or covetousness, than to congratulate him in his joy, the apostle mentions the rejoicing first.

16. "The same mind one toward another." A family virtue again in which there is a common regard and a common understanding. Each thinks affectionately well of the other. "Mind not high things." Diotrephes missed this (III John 9). So did Absalom in his yearning, "Oh, that I were made judge!" (II Sam. 15:4.) So does everyone who seeks for place above his fellows (Mark 10:44, 45). The rose by the dusty wayside is as sweet as the rose in the king's garden. The human regard worth having is given for what one is rather than for where he is.

"But condescend to men of low estate." The original is not decisive as between lowly things and men that are lowly. On the whole, the latter is preferable. "Condescend" is an unfortunate word and must be rejected; condescension has no place in the Church. Some render, "be carried away with" the lowly —give yourself to them. The world neglects and despises them; Christ loves them and died for them. There is often more genuine worth and manhood in the alleys than in the avenues; and Christian love goes where love is most needed. It is "carried away" in the service of need. Christ in help to one lowly woman was so "carried away" that He had no desire to eat (John 4:31, 32).

"Be not wise in you own conceits." The word "wise" is the same which we have had twice before in the verse—"mind"; but it cannot be shown readily in a translation. Think the same things toward one another; think not on high things; think not highly of yourself. Self-conceit, too high an estimate of one's self, is the chief hindrance to the three duties enjoined just before. The man who complacently reflects on his own abilities or exaltation is feeding on his own vitals. He will grow lean. He who in self-forgetfulness is carried away with the lowly grows large of heart. The man who is above doing what Christ did for men is far beneath His approval.

17. "Recompense to no man evil for evil." Verse 14 forbade the feeling, this the act; it is only love that can obey either.

"Provide things honest in the sight of all men." Have a care, see to it, that all your life is such that you do not awaken the prejudice or contempt of men; let your conduct commend itself to them. This verse looks at the behavior of the Church with reference to those outside. This is not subservience to public opinion. Jesus would not "offend" others (Matt. 17: 27). It is a part of Christianity to commend itself to the world by a well-ordered life. The word "provide" in its modern narrow sense of furnishing or supplying is misleading. The injuction refers not to acts, but to the prudence which regulates them.

18. "As much as lieth in you, live peaceably with all men." Seek peace. The other party may not yield, but let it be no fault of yours if he does not. You are not guiltless until you have exhausted every means to bring about reconciliation. How could church quarrels florish if men heeded this?

19. "Dearly beloved [by God], avenge not yourselves." You need not, since you are his dear children (Luke 18:7; Rev. 19: 2). The sentiment of verses 14 and 17 is brought up a third time. Bless him that wrongs you (v. 14); do him no evil (v. 17); do not seek his punishment before the court or otherwise (v. 19). The desire for revenge is not Christian.

"But rather give place unto [the] wrath" of God in the day

of judgment. That the taking of vengeance does not belong to man as man, but that it will surely be meted out to the wrong-doer, is enforced by a crisp couplet from Scripture enforcing these two points. Vengeance is God's prerogative; he will not fail to inflict it (Deut. 32:35).

20. "Therefore if thine enemy hunger." The "therefore" in all modern revisions gives place to "but." The verse is not a deduction from what precedes, but states a course of conduct for the wronged man the opposite of that which the flesh would prompt. Instead of taking vengeance on his enemy, he is to feed him and give him drink if the opportunity presents itself. The verse is a quotation from the Scriptures again (Prov. 25:21, 22).

"Heap coals of fire on his head." This is the only venge-ance you are to inflict, the coals of red-hot love. God's venge-ance is of another sort. This is the only kind allowed you. The explanation that kindness shown the wrongdoer will awaken burning shame in him seems overdrawn.

21. "Be not overcome of evil," as you would be if you cried for vengeance; you would be conquered then; "but overcome evil with good," the only weapon in your hand, and a most effective one. For he who cannot be moved from the basis of love is a victor even though he cannot win his enemy. To win himself is a much greater triumph. This verse looks not alone at the one just before it, but also back over the whole section. The section looks like a cluster of rules or precepts; but it is not such. Its one keynote, its theme through all the variations of the different verses, is love. It is I Corinthians 13:4-7 put in another form for the less ideal, but more practical, Romans.

CHAPTER 13

CIVIL DUTIES OF BELIEVERS

THERE ARE OBLIGATIONS flowing from the endowments of certain gifts, and other obligations flowing from fraternal relations, obligations of love. The former were discussed in 12:1-8 and the latter in 12:9-21. These are all purely spiritual obligations having their source in the relation to Christ. But the Christian has another relation, a natural relation, having its origin not in Christ, but in God. The former chapter is spiritual or Christian; the one before us is divine. These are clearly distinct. Confusion here makes church and state one, and reduces Christianity to sociology. It is easy to distinguish between what is spiritual and what is divine. The Holy Spirit has brought about institutions and relations unknown to nature. The Church with its various functions is the sum of these, and they had no existence before Christ came. But there were men and relations long before. God instituted the latter not for the Church, for there was none, but for men. They are divine, but not spiritual.

One of them is marriage. God gave it. Unregenerate men without the Spirit enter this relation and are under solemn obligations to preserve it inviolate. The Sabbath is another. It was given to man, and as such he is bound to keep it. The state may enforce its obligations, as it does that of marriage, and it would but for the hopeless confusion into which the Church long ago fell on this point. The state is the sum of divine institutions as the Church is of the spiritual. A Christian is a citizen of the world as clearly as he is a member of the Church. Union with the body of Christ absolves him from no duty that belongs to men as men. On the other hand, Paul enforces these duties on the believer by his relation to Christ.

214

When the natural man violates a divine institution he sins against God; but the same violation in a believer would in addition be a sin against Christ.

The consideration of these matters falls under three heads: (1) duties to the state (vv. 1-7); (2) to the citizens of the state (vv. 8-10); (3) the Christian enforcement of these civil duties (vv. 11-14).

1. "Let every soul [none is exempt, not even the pope] be subject [submit himself] unto the higher powers," the civil authorities that are over him. This is the broad general principle; its essence is submission (I Pet. 2:13-17). Within this limit it does not forbid teaching and agitation for better government if these do not lead to resistance, but under this principle it is hard to see how a Christian can lead in a rebellion. Paul's words are unmistakable, and yet there stand Cromwell and Washington!

"For there is no power [no civil authority] but of [from] God: the powers that be are ordained of God." Or, "And those that are have been ordained by God." This is said to enforce ("for") the injunction of submission. Civil government has its source in God, and all constituted power is appointed and ordained by Him. The cruel abuses in governments are no necessary part of them and do not invalidate their divine charter any more than the abuses of marriage rob it of its sacredness. Any government is preferable to anarchy, just as poorly enforced marriage laws are better than none. Man abuses all God's gifts.

In this Paul was writing to a point. Only a few years before the Jews in Rome had rebelled and were expelled from the city (Acts 18:2), Priscilla and Aquila among them. In their daily toil in Corinth in making tents, Paul and Aquila must have often discussed this expulsion. The apostle knew those of his own flesh to be very restive under the Roman yoke. Statesmen that he was, he may have forecast the destruction of the Jewish nation, which occurred within little more than a decade from the time that this chapter was penned. He knew that Jews everywhere disputed the authority of Rome, and that they held the fanatical doctrine, sometimes appearing sporadically in more modern church history, that God's child is directly responsible to God alone and that the king's authority is a usurpation. That a Gentile prince could have divine authority was a doctrine hard for a Jew to accept, especially when that authority was exercised over him. If Paul was hated for this teaching, as he must have been, by the Jewish nation, Titus gave him a thorough vindication twelve years later. The disregard of this verse was the Jew's national ruin.

2. "Whosoever therefore resisteth the power [it ought to read, "So that he that sets himself against the power"], resisteth the ordinance of God." This is the logical and necessary result in rebellion, for government is not man's, but God's.

"And they that resist." Paul changes from the singular to the plural in passing from the statement of the principle to the consequence on those who violate it. This consequence is not "damnation," but condemnation. Damnation suggests future eternal punishment, which is not meant here. The condemnation is from God through human instrumentality. Godet remarks that Paul reproduces Jesus here (Matt. 26:52).

It is not intended to be taught here that the subject must do at the command of the governor that which is morally wrong. God has sometimes honored His people by allowing circumstances to arise in which they could suffer for His name's sake and conscience' sake. One can refuse to do wrong and undergo the penalty without resisting the power.

3. This verse looks back to the first and gives an additional reason "for" subjection to the "higher powers." Rulers, with few exceptions, have punished only evildoers. The Roman persecution of the Church was not malicious, but arose from the mistaken notion that the peace and safety of the state were imperiled by the Christians' refusal to honor the gods. More than once Paul found protection in Roman law (Acts 18:12-17; 19:35-41; 22:25). The so-called church itself has been the worst persecutor.

"Wilt thou then not be afraid of the power?" Do you wish to live without fear of the state's authority? Do right and you will have no cause for alarm. Rulers have troubles and anxieties enough, and the Church ought so to live that the governors could say they have none from it.

4. This verse bears logically on the last. There is no fear of the ruler when you do good; "for" he is God's minister to thee for "good." God gives rulers in His people's behalf. Therefore, to caricature them in public prints is grossly irreverent and promotive of lawlessness, and to fail to pray for them "first of all," a failure all too general, is an express violation of God's Word (I Tim. 2:1-3).

"But if thou do that which is evil," then fear; for God did not put the sword in the ruler's hand "in vain," as a meaningless symbol of power. That sword has a solemn purpose. The governor's office has two sides: on one, it defends the good; on the other, he is "a revenger to execute [God's] wrath upon him that doeth evil." Punishment is usually meted out in the the name of the state. A higher position might be taken. It might be inflicted in the name of God. Civil penalties, including capital punishment, are an expression of His will. Twice in this verse the ruler gets a very solemn title, "minister of God"—twice because of his twofold office. The state and the Church have each a place in the world. If God's appointed and established order is preserved neither will invade the function of the other.

5. "Wherefore [as civil government is God's appointment] ye must [necessity] be subject [be in submission to it], not only for wrath [not only in fear of the sword], but also for conscience' sake." Resistance is not merely inexpedient; it is morally wrong.

6. "For for this cause." Better, "For on this account." By the first "for" it is shown that this verse confirms the last one. On this account, there is a moral necessity for submission to authority, "tribute," or tax, is regularly paid. Instead of "pay ye" it ought to be "ye pay." Taxes are not merely an imposition of the government, but are made necessary by its divine character.

"For they [magistrates] are God's ministers." Paul uses now a very different word for minister. In verse 4 the word means servant. Here it means one of a priestly character. Government is God's, and the magistrate is his sacred official through whom he administers it, "a divinely consecrated sacrificial service" (Meyer). "Attending continually upon this very thing"—of administering this sacred governmental office for God. As it is not an occasional, but a continuous duty, God has appointed by taxes that rulers should be paid. It is the divine decree that to every office, the Jewish priesthood, the magistracy, and the Gospel ministry, there is attached a remuneration. "The laborer is worthy of his hire" (Luke 10:7).

7. "Render therefore to all [in authority] their dues." Omit "therefore." Four specifications are given: render "tribute," personal or property tax, to him to whom it is due; "custom," import or export dues, to him to whom it is due; "fear," reverence (Meyer says "veneration"), to him who bears the sword for God; "honor" to all his subordinates.

In this discussion Paul has so framed his language (1) that it is applicable to every form of government without recommending or condemning any. (2) He does not subordinate the Church to the state nor the state to the Church. They are different in their character, the one natural, the other spiritual, and their aims are different. The state promotes moral living, the Church spiritual living. (3) Paul must have been aware that many rulers, too many, were immoral and selfish men, and that many of their enactments were arbitrary and oppressive; but in such cases neither he nor the Bible has one word of advice for the believer, or but one—submission. David when cruelly persecuted by Saul refused again and again to use the advantage that fell to him against the king. He constantly yielded, and trusted to God for his rights (I Sam. 26:9, 10). God appoints governors for a good purpose, and when they fail to serve it He removes them by His own means (Acts 12:23). (4) Paul seems to say nothing for the sentiment of patriotism; and yet he does. The law-abiding citizen is the loftiest patriot.

8-10. Having shown the believer's duties toward magistrates, Paul naturally comes to civil duties toward all men. (See (2) above.) The very first injunction, "Owe no man," shows that we are outside the Church. This section is not a resumption of the last chapter, where we had the spiritual relation of brother to brother in the Church. The believer occupies also another sphere in his relations with his fellow-believers and with all men in the world. While the Spirit rules in the Church, the world is a world under moral law. Hence law is not mentioned in the last chapter, but here it is again and again exalted as a matter to be fulfilled, and the second table is quoted. Neither is the word "brother" used here, but the civic term "neighbor." Paul in reminding his readers here of their duty to fulfill moral law does not contradict what he said in 6:14 and 10:4. The Christian's relation to God is not legal; his relation to the world is nothing else. "Christ is the end of the law for righteousness" in the spiritual sphere, but in the world law holds; and it holds all who are in the world, else why does Paul here enjoin it?

But God demands much more of the believer than the state asks. The latter says, "Thou shalt not injure thy neighbor." God says, "Thou shalt love him as thyself"; and short of this love the civil law is not fulfilled. Love is not the "fulfilling," but the fulfillment, of the law. This is impossible to men in their natural state, but not to him whose heart is made like God's. It is by this simple but powerful principle of love that the Christian not only fulfills the law, but finds his freedom in it. Love takes the place of the letter and makes all moral duties not only light, but a delight. He that loves will not continue to be owing any man anything but "to love one another," a debt which cannot be discharged. Paul says "one another" because at first he has no one in view but believers. Love will restrain a man from making debts which he cannot pay, and thus save the Church from much scandal. Love will restrain a man from adultery, murder, theft, false witness, covetousness. These are not all, but only instances, for Paul adds the sweeping words, "If there be any other commandment," love will fulfill it. And love alone can keep law. The state must use the sword, because, though it can make good laws, it cannot inspire the love that heeds them.

11. "And that, knowing the time." Here begins an enforcement of what was just said, followed by some exhortation

against fleshly indulgence. (See (3) above.) The principal argument is in the imminence of the consummation of their hope.

"And that" should be "And this." "And this do [viz., "owe no man anything, but to love one another," which love is a fulfillment of the law]—this do, knowing [as you do] the season ["time" (I Thess. 5:1)], that now it is high time to awake out of sleep [to cast off inactivity in worship, and work]." Be active. "For now is our salvation nearer than when we believed." This is the reason for awakening from sleep, a reason so often given in the New Testament (Heb. 10:37; Phil. 3:20, 21; Gal. 6:9). The salvation is not that from sin, which the Romans already had (I Pet. 1:9), but the completion of it in the glorification awaiting them at the coming of Christ (I Pet. 1:5, 6). When Paul says that this salvation is "nearer" he is not speaking chronologically, nor is he implying an expectation of it in his day. He did not know the date of the appearance of Christ. Just as one might say death is always near and live in the power of such a sentiment, though the death is long postponed. Paul's language here, as elsewhere on this topic, is adapted to every generation of believers, who, not knowing the time, can at least say salvation is "nearer."

12. "The night [of the Lord's absence] is far spent, the day [to be ushered in by his appearance] is at hand." It was Christ who imposed this attitude of alert expectation on His followers, and the apostolic Church seems to have had no other (I Thess. 1:9, 10). He also warned against a seeming delay (Matt. 24: 48). It belongs to the servant to watch at all times, for the Master comes in His own time. "Therefore" the works befitting only darkness are to be "cast off" as an unclean garment, and the "armor" (Eph. 6:13) suitable to the light when it dawns is to be put on.

13. "Let us walk honestly, as in the day." They are not in the day, but they are to live as if they were in it. This is the emphatic phrase in this sentence. The lightning flash that ushers in the day will not change a man's walk; it will merely show what it is. Therefore let us walk becomingly ("honestly") now. Boise translates the remainder of the verse thus:

"Not in carousals and intoxications, not in licentious acts and debaucheries, not in strife and jealousy." It is to be noticed that strife and jealousy are classed with these coarse indulgences of the animal nature and made their climax. The contentious, envious man ranks with the drunkard and the debauchee.

14. "But put ye on the Lord Jesus Christ." He is first put on in baptism (6:3; Gal. 3:27), and then put on daily in living in the obedience, disposition, and hopes suggested by his threefold name, Lord Jesus Christ. As Lord He rules; as Jesus He lived; as Christ He is the surety of all hopes (Phil. 3:20; Eph. 4:24; Col. 3:12). To put Him on is to walk in the power of His life (8:2).

"And make not provision for the flesh, to fulfill the lusts thereof." "Provision" here is misleading. (See on 12:17.) Literally translated, the sentence reads, "Take no forethought for the flesh, for [its] desires." The flesh here, as usual, is the whole man viewed apart from his relation to Christ. It is the seat of all the sins mentioned in the last verse, and is a bundle of desires ("lusts"). No forethought is to be taken for these. (See on 6:12.) The heathen went astray by them (1:24). They drown men in destruction and perdition (I Tim. 6:9). And they that are Christ's do not take forethought for their gratification; Christ's followers "have crucified the flesh with the affections and lusts" (Gal. 5:24). They that are His have daily needs for which the heavenly Father has made bountiful provision (Phil. 4:19; Matt. 6:8, 33; Luke 12:30), but none for their own desires, for these are all sinful.

This is the Christian citizen's chapter. He is to be loyal to the government, just toward his neighbor, and clean in his personal life. The means for all this is Christ, and the root of failure is self—forethought for desires.

CHAPTER 14

FRATERNAL DUTIES IN MATTERS
OF CONSCIENCE

FROM SPEAKING of those who were too lax in the indulgence
of natural appetites, the subject passes mainly to those
who are too scrupulous. The object is not to remove these
scruples, but to show those who have them and those who
have them not how to live in Christian peace. The discussion
runs to the thirteenth verse of the next chapter, and comes
under three heads: (1) conscience in the matter of eating and
drinking (14:1-12), an exhortation for the most part to the
weak; (2) the right use of liberty by the stronger brethren (14:
13-23); (3) Christian forbearance is the will of the Lord in
accordance with his work for common worship (15:1-13).

Conscience in matters of eating and drinking did not origi-
nate with Moses. It is deeply ingrained in human nature,
and existed long before his time. By codifying and making
authoritative dietary laws he probably relieved more than he
burdened the conscience of his day. Paul was given a deep
insight into the religious heart to write this chapter. The
experience of the centuries, the present as much as any, has
shown that the church can be disturbed by dietary questions
quite as much as by those that are purely spiritual. Paul lays
down no rule for the Romans in this matter. He insists mainly
for the guidance of the stronger brother that he direct his
conduct at the table by love, the principle that guides also in
the matters considered in the last two chapters.

The question was not as serious in Rome as at other places.
It was not one of eating that which had been offered to idols
(I Cor. 8); it did not touch the doctrine of justification (Gal.

2:12-21), nor was it raised by the Judaizers (Col. 2:16). It does not seem to have been a question wholly between the Jewish and the Gentile element in the church. The weak Gentile was as likely to have scruples as his Jewish brother. They arose then, as they do now, from a natural infirmity of the understanding. Grace sanctifies the heart much more easily than the head.

1. "Him that is weak in the faith." Omit "the." Faith is weak by lack of moral discernment and understanding. It has no breadth. It knows that Christ saves from sin, but it does not perceive the relations of this salvation to living, and so is full of small scruples, whose observance it invests with the highest importance. At the same time it is blind to real piety. It would not eat meat, but it would condemn harshly the man who does, exalting its own abstinence far above Christian love.

But this weak believer, weak in his faith, but correspondingly strong in his scruples, is to be received into Christian fellowship, but not to be disputed with about his thoughts. This seems to be the meaning of the phrase "not to doutbful disputations." He cannot be argued out of his views; argument would only confirm him in them. He must grow out of them, and meanwhile he is not to be criticized and judged, but loved. This verse is addressed to the stronger brethren, and may imply both that they are right and are in the majority.

2. Omit the "for." This verse, however, shows to what the first one points.

3. The man who sees that there is no piety in the kind of food he eats may look with contempt on his poor narrow brother over his dish of vegetable food; for there is nothing on which a man prides himself more than on his superior knowledge of truth. On the other hand, the weak brother, seeing the other with his meat and wine, may condemn him as no saint, for the table is the narrow bound of his field of morals. The weak man is not to judge the strong in the exercise of his liberty, because God has "received" the latter. The reference is to the time of his conversion.

4. This verse is a sharp thrust at the vegetarian. It utterly denies his right to judge. The man who has confidence to eat meat is the Lord's servant, not the weak brother's. And he stands or falls to his "own" Lord, who is Christ. There is point in the word "own." But he will not fall in the exercise of Christian liberty. "Yea, he shall be holden up: for the Lord [not "God"] is able to make him stand." The reference is not to the final judgment, but to his daily walk, from which the weak brother is sure that he will decline because of his meat. Here is an assurance to liberty which the abstinence of a weak brother lacks. He has no promise to be holden up; rather a stern rebuke that he has forgotten Matthew 7:1-5. It is also plainly implied that the strong brother is not responsible to the church in the use of his liberty, but only to the Lord. The church has not a shred of authority in this matter; it may not say what diet a member shall or shall not eat. Christ cleansed all foods (Mark 7:18, 19).

5. "One man esteemeth one day above another." Closely connected with this question of food is that about holy days. It is impossible to say that this general language does not include the Sabbath. There is a Sabbath and it is divinely instituted (Mark 2:27, 28), but there is not a line nor a word in the New Testament about how it is to be observed. In Judaism the law of observance was plain enough (Exod. 35:2). May the church or any man in it prescribe how a holy day shall be kept? Paul's rule is, "Let every [each] man be fully persuaded in his own mind." He leaves it to that which Rome condemns, private judgment. He uses the word "mind" because it is a question for an enlightened understanding.

6. "He that regardeth the day, regardeth it unto the Lord." And since he is honoring God in his observance he is neither to be despised nor hindered. Paul has said nothing here about the nature of the day; it is purely a question of regard for it. One believer is devout on every day; another believer is more devout on special set days than on others.

The second sentence in this verse is omitted on strong evidence by most modern editors.

The discrimination in days is of the same character as the

discrimination in food. The root of it in either party is regard
for the Lord. It is "unto the Lord," in deference to the relation held with Him. Therefore there should be no despising
and no judging. Each party is serving the same Lord, but in
different ways. The proof that it is service to Him is that "he
that eateth" meat gives God thanks for the meat; and "he
that eateth not" meat, but dines on vegetables, does so out of
regard for the Lord, for he too gives thanks to God for the
vegetables. This consideration goes to show that there is little
merit in mere breadth of view, and little demerit in narrow-
ness. The merit lies in the thankfulness with which each man
partakes of his own particular kind of food, and in the matter
of thanks they stand on the same level before the Lord. A
man's views about these minor morals have little to do with
that standing.

It must be noted on this verse that the Roman Christians
were in the habit of giving thanks for food at the time of eating; they had Christ's example (Mark 8:6, 7).

7, 8. These two verses bear ("for") on the assertion that
eating is not a private and personal act, but one regulated by
regard to the Lord. No Christian lives out of regard for himself alone. He has the Lord's honor and will always in view.
He glorifies Him even in death (John 21:19). Living or dying,
then, we are the Lord's and not our own to make our own
notions stand, be they broad or narrow.

9. This verse ought to read as in some recent versions: "For
to this end Christ died, and lived [again], that he might be
Lord of both dead and living." It preserves the correspondence of the words and ideas. It shows ("for") how Christ
became Lord. He died to redeem His people (I Cor. 6:19, 20);
He rose that He might reign. By death and resurrection He
acquired Lordship of both the dead and the living. Hence the
brother weak or the brother strong who would insist on his
own method of living as the rule for all strikes at the very
Lordship of Christ. Scruples may be observed and liberty en-
joyed, but let every man beware how he thrusts them in the
place given to Christ by the cross and the opened tomb. The
resurrection not only gives life, but regulates living.

10. "But why dost thou judge thy brother?" The King James Version obscures the emphasis. "But thou [the abstemious man], why dost thou judge thy [liberal] brother? or thou again [the liberal meat-eating man], why dost thou set at naught [treat with contempt] thy [abstemious] brother?" These questions are solemnly pertinent, because ("for") we shall all, strong and weak alike, stand before the judgment-seat of Christ, or God, as some read (II Cor. 5:10). The right and the wrong in a brother's conduct are to be determined at that bar and not by individual opinion. In that solemn tribunal no man will judge his own case, much less his brother's. The "judgment-seat" is that of the great and appointed day (Acts 17:31). As to the matter of acceptance, it only confirms; but as to conduct, it exhibits and awards.

11. A solemn scriptural (Isa. 45:23) confirmation of the "all" in the preceding verse. All shall stand in judgment, for God has sworn not only that there shall be universal submission to Him, but confession of His right to judge. This admission must be made even by those to whom the judgment brings nothing but condemnation.

12. "So then every [each] one of us." This is the conclusion drawn from the two preceding verses. The emphasis is not on "himself" and not on "God," but on the words "each one of us." Godet gives the sense of these three verses thus: "The preceding context [v. 10] signifies, 'Judge not thy brother, for God will judge *him*; judge thyself [v. 12], for God will judge *thee*.'"

So far, then, Paul has neither approved nor condemned any kind of food; he has neither given nor withheld his sanction of sacred days. What a man may do in reference to both food or days is in itself nothing, but what he may think about his own or his brother's doing in these cases is all-important. This is the first point in the chapter.

But what one does, though indifferent in itself, is sure to provoke thought and feeling. Hence Paul's second point (see (2) above) about the right use of liberty. This is addressed first of all to the strong brother.

13. "Let us not therefore [in view of the fact of God's

judgment] judge one another any more." Such judgment is doubly wicked because it anticipated God's, and assumes His place (2:1). "But judge this rather." Note the emphatic turn in the meaning of the word "judge."

"That no man put a stumbling-block or an occasion to fall in his [a] brother's way." For Paul's own comment see I Corinthians 8:8-13. In eating and in drinking a man must be directed not by what he thinks, but by the thought his act will provoke in the mind of another.

14. All food is clean; but it is only clean to him who has the enlightening grace to see it so. Many have not this grace. With Moses' law about clean and unclean meats ever before them, and unable to comprehend the liberty in Christ Jesus (Gal. 5:1), many saints could not say that there is "nothing unclean in itself." Their inability was not a moral defect, and must not be despised.

15. "Grieved with thy meat." Today the question centers about drink. Even yet there are Christian men who practically insist on their right to use wine. The cause of temperance, as it is called, has suffered irreparably at the hands of its advocates because they have been wiser than Paul and based it on other grounds than his. He would surely write today about wine what he wrote about meat: that, while it is not morally unclean in itself, except to him who so esteems it, yet he who uses it is not walking according to love ("charitably"), inasmuch as his use of it is a grief to many and leads others to fall. Paul's plea, which is the Holy Spirit's, is unanswerable and irresistible. To deny the liberty is to take all the virtue and force from the abstinence. To refuse to do for the good of others what one has a right to do is love of the highest character—it is Christlike. But if meat and drink are in themselves morally evil there is no virtue in abstinence. There is no credit in refraining from that which is sinful; it is duty, not love.

"Destroy not him with thy meat [or drink], for whom Christ died." The exercise of that liberty at the table which may cost the soul of one of Christ's own is characterized by Himself in Matthew 18:6.

16. "Let not then your good be evil spoken of." Broad views, clear perception of the liberty and freedom in Christ, are a "good." But he is an enemy of freedom and of liberty in matter of food who brings them into disrepute by his manner of living. Paul is an advocate of liberty, but only love knows how to indulge it. The address is to the strong brethren. Meyer takes a different view. The address is to the whole church. The "good" is the Gospel, which may be despised by the heathen if believers wrangle in such a way over meat that the faith in Christ must seem to be concerned about nothing else. The reason for this view is that the discussion passes from the singular in verse 15 to the plural here—"your" good.

17. "For the kingdom of God." This verse gives a substantial reason against conduct which would lead to a wrong view of the kingdom of God. The Romans were subjects of this kingdom. If they spend their time and energy on sumptuary questions, are they not perverting the kingdom?

The phrase "kingdom of God" occurs only here in the epistle. God rules everywhere, but there is a realm where He governs by spiritual forces or laws alone. All who submit to these are in the kingdom and are themselves spiritual in character (Matt. 5:3-16). This kingdom, then, cannot in its essence be eating and drinking, which pertain to nature. The kingdom is the product of the Holy Spirit (John 3:3; 18:36). It is founded on the atoning sacrifice of Christ, and in its essence is "righteousness and peace and joy in the Holy Ghost." "Righteousness" is not merely moral rectitude, but, as Paul has used it in the epistle, embraces justification and sanctification, deliverance from the guilt, the power, and the presence of sin. "Peace" is peace with God (5:1); and the joy is not that which flows naturally from the heart, but is awakened by the Holy Spirit. He that is manifesting these is manifesting the kingdom and showing men what that kingdom is. And this will bring together the two views of the "good" given above. Men will neither blaspheme the liberty of the kingdom nor the kingdom itself when it is seen in the life of those really in it, a life not concerned with eating and drinking, but with righteousness and peace and holy joy.

18. "For he that in these things." The Revised Version wrongly rejects the words "these things." The verse confirms that character of the kingdom which Paul has ascribed to it. It must be "righteousness and peace and joy in the Holy Ghost," for he who serves Christ in these three not only finds himself "acceptable to God," but also cuts off occasion for evil speaking on the part of men and is "approved" by them.

19. An exhortation. "The things which make for peace" and which are to be followed are the three mentioned in verse 17. There is enough in these to engage all hearts for all time, and he who gives himself to them is in the way to "edify" another. Attention given to minor morals has in times past distracted the church and pulled down instead of building up. To be right in anything, one must first be exactly right with God through Christ.

20. "For meat destroy not the work of God." The word "destroy," or pull down, is the opposite of "edify," or build up. This verse is an advance on the fifteenth. There it was a question of grieving the brother and destroying him; here it is a malign work of fighting against God in pulling down the gracious work which He has done in the weak brother.

"All things [in the way of food] indeed are pure." But there is more than this principle involved in the question, and this one alone cannot settle it; for even the pure food is evil to him who eats it with offense of conscience. If, in imitation of the strong brother, one partakes of food which his conscience does not allow, he has stumbled; his fellowship with God is broken, and the strong brother who led him to this is responsible; he has destroyed God's work.

21. "It is good neither to eat flesh . . ." This maxim, addressed to the strong, covers the whole matter in question. It is made the more pointed in that it follows the last verse without the intervention of a connecting word. It is a flash of light. The italic words in the King James Version do not bring out the whole thought. It is good, morally excellent and wholesome, to eat no flesh, and to drink no wine, and to do nothing whereby thy brother stumbles, or is made to halt, or is weak. The phrase "and to do nothing" is sweeping and embraces all matters of conscience. The King James rendering, by omitting the necessary word "do," narrows the sentiment to the single item of drink.

22. "Hast thou faith?" Have you such confidence in the justifying work of Christ that you see your freedom in matters of food and drink? "Have it to thyself before God." Keep it to yourself; do not parade it in the exercise of it in eating and drinking and in your treatment of the Sabbath. Paul here clearly sanctions the broad and liberal view of the strong brother. He has tacitly done the same thing all through the chapter. But it is the very man who is sure of his freedom in these things in Christ, just as it is the man who has real wealth or real learning, that makes no offensive display. And this leads to the next assertion, "Happy is he that condemneth not himself . . ." There is a danger in this liberty too. A man may not be as well grounded as he supposed himself to be. He may "allow" himself an indulgence for which his own conscience will afterward condemn him. In the eagerness to exhibit or indulge his liberty in matters which he approves or allows, he may subsequently have to sit in judgment upon himself and pronounce a verdict of self-condemnation.

23. "And he that doubteth is damned if he eat." The word "damned" is misleading. The man is condemned by his own conscience. Mere hesitation or uncertainty leads to this. Conscience must have the benefit of every doubt, for in all matters in which the Bible is silent it has God's authority. It may not usurp the function of His revealed will, but there are many things arising in daily life on which God's mind has not been made known except in a general way. Here conscience must be heeded, or it utters its condemnation and the man passes under the dark cloud of God's displeasure.

"Because he eateth not of faith." Better, "It is not of faith." His act did not flow from his trust in Christ; he was not sure that his justification by God permitted this, and therefore he felt condemned in eating.

Paul closes this second point with the principle underlying all Christian conduct: "And [the "for" of the King James Version is wrong] all that is not of faith is sin." "All" is better

than "whatsoever." Christ has certainly redeemed the believer
from every sumptuary and ceremonial observance. But distrust of Christ in these matters binds the conscience just so
far as the distrust extends. To violate this bond is sin.

It must be carefully noted that Paul is not speaking here of
absence of saving faith, but of defect in it. Hence this is not
a general but a Christian principle. Paul is prescribing for
what is before him in the church and not for mankind.

This principle thus limited is the major premise of a syllo-
gism: all that is not of faith is sin; eating in doubt is not of
faith; therefore it is sin and brings condemnation. In these
matters a man's conduct must be limited by his faith.

Jesus taught with sunlight clearness, "There is nothing from
without a man, that entering into him can defile him" (Mark
7:15). The word "nothing" is decidedly emphatic and embraces what is drunk as well as what is eaten; and the weak in
faith must remember this before they condemn the saints who
take the liberty here given them.

On the other hand, Paul teaches that this liberty will limit
itself by love. There has not been a time since he wrote when
it was more necessary to heed this than today. For now there
is abundant teaching in zeal without knowledge that contra-
dicts and nullifies the principle laid down by Christ. This false
teaching binds without enlightening the conscience. The result is the weakness of a mere sense of duty in this matter in
the church instead of the strength of the liberty in Christ that
may exhibit itself in love like His. Therefore all the more must
the strong be abstinent, patient, and loving. Paul does not in
the least, as we have seen, set at naught Christ's words recorded
in Mark, but he shows how they were intended to be used—
in love. So used, they, like all others in the Book, are seen to
be uttered "not to destroy men's lives, but to save them"
(Luke 9:56).

CHAPTER 15

DISCUSSION OF FRATERNAL DUTIES CONCLUDED, AND PERSONAL MATTERS

THE ARGUMENT OF THE EPISTLE concludes at the thirteenth verse of this chapter. (See under (3) in introduction to last chapter.) Paul gives what he has to say about eating and drinking and like matters under three heads. The third one is the first (1) section of this chapter (vv. 1-13), in which Paul shows (a) that the strong must act in the spirit of Christ, that there may be union in worship (vv. 1-6); (b) that they must receive one another in the spirit of Christ (vv. 7-12); and (c) pronounces a benediction (v. 13). Christ's attitude toward God and toward them indicates His will, which the strong should follow.

In the second (2) section of the chapter (vv. 14-33), a section entirely epistolary, like that in 1:8-15, Paul (a) justifies his writing to the Romans (vv. 14-16); (b) gives his rule in choosing his field of labor (vv. 17-21); (c) speaks of the delays in visiting them (vv. 22-29); (d) but hopes to come, and asks for their prayers that the way may be kept clear (vv. 30-33).

Because a few authorities, though from these all the great Manuscripts and the Latin fathers must be excluded, place the benediction (16:25-27) at the close of chapter 14, the higher criticism, beginning with Semler, has called these last two chapters in question. Paul was supposed to be the author of the whole, but originally these two chapters, the benediction excepted, were not intended for Rome. Baur was the first to assail their Pauline authorship. The difficulties are only slight and have been much magnified. Meyer, who gives a brief history of the discussion, concludes: "This entire hypothesis turns upon presuppositions and combinations, which are partly arbitrary in themselves and partly without any solid ground or support in the detailed exegesis." So that it may be safely said with Kerr (*Introduction to New Testament Study*), "Despite these objections, the integrity of the epistle as it now stands is certain."

1, 2. "We that are strong." Paul places himself among the strong. "The infirmities of the weak" were a burden to be borne, a heavy weight, except where love gave strength to carry it. He does not say that the weak should reflect on the load which they are imposing on others; for if they had the power to reflect they would not be weak. To eat meat and to drink wine may please the palate, but the justified man does not live to please himself, but to please his neighbor. The neighbor may be pleased to his hurt, so Paul adds that he must be pleased "for his good to edification." To afford him religious pleasure which does not build him up is not for "his good."

3. "For even Christ pleased not himself." He is not presented as an example, but His manner of living affords an argument. If it should seem burdensome and grievous to some strong Roman to live narrowly for the sake of the weak, the consolation and the dignity of such a life are that Christ also lived it. The phrase "for even Christ" would better be rendered, "for Christ also." The Scriptures are not in the habit of holding up Christ as an example, for men are neither saved nor sanctified by an example.

That His life was one of not pleasing Himself is in accord with that which was predicted of Him in Psalm 69:9. Reproaches fell on Christ because He pleased not Himself, but lived to please God in the work of saving men. If self-pleasing had been the guide of His life He would have escaped the reproach and shame cast upon Him by the Jews; but living as He did to please God, to serve His will for the salvation of men, these reproaches came, and thus were God's. This was Christ's honor, and should anyone complain who has the opportunity to gain like honor in denying himself for the good of others?

It is startling to read that "Christ pleased not himself." His life was one of pain and suffering; and yet He spoke about His "joy" (John 15:11). And we feel that it ought to have been only a delight to a perfect man, as He was, to serve God. It was. And the solution of the apparent contradiction is that in the service of God pain is only pleasure, while self-pleasing is only pain. The Christian lives only when he dies, and this is the joy and consolation in dying daily (I Cor. 15:31). It is only sorrow that can be turned into joy.

4. "Written for our learning." This one verse, culled from the Old Testament, moves Paul to say that every part of that same Testament was written for this purpose, our teaching or "learning" (II Tim. 3:16). Paul gives here one chief object of the existence of the Old Testament. It abounds in instances of a self-denying life redounding to the glory of God, and thus stimulates the "patience" and gives the enheartening or "comfort" which such a life needs. The record of these instances is authoritative and so becomes a proof that as God dealt with His servants then so will He deal now; He does not change. It is by means of this "patience and comfort" derived from the Scriptures that settled hope arises. Paul has already (5:3, 4) shown the relation of patience and hope.

5, 6. The apostle virtually prays that all parties in their use of the Scriptures may have granted to them by God their patience and comfort. These graces are, after all, the gift of God, but given by Him through His Word. It is by these two Christian qualities, also, that God will make them "like-minded" toward one another, a mind according to Christ's, described above. This does not mean, then, that they will come to a common view on meats and wine, but to unanimity in loving intercourse, so that "with one mind and one mouth" they may glorify God. They may be divided in their dietary views; this in itself is a small matter; but they must not be divided in their worship and praise of God. For the patient and comforted mind can join in praise with those from whom there is dissent of opinion. This is true Christian union. "Even the Father of our Lord Jesus Christ." Translators are divided, some rendering "and" instead of "even," making the sentence read, "The

God and Father of our Lord Jesus Christ." In either case Paul's point is the same. God is to be glorified not only as God, but also in His relation to Him through whom all are saved, Jew and Gentile, the liberal and the narrow man alike.

7. "Wherefore receive ye one another." A deduction from the desirability of union in praise. It is not now an exhortation to the strong to bear with the weak (v. 1), but strong and weak alike are addressed. They are to receive one another into fellowship and favor, just as Christ had taken them into His. Some read "us," others "you." Christ accepts men, whether broad or narrow, whether Jew or Gentile, whether bond or free. Beyond a genuine belief of the Gospel He makes no other demand. If He accepts men in all their weaknesses and without any regard to their views about secondary matters, well may we. "To the glory of God" might be joined with "receive ye," but may possibly go with what just precedes. Christ received us that God might gain glory. If we do not receive one another His gracious purpose is marred.

8. "Now I say." The true reading is, "For I say," the "for" introducing the long passage following to show how Christ received both parties. The word "meat" and the words "strong" and "weak" are not again used; but instead the two nationalities in the church appear, the Jew and the Gentile, showing that the division in dietary matters ran in the main between these two. The Jew would be the weak man, the Gentile the strong; but there were doubtless exceptions on both sides.

This conclusion of the whole argument is based anew (a) on the work of Christ in behalf of both parties, in which, however, the Jew holds a priority, and (b) on the Scriptures. The privileges of the Jew are seen in the fact that Jesus Christ was Himself circumcised, and this to fulfill the promise made to the Jewish fathers. The Gentile had no direct promise. The Jew's salvation came "for the truth of God," the Gentile's "for his mercy." Here again, as in 11:17-20, the Gentile is plainly reminded that so far as his nationality goes he has not the same foundation as the Jew.

"Jesus Christ was a minister of the circumcision." Omit

"the." "Circumcision" is not "abstract for concrete" (Boise) and does not signify Israel. Paul does not mean that Jesus Christ was a minister, an attending servant, to the Jews, or that He belonged exclusively to them. The word has its simple meaning in which it stands for a religious system. Christ was a minister of circumcision in that He fulfilled the whole Mosaic requirement in His person and in His work. It would be little to the point to say here that Jesus served the Jews. It is everything to say that He was the minister of a covenant that brought salvation to the Jews and through them to all men. Galatians 4:4, 5, is a good comment on this phrase.

"For the truth [in behalf of the veracity] of God." Christ was such a minister of circumcision "to [or "that he might"] confirm the promises made unto the fathers," Abraham, Isaac, and Jacob. The promises all lay within the limits of the covenant of circumcision (Gen. 17:7, 14, 21), and Christ came, Paul does not say to fulfill, but to "confirm," them. "Confirm" means to make firm, to establish, to make sure; and therefore Israel may praise and glorify God for His faithfulness.

9. "And that the Gentiles might glorify God for [in behalf of] his mercy." Christ's coming was to the Jew in the way of God's truth, to the Gentile in the way of His mercy. The former can praise for fidelity, the latter for grace.

There is a question about the grammatical dependence of these two verses. Godet makes verse 9 depend on "I say" in the previous one. Sanday connects the ninth verse with Christ's becoming a minister of circumcision, so that this ninth verse gives a second and subordinate object of that ministry. The latter seems to be more logical, but whichever connection is taken, the main thought is clear that the call of the Gentiles, as well as the fulfillment of the promises to the Jews, both depended on Christ in His ministry of circumcision. It was by this ministry that He received us to the glory of God, that He might be praised by the Jew for His truth and by the Gentile for His mercy. Jacob worshiped for both (Gen. 32:10).

"As it is written." Four quotations follow, one from the law, two from the Psalms, and one from the prophets, in confirmation of God's purpose that Gentiles are to glorify God.

This first one (Ps. 18:49) shows Christ among the heathen praising God. Of course He gives the praise through them. Therefore the quotation implicitly declares the conversion of those who praise.

10. "And again he saith," quoting Deuteronomy 32:43, that Gentiles are to join in praise with "his people," the Jews.

11. "And again, Praise the Lord" (Ps. 117:1). This little psalm of but two verses shows that God would bring Gentiles generally to His worship. "All" occurs twice. "People" is plural, mean Gentiles.

12. "And again, Esaias saith" (Isa. 11:10). The Septuagint Version is quoted. The prophet declares that He who comes in the Davidic line, the root from Jesse, shall also be King over Gentiles. "In him shall the Gentiles trust"; or better, "In him will Gentiles hope." It is significant that not only here, but in all these four quotations, the article is omitted before the word "Gentiles." The Gentiles, all of them, according to chapter 11, will one day be brought to Christ. But in Paul's day and to this day only some have come. If he had said "the" Gentiles the facts around him would have disproved his assertion; but Gentiles had come to Christ in his day, first fruits of the coming harvest, and he quotes in a way to embrace just these first fruits and for the present, no more. The Revised Version in its translation of these citations is not critical.

This last quotation shows the union of Jew and Gentile under Christ in a common hope, by which word Paul has come around again to the idea of verse 4: "That we through patience and comfort of the Scriptures might have hope."

13. "Now the God of hope [the God who has laid in Christ the foundation for it] fill you with all joy and peace in believing"—the opposite of painful contention and disputing. In the discussion Paul has had much to say about bearing and forbearing, about love and service. He now uses the word which embraces because it gives the source of all these. All joy and peace come "in believing." Paul longs for their joy and peace, that they "may abound in hope [of eternal life], in the power of the Holy Ghost." His fruits come in clusters (Gal. 5:22, 23), only one of which Paul names—hope. Strife drives away

the Holy Spirit; joy and peace detain Him, and He makes hope
to abound.

Paul closes the argument with two practical ideas, praise
and hope. The two are really but one—praise. Every line and
thought from the beginning of the epistle has led up to worship. "The harmonious glorification of the God and Father of
our Lord Jesus Christ by the whole body of the redeemed, as
it is the most exalted fruit of the scheme of redemption, so it
is the last end of God in it."

14-16. In this epilogue Paul, first of all, in these three verses
apologizes for writing to the Romans. It is not because they
are not "full of goodness," but because they are. The case is
not as in Jude 3, but more like that in I John 2:21, 27. He
writes not so much to instruct, as to "put them in mind" of
what they already know. For Christian argument and admonition are of no value except where Christianity already
holds sway. He thus writes because of the apostolic "grace"
(1:5; Eph. 3:8) given him by God that he should be a minister, a spiritual priest, to the Gentiles, not to offer a sacrifice
for them, which was already done, but to minister to them the
Gospel, that they themselves might be an acceptable "offering".
to God (Eph. 5:26, 27; II Cor. 11:2). The offering is acceptable because it is sanctified, made holy, by the presence of the
Holy Spirit. Paul gave men the Gospel, and God gave such
of them as believed the Holy Spirit, and by these two means
they became a fit offering to God. The Christian priest is just
a preacher of the Gospel; for Paul's language on this point is
highly figurative.

17. This verse forms the transition to what the apostle has
to say about his field of labor. "I have therefore [as one ministering the gospel of God] whereof I may glory in [not
"through"] Jesus Christ" as to things pertaining to God. This
glorying was worthy. It had its basis in Christ, and it was about
God's affairs, the spread of the Gospel.

18, 19. This glorying was Paul's own, as is shown by the
somewhat emphatic "I have." In attestation ("for") that it
is his, he "dare" not speak of what God did not do by him to
win Gentiles to obedience; but passing to the positive, he

mentions the great works done through him from Jerusalem, the starting point of his ministry, "round about unto Illyricum," northwest of Macedonia. This country is not mentioned in Paul's history as given in Acts, but many other events belonging to his history find no record there (II Cor. 11:23-25). Through this wide extent, he says, "I have fully preached the gospel of Christ"; literally, "I have fulfilled the gospel of Christ." Just how much this means cannot easily be told.

20, 21. "Yea, so have I strived," or, "Yea, making it my ambition so to preach," making it a point of honor not to go where anyone had gone before me. He considered that his work was to lay foundations (I Cor. 3:10) and to let others do the building. He seems to have had as a motto to guide him the Scripture found in Isaiah 52:15, after the Septuagint. But why, then, does he wish to visit the Roman church already founded? It is hard to say. It may be that the Gospel was never officially preached there (Acts 19:21; 28:22); or it may be that, having fulfilled the Gospel of Christ, he did not consider his rule any longer binding. It was not a hard and fast rule. He preached a year at Antioch in Syria after the church was unofficially gathered (Acts 11:25, 26). And finally, he was only going to call on the Romans on his way to Spain (v. 24), a far-distant new field. Paul interpreted the commission, "Go ye into all the world, and preach" (Mark 16:15), to mean, for him at least, not that he should go after someone else had opened the way to the heathen, but that he should go first. He was a pioneer.

22-24. "Much hindered," or often hindered by abundance of work. Blessed hindrance! But Paul had removed the obstacle by doing all that was to be done "in these parts," or regions over which he had been traveling about fifteen years. He had a "great desire" to see the Romans. "Many years" is indefinite. The city lay on the highway to Spain, to which distant land he was going. He hoped to see the Romans on this journey, and "to be brought on the way thitherward." This phrase, "brought on the way," or sent forward, refers to a semi-official custom of the apostolic churches in furnishing an escort to go some or all the way with a departing minister or missionary. Paul is here most likely asking that one or more of the Roman brethren be sent with him to Spain. (See Acts 15:3; 20:38; 21:5; I Cor. 16:6, 11; II Cor. 1:16; Titus 3:13; III John 6.) The original word is technical and is used only in reference to this custom.

"If first I be somewhat filled with your company." He anticipated much spiritual enjoyment in his visit to Rome; but in the word "somewhat," or "in a measure," he intimates that he may not be able to stay long enough to be fully satisfied with such blessed "company." We know from the Book of Acts how he got to Rome, how eager the brethren were to meet him (Acts 28:15); but there is no other mention of the church there, and it is not known whether he ever reached Spain.

25-27. But Paul cannot come directly to the Roman brethren; he has yet one duty to perform: "to minister to . . . the poor saints which are at Jerusalem." The epistles to the Corinthians show how Paul's heart was set on this contribution. Macedonia did its part (II Cor. 8:1-5); Corinth had been urged to attend to the matter; Galatia, not mentioned here for some reason, contributed (I Cor. 16:1). It may be that the Galatian funds had already been forwarded to Jerusalem.

"It hath pleased them." This cause is repeated from the twenty-sixth verse, that Paul may show that there is another side to this act than mere benevolent pleasure. A man is not simply "pleased" to pay what he owes; it is his "duty." This contribution was a debt due from the Gentiles to the Jews for the reason here given. And that debt is still due these same Jews. But for their unparalleled sufferings in all time, the world would have had no Bible and no Gospel. The word "minister" is an official word. It was the Gentiles' duty not merely to give their "carnal things," but to minister as priests. This gave the contribution a spiritual character. The word "minister" occurs in only two other places, which shed light on this act here (Acts 13:2; Heb. 10:11).

28. "When therefore I have...sealed to them this fruit." The money contribution was the fruit of the Gospel among the heathen; it showed the effectiveness of that Gospel (Col.

1:5, 6). To seal is to authenticate, to make one's own. Paul would turn the money over to the Jewish church and thus seal it theirs. This verse by means of the word "therefore" resumes the topic of verse 26 after the digression in the verse intervening. He says, "When I have performed this." The emphasis is on "this," as if the carrying up of the contribution were the only thing left, the final hindrance to his visit. The word "performed" is a religious word akin to the word "minister" just above (Phil. 1:6; Heb. 9:6). "By you" is possibly "by means of you."

29. "And I am sure," or, "I know." The phrase "of the gospel" is not genuine; possibly added by some one to make Paul's statement harmonize better with the painful history of his coming in chains to Rome. Paul did not know when he would come; he did not know the suffering that would overtake him; but he was sure of the condition of his heart. So far every true saint may know his own future—that to the end he will be attended with the very "fullness of the blessing [or "benediction"] of Christ." "The Lord is my shepherd; I shall not want" (Ps. 23.).

30, 31. "Now I beseech you," or, "I exhort you." Paul knew what Jerusalem was, and he was aware of the prejudice against himself. He asks the Romans that, through the Lord Jesus Christ, and through that love which the Spirit gives the saints one for another, they would strive—a word from the gymnastic contests—along with him (1:9, 10) in their prayers to God for him. They were many, many miles from him, and they could not know any day just where he was or under what circumstances; but God knew, and their prayers would be effective. And so prayers for missionaries in foreign lands are offered today, while their trials and needs are known only in a general way.

Two things are to be prayed for. Paul is God's great apostle and is doing His will, but is not exempt on that account, any more than Christ was, from the hatred of men. His fear is twofold: the unbelievers in Judea may seek to destroy him, and the saints may refuse his gifts from the heathen. To look at the history of Paul's visit to Jerusalem in its rough outward aspect, one might say the prayers were not answered. But the rough handling which the apostle received shows most strikingly how he was delivered, and affords a useful lesson on the way that God answers prayer. How shrewdly Paul helped himself! (Acts 22:25; 23:6; 25:11.) And how came it that his nephew discovered the secret plot to slay his uncle? (Acts 23: 16.) The dangers he encountered were many, his life was in constant peril, and yet he was spared and saw Rome. While the record about the gift for the saints is almost silent, the fair presumption is (Acts 21:17-20) that it was acceptable. In answer to the prayers, God did not keep Paul out of the dangers, but He preserved him in them. He had to enter the lions' den, but God closed their mouths.

32. "Come unto you with joy." This must not be hastily misread as if Paul wrote, "And that I may come." There is no "and"; otherwise his prayer would be threefold. His prayer was for two things as above: to be delivered at Jerusalem, and to have his gift accepted, "that I may come unto you with joy." His joy in coming was in what was behind as well as in what was before him. He came to Rome a prisoner; but who shall say that, having escaped Jerusalem with his life, and having now Rome and Spain before him, the latter for evangelization, he did not come with joy?

"By the will of God." This was the main source of Paul's hope—the will of God. "May with you be refreshed" by a common interchange of faith and its fruits (1:12).

33. "The God of peace be with you." In verse 13 he was called the God of hope, here the God of peace, not as an empty pious wish. Paul had fears, but his reliance on God was such that these did not disturb the deep current of his peace. The Romans would have fears for him. May the God of peace save them from pain in their fear!

Chapter 16

LOVE WITHIN THE CHURCH

THE LOVE OF THE SAINTS shows itself (1) in a commendation (vv. 1, 2); (2) in sundry hearty greetings (vv. 3-16); (3) in a solicitous caution about false teachers (vv. 17-20); (4) in further greetings (vv. 21-24); (5) the doxology (vv. 25-27). There is no formal arrangement, for Paul closes in the free and unstudied manner of an epistle. Hence in the midst of his salutations he inserts the caution against the false teachers, and then resumes the salutations. There is no marked logical connection unifying the chapter.

Thirty-five persons are named in this conclusion. These names may be classified as follows:

With Paul:	At Rome:		
	MEN		**WOMEN**
Timothy	Aquila	Rufus	Priscilla
Lucius	Epænetus	Asyncritus	Mary
Jason	Andronicus	Phlegon	Junia
Sosipater	Amplias	Hermas	Tryphena
Tertius	Urbane	Patrobas	Tryphosa
Gaius	Stachys	Hermes	Persis
Erastus	Apelles	Philologus	Julia
Quartus	Herodion	Nereus	
Phebe		Olympas	

Thus it is seen that there were nine persons with Paul when he wrote—eight men and one woman, Phebe; that there were twenty-four persons at Rome who were greeted—seventeen men and seven women. Besides these, there are two households in Rome that are mentioned, that of Aristobulus and that of Narcissus. The names of those in the households are not given. There are also some unnamed "brethren" referred to in verse 14. And finally there are two unnamed women, the "mother" of Rufus (v. 13) and the "sister" of Nereus (v. 15). Riddle says of this list of names that it shows "(1) Paul's personal regard; (2) the high place he accords to women; (3) the great influence he exerted, since so many friends were present in a place he had never visited; (4) the undying name received from his friendly mention is a type of the eternal blessing which belongs to those whose names are written in the Lamb's book of life."

The objection that Paul, after having traveled and made converts all over the eastern section of the empire, could not have known so many persons in Rome, a city that he had not visited, is not worthy of an answer. Did Paul write this epistle, with all its freedom and fraternal spirit, to these Roman brethren while unacquainted with them?

1. "Phebe our sister." That she was the bearer of the epistle is "a supposition which there is nothing to contradict" (Meyer). The commendation rests on two grounds: she is "our sister," and she is a "servant," or deaconess, of the neighboring church of Cenchrea, nine miles from Corinth, and its seaport. The word "our" is indefinite, giving but little hint of how much it includes. (But see below on vv. 8 and 9.) She was a servant not in, but of, the church of Cenchrea, holding an official capacity.

2. The aim of the commendation was twofold: first that the Romans might "receive" her in a manner worthy of themselves as saints. What lies back of these earnest words, "that ye receive her in the Lord, as becometh saints"? Was it because of her relation to the church at Cenchrea as deaconess that Paul thus spoke? Was it because she was a woman traveling alone? Again, she was commended that the Romans might "assist her in whatsoever business she hath need of you." From the technical language here employed many have supposed that her business at Rome was legal. Paul tells why ("for") she is to be assisted: because she has assisted many, even the great apostle himself. The language is general. How she helped

Paul or anyone else is not told; but because she aided others she is worthy of aid. What a charitable free-masonry existed in the church! Her "business" was her own, but Paul does not hesitate to call on the whole Roman brotherhood to stand by her in it.

3. "Priscilla and Aquila, my helpers in Christ Jesus." These two were not apostles, not prophets, not even called teachers; just helpers, fellow workers. Their tent-making belonged to their work "in Christ" just as Paul's also did (Acts 18:3), for their hands were busy only that the Gospel might be spread. They appear in the history first at Corinth about the year 52 A.D. (Acts 18:2); they move to Ephesus two years later (Acts 18:18, 26; I Cor. 16:19); they are now in Rome, and at a later date are again in Ephesus, II Tim. 4:19). The latter remark, however, depends on the date assigned to II Timothy. It is worth noting that in four of the six mentions of the names of this couple Priscilla's stands first. The order in the King James version (Acts 18:26) is not correct.

4. "Who for my life laid down their own necks" on the executioner's block. Whether this means literally, the stroke having been in some way suspended, or whether they only incurred imminent peril in Paul's behalf, is not certain. In some way at the hazard of their lives they saved Paul's, and so won not only his thanks, but those also of all the Gentile churches, whose apostle was thus spared. Christ died for them; they were ready to die that His great servant might live.

5. "The church that is in their house." They had had a church in their house at Ephesus (I Cor. 16:19); Nymphas, whoever he was, maintained a church in his house at Colosse (Col. 4:15). (See also Philem. 2.) Paul had never been at Colosse, but he knew of Nymphas' church just as he knew of this one with Priscilla and Aquila. Paul was not ignorant of details, but carried "daily the care of all the churches" (II Cor. 11:28). The apostolic churches in the various cities do not seem to have had a permanent meeting place where they could come together regularly, but the brethren met in groups in the houses of the brethren as here. Such a group regularly meeting was called a "church." But all believers in any one city must have also come together often (I Cor. 5:4; 11:20; Acts 20:7, 8).

"Epænetus, who is the first-fruits of Achaia." Read "Asia" for "Achaia," not the Asia of today, but the Roman province of that time so called, with Ephesus as the chief city. This man by his promptness in yielding to the Gospel, so that he was the first to believe when Paul came to Asia, earned a deathless honor in Christ and is remembered by Paul. The apostle had not forgotten the heart thrill of joy he himself felt when this first convert accepted Christ.

6. "Mary." There are six of this name in the New Testament. "Much labor on us" ought to be "much labor on you." What this woman's labor on the Romans was we do not know, except that it was abundant.

7. "Andronicus and Junia." Brother and sister or husband and wife. But some read "Junias," a man's name, instead of "Junia." They were relatives of Paul and so Israelites of the tribe of Benjamin. When or where they had been fellow-prisoners (II Cor. 11:23) is unknown. Paul was often in prison. These two were well known by the Twelve in Judea, who held them in high esteem. But some think that the word "apostles" here is to be taken in the wider sense of II Corinthians 8:23 and Philippians 2:25, where it is rendered "messengers" of the churches. In the latter case we must read "Junias," and understand that these two were distinguished among the messengers of the churches. Paul adds a fourth note about the two: "Who also were in Christ before me." They were Paul's seniors in the divine life. No doubt their prayers had been again and again offered for his conversion. This note, together with that about Epænetus in verse 5, shows that regeneration, or the state in which one can be said to be "in Christ," is a matter of definite date. Between the condition of condemnation and that of "not condemned" (John 3:18) an appreciable interval of time is inconceivable. It is God that justifies, and He does not justify by a process, but by a judicial sentence. If He justifies at all He justifies "from all" (Acts 13:39). But Paul in saying that these were "in Christ" before him must be speaking objectively. He recalls the time

when he, a persecutor of the saints, learned with bitterness of spirit that his relatives, Andronicus and Junia, were "baptized into Christ" and thus publicly proclaimed their renunciation of good works as a ground of salvation and their acceptance of Christ.

8, 9. Nothing is known of these three persons, Amplias, Urbane, and Stachys, except the record here given. The phrase "in the Lord" shows that Paul's love for Amplias was distinctively Christian. He calls Urbane "our helper in Christ." As he had just used the singular, this plural "our" must include Paul's fellow laborers. Urbane, though not an apostle, did apostolic work. Hence note the nice shade of difference in changing from "beloved in the Lord" to "helper in Christ." The latter is more specific. Stachys is simply "my beloved."

10. Apelles had stood, no doubt, one or more severe tests of his faith, and so can be greeted as "approved in Christ." (See on 5:4.) He was a tried believer. Of Aristobulus, whether he was dead or alive, a saint or a sinner, these words give no hint. It is those belonging to his household, possibly slaves, who are greeted. If the master was alive he was not in Christ or he would have been greeted also. If dead he may have been a believer.

11. Herodion was a "kinsman" of the apostle. As nothing more is said about him, he may as a believer have been distinguished for nothing else.

"Them that be of the household of Narcissus." The same remark must be made of this man as of Aristobulus. But a note is added about his household, that they "are in the Lord." Meyer dispatches the phrase with one word, that it is written "redundantly." How many difficulties might be gotten rid of with this word! But this is not exegesis. Paul does not pen superfluous words. Every person named in this chapter was "in the Lord." Many of them were something more. Those in Narcissus' household were no more. The phrase gives the ground, the only but ample ground, on which they were greeted.

12. "Tryphena and Tryphosa." These two women with "the beloved Persis" are hailed for their labor "in the Lord."

The first two were still engaged in it; Persis for some reason —she may have been disabled in some way—had ceased, for note the tenses. Persis "labored much," which may indicate length of service. Observe that while Paul in speaking of men says "my beloved," he now delicately omits the pronoun before this woman's name. How much did all these women contribute to the world-wide reputation of this church? (1:8.)

13. "Rufus,...his mother and mine." This may be the Rufus of Mark 15:21. That the evangelist wrote his Gospel at Rome (Col. 4:10) is generally admitted. He refers to Rufus as one well known. Paul calls him "chosen in the Lord." But all are chosen, and so the word must have here a special sense —distinguished, excellent. For some tender service Paul beautifully calls Rufus' mother his also. This service, Godet thinks, was rendered while Paul was a youth studying in Jerusalem, and that he made his home in this family. This is mere conjecture.

14. The five names mentioned here, together with "the brethren which are with them," indicate some kind of an association, possibly one of the house churches again.

15. Here are five persons more, two of them women, "and all the saints which are with them." He says "saints" now instead of "brethren," because this term can include both sexes. Is this another house church, differing from the last one only in embracing both men and women? The word "with" in both verses implies an association. Paul knew of these. He knew the leaders of them by name and salutes the rest in each group by the terms "brethren" and "saints," so that, with verse 5 above, he seems to greet everyone in the church at Rome.

16. "Salute one another with a holy kiss." The kiss in that day, like handshaking now, was a common token of respect among friends on meeting. Jesus rebuked the Pharisee, Simon, for neglecting to kiss him (Luke 7:45). Paul here means that when they receive the letter from Phebe, and come together to learn its contents, and have now read these salutations, they shall greet one another as brethren in Christ by this token. To employ the kiss as such a recognition makes it "holy." This

act marked the reception of a letter from an apostle. (See I Cor. 16:20; II Cor. 13:12; I Thess. 5:26; I Peter 5:14.) That Paul intended to establish a permanent custom or ordinance of the "holy kiss" is in violation of the context. The reception of his letter and of his greetings was to be marked by their greeting one another, just that and no more.

"The churches of Christ salute you." It ought to read, "All the churches." Paul had just been visiting many of them, making known his intention to go to Rome, and how natural that these churches should ask to be remembered to the Roman brethren! Paul conveys their greeting in the letter. The "all" was possibly dropped by some later copyist in the supposed interest of truth.

17. "Mark them which cause divisions and offenses," or occasions of stumbling. Paul "beseeches" the Romans to "mark" these false teachers, that is, to keep an eye on them. They would divide the church and put stumbling-blocks in its way by their nonconformity to the "doctrine" or teaching which the Romans had formerly learned, and which Paul has now confirmed in his letter. The Romans must have had the Pauline type of doctrine from the very first. The tense shows that these disturbers of the peace were at work when Paul wrote; and what is the remedy prescribed? Excommunication? Imprisonment? Torture of the heretics? No; simply "avoid them," turn away from them, freeze them out by not listening to them.

18. The reason for steadily refusing these men a hearing is that they are not serving the Lord, "but their own belly." They are making a living by false teaching. False doctrine and sensuality often accompany each other, as the first chapter shows.

These men are bright speakers, full of pleasing eloquence, and their "good words and fair speeches [II Sam. 15:1-6; Matt. 7:15] deceive the hearts of the simple." For how could they talk so seraphically if not saints! The "simple" have no shield against the eloquent tongue of the deceiver (Gen. 3:1, 4, 5; II Cor. 11:3), that speaks not from his heart, but, as Paul suggests, is a ventriloquist. Therefore the church must not listen to these men, but turn away from them.

19. "For your obedience is come abroad." The "for" is difficult. It introduces an antithesis between the "simple" and the Romans, who, Paul wishes to say, were not so, "for" they were obedient. The word "simple" has not a bad sense except as it indicates a negative quality of character. The emphasis of the sentence is on the word "your." I say simple, and so do not mean you, "for your obedience is come abroad unto all men," and their faith likewise (1:8); for faith and obedience cannot be disjoined. This last chapter links in with the first. "Over you," therefore, I am glad, because of your obedience. The emphasis is on "you," showing anew the antithesis against the simple. But while "glad," Paul urges wisdom as to "that which is good." The seducers seem to be wise. The shield against them is the true wisdom, unmoved faith in the Gospel. "And simple concerning evil." The word for "simple" here is not the same as in the last verse, but means harmless (the word in Matt. 10:16) or free from evil. "Be deep in the wisdom of humble faith; be contented to be unacquainted with a wisdom which at its root is evil" (Moule). For a man need not be evil, and needs no personal experience in the practice of it, to be wise about it. The pure life begotten of a pure faith knows best what sin is. Darkness cannot reveal darkness.

20. "And the God of peace." He is so called to show how contrary to Him are those who cause divisions and deceive the hearts of the simple. It is the "God of peace" that shall "bruise Satan" under their feet "shortly." This last word does not mean "soon," as is clearly shown in Luke 13:8, where it is translated "speedily." God will "bear long" with His elect that cry day and night unto Him, but avenge them "speedily." The long-continued patience is contrasted with the rapid course of vengeance when the latter once begins. In no instance of the seven in the New Testament does this word mean "soon." In this whole exhortation, beginning at verse 17, Paul has Genesis 3 clearly in mind. He quotes now the very word, "bruise," found there. Just such false teachers as these now

troubling the Romans Paul calls elsewhere "ministers" of Satan (II Cor. 11:15). They are the embodiment of his spirit. If the Romans will be "wise unto that which is good" and avoid these men, God will bruise Satan in destroying the influence of these emissaries of Satan. A church at peace and in unity has Satan under its feet. By means of the word "bruise" from Genesis 3:15, and the word "Satan," Paul flashes a double ray of light on the character and inspiration of these seducers in Rome in a manner as adroit as it is vivid.

An end to the epistle is now reached, and so Paul pronounces a benediction.

21-23. But would this epistle be dispatched to Rome without first being read to the church in Corinth, where it was written? And when so read the Corinthian hearers must have their greetings subjoined, first among whom comes Timothy, Paul's "work fellow," and, besides several others, another kinsman, the fourth one in the chapter.

The amanuensis, Tertius, who in some quiet chamber had been writing down what Paul dictated, and would not disturb the apostle or add a word of his own there, now that an end is reached and others are present and giving their salutations, adds his own. Paul certainly did not dictate "I Tertius."

"Gaius," in whose house the letter was written, as must be supposed, is doubtless the man alluded to in I Corinthians 1:14. He was now Paul's "host," as Priscilla and Aquila had been some years before (Acts 18:3), and the host "of the whole church." There is no reason for diluting this statement as some commentators do. The entire Christian assembly met within this man's gates and may have been present when this was penned. But why do we not read, "The church of Corinth salutes you"? Because their salutation is to be found in verse 16 above. A city officer, Erastus, the chamberlain, salutes. His faith in Christ did not debar him from a civic function. The view that a Christian cannot hold an office of the state wrecks on this passage. "And Quartus the [not "a"] brother." The Romans would especially appreciate this last salutation, for they knew Quartus and all about him, as the word "the" indicates We are in entire ignorance of him.

24. The epistle having officially ended with verse 20, this fraternal postscript was appended, not being suitable earlier, and now again a benediction is pronounced. The doubt of its genuineness (the Revised and many other modern versions reject it) arose from a failure to see the structure of this closing portion. As the benediction of verse 20 closed the epistle officially, so this one closes it fraternally. Meyer skillfully defends it.

25. We may now conceive of Paul as taking the pen from the amanuensis Tertius, and adding the doxology in his own peculiar (Gal. 6:11, R. V.) hand, not only to authenticate the epistle (II Thess. 3:17) to the Romans, but also to bring the whole to a worthy and exalted close.

25-27. "Now to him that is of power to [e]stablish you." Paul began the epistle with this thought (1:11). He wrote about his desire to visit them and to impart to them some spiritual gift, to the end that they might be established. And now he refers them to God, who "is able" to do this.

"According to my gospel." "According" does not mean either "in" or "by" or "in respect to." The word expresses a correspondence. When in building a house it is set and established according to a fixed street line, there is an agreement between the house and the line, such a harmony that each measures the other. When the Romans became finally fixed and settled in their faith Paul hoped to see that faith in exact parallel with his Gospel. He has already called the latter a "form" or mold (6:17). God is able to put its stamp upon their thinking, feeling, and living, so that in all these there will never be any divergence from the Gospel. A church is "established" when it reverently believes and says of everything —sin and Satan, Christ, death and life, the past and the future —just what the Gospel reveals about these things. The heart is so unstable, there is so much inadequate and even false teaching, and Satan is so constantly seeking to undermine, that God alone is "of power to establish" so that there be no swerving. The Romans are joyfully firm now, Paul knows, but divine power alone can preserve them in that firmness.

"My gospel"—the Gospel as I preach it. (See remarks on

2:16, and compare II Thess. 2:14; II Tim. 2:8; Gal. 2:2.)
There was no conflict between Paul's Gospel and Peter's, but
Paul's shows a much wider development.

"And the preaching of Jesus Christ." Subjoined to show
without fail what Paul's Gospel is in its substance and contents. It is a proclamatio nabout Jesus Christ.

"According to the revelation of the mystery." The word
"according" has the same meaning as in the first instance in
this verse. The question here is about the connection of the
phrase introduced by it, whether to join it with the verb
"stablish," thus making the two "according" phrases parallel,
or to affix it to the words "preaching of Jesus Christ." Practically the two connections come to the same thing. The
preaching of Jesus Christ accorded with the revelation by God
to Paul of a "mystery." A mystery is a spiritual truth which
could not be known to exist except by direct revelation. But
after it is revealed it is still called a mystery. Some part of
the one alluded to here was given in 11:25—a part, for the
Romans surely knew the whole as it is given in Ephesians 3:3,
6. The sum of the mystery was the union of Jew and Gentile
on the same level in Christ "until the fullness of the Gentiles
be come in," when the Jew should again come to the front and
receive his headship. The relation of Jew and Gentile was the
burning question in the church in Paul's day. Nothing could
be settled till it was settled. This question was the foe of stability and well-nigh wrecked the churches of Galatia. And Paul
knew the might of the disturbing currents sweeping around the
churches, and that nothing but God's power could establish
the Romans conformably with a preaching that accorded with
this mystery, so hateful to the zealous but unbelieving Jew,
who knew Moses, but had only hate for what Peter calls "the
present truth" (II Peter 1:12).

"Which was kept secret since the world began." About
this mystery there was a hush during eternal ages. The end
of these silent times came in Paul's day. God knew from all
eternity that Jew and Gentile were to be saved alike by a common faith in Christ, but He did not reveal it till He raised up
the apostle to the Gentiles (Gal. 1:11, 12, 15). Judaism

neither revealed nor embodied this mystery. Judaism was quite subordinate, and served its own divinely given purpose until God's plan for the world should be made known.

"But now is made manifest." The "now" is in pointed contrast with the time in which the mystery was kept secret, "which in other ages was not made known unto the sons of men, as it is now revealed unto his holy apostles and prophets by the Spirit" (Eph. 3:5). The contrast here, as Colossians 1:26 shows, is between the other ages and "now." It may be further remarked on this Ephesian passage that the "as" does not give a comparison between degrees of revelation in the former time and "now." It denies that there was any revelation at all of the mystery in that former time; just as if one should tell a man born blind that the sun does not shine in the night as it does in daytime. It does not shine at all by night. Certainly there is no comparison by "as" in Acts 2:15; 20:24. "As" with a negative in the preceding clause has not received the attention which it deserves. It is sometimes almost equivalent to "but" (I Cor. 7:31).

It may be remarked also on the Ephesian passage that it is generally admitted that in the phrase "holy apostles and prophets" Paul is referring exclusively to the New Testament prophets. Paul was both an apostle and a prophet.

"And by the Scriptures of the prophets." This very faulty rendering of the King James Version is, strangely enough, followed in the Revised Version, but not in some other equally good modern translations, that read "prophetic writings" instead of "Scriptures of the prophets." In the original there is no article with either word, as there would be if it referred to the Old Testament; nor is the word rendered "prophets" a noun, but an adjective. The commentators generally (Godet is an exception) make this mistranslated phrase refer to the Old Testament.

But how strange that Paul should say that this mystery was kept secret until his day, as the commentators admit that he does, and that then he should contradict himself by saying that it was "made known" "by the Scriptures of the prophets"! These prophetic writings were chiefly Paul's own. He claims that this mystery was made known to him by revelation and that he "wrote" about it in "few words" (Eph. 3:3). The apostles needed to have their understandings opened to understand the Scriptures, but this cannot be called a revelation. This mystery of the union of Jew and Gentile on the common level of the church is utterly wanting in the Old Testament. The angels did not know it (Eph. 3:9, 10). Repeated visions were necessary to lead Peter into an acceptance of it (Acts 10; 11).

The Old Testament bears witness to the life, death, resurrection, and ascension of Christ, as well as to the doctrine of justification by faith, as Paul has been careful all through this epistle to show abundantly. It testifies clearly, too, that the Gentiles are to be saved; but beyond this, instead of predicting that Judaism should for a time be set aside, it declares its exaltation in Christ in innumerable places, and instead of foretelling the equality of Jew and Gentile, it invariably predicts the latter's subordination in the time to come. The expositors miss the meaning of this phrase, "Scriptures of the prophets," first, from faulty presuppositions; second, from a hasty following of the ancient commentators, whom they quote with one consent, especially Theodoret (see Alford and Ellicott); third, from an inadequate conception of the historical situation; and, fourth, from not seeing the climactic relation of this doxology to the peculiarity of the epistle. As no other this epistle breaks down the barrier between Jew and Gentile, while admitting the "advantage" of the former (3). Chapters 9-11 are peculiar to it. And Paul looks now to God to establish them, not in accord with the Old Testament, but according to this new revelation, "according to my gospel," "according to the revelation of the mystery."

"According to the commandment of the everlasting God, made known." The mystery of the oneness of Jew and Gentile in Christ was not only manifested to the apostle, but made known authoritatively. There are four qualifying clauses about the mystery: it was made known (a) by means of the prophetic writings; (b) because of the command of the everlasting God (it was Christ who commanded the Gospel to be preached;

God commanded the mystery to be made known, significantly called the "everlasting" God); (c) the aim in making it known is "the obedience of faith" (see on 1:5); (d) and the extent of this knowledge was "to all nations."

"To God only wise." The translation of the Revised Version is preferable: "To the only wise God, through Jesus Christ, to whom be the glory forever. Amen." Paul, with no strict grammatical connection with what precedes, closes with an adoring look upward in an attitude of worship. The phrase "through Jesus Christ" seems to go with the word "God," who, through Jesus Christ, is manifested as the alone, as the absolutely, wise. "To whom [God] be the glory"—the praise, worship, and honor for all that is done for men in Christ. "To whom be the glory forever. Amen." Bengel adds: "And let every believing reader say, 'Amen.'" The subscription of the King James Version, while not genuine, is undoubtedly correct.